Wind and Ice

One Hundred Years (almost) of Kamloops' Hockey

by Glen Cowley

rockface books
Kamloops, British Columbia

rockface books
7189 Paul Lake Road
Kamloops, B.C.
V2H 1N9
(fax 250 573-5193)

Canadian Cataloguing in Publication Data
Cowley, Glen, 1949-
Wind and ice: one hundred years (almost) of Kamloops' hockey
Includes bibliographical references.
ISBN 0-9686331-0-2

1. Hockey--British Columbia--Kamloops--History. I. Title. II. Title: Wind & ice.

GV848.4.C3C69 1999 796.962'09711'72 C99-901539-7

Cover design: Wilf Schmidt
Cover photograph courtesy Kamloops Museum & Archives
Back Cover photograph courtesy KMA

For Special Orders:
Wind & Ice (Glen Cowley)
Box 435
Kamloops, B.C.
V2C 5L2

Printed and bound in Canada by Hignell Printing Ltd.
Winnipeg, Manitoba

Table of Contents

Part One - In the Beginning

Part Two - Heyday of the Seniors

Part Three - The Rise of the Juniors

Acknowledgements

Putting together a book like this takes the support and cooperation of many.

The patience and assistance of Elisabeth Duckworth, Susan Cross, Cindy Gourd and the late Myles Morrison of the Kamloops Museum and Archives is greatly appreciated.

Wilf Schmidt's direct help with the mechanics of putting the whole thing together and attending to the photography was invaluable. His experience and knowledge made the project viable. Ken Alexander, editor of Kamloops This Week, provided the polish that made the final product presentable. A special appreciation goes to Doris Rubel, the mother of all hockey mothers, and Ted Desireau, of the Wall of Fame, who assisted with the provision of numerous photographs.

Numerous others afforded time and information that have helped expose a legacy that is as much a part of Kamloops' history as the railroad and the fur trade.

I hope that the product is worthy of that support and provides the information and enjoyment for which it was intended.

Dedication

To the players, organizers, coaches, parents, media and fans who have made Kamloops a hockey town with a story to tell.

Introduction

I have been a hockey fan for as long as I can remember.

Growing up in Southern Ontario, the annual battle between the Montreal Canadiens and the Toronto Maple Leafs consumed my winters. Saturday Hockey Night in Canada was as regular a routine as brushing my teeth. It was a routine shared by many Canadians.

When the fates dictated Kamloops become my home in 1985, I continued the routine until fortune had it I was introduced to junior hockey and the Kamloops Blazers. Life has not been the same since.

Taking an interest in the Blazers led me to seek out information on the history of the sport in this sagebrush city. I was certain the depth of hockey interest and the local talent had to have roots even deeper than the Blazers. When I found virtually nothing on the subject on the library shelves, I had to look elsewhere. This led me to the archives and the decision to bring back to life the vibrant history that is the story of hockey in Kamloops.

It is a story which faint beginnings start prior to the turn of the century and which reached a natural turning point when the history of Kamloops' hockey and the franchise that was to become the Kamloops Blazers converged in 1981. Like the meeting of the North and South Thompson rivers, the franchise and the depth of Kamloops' hockey met to form a mighty river that continues to flow. This union of the legendary franchise from Humboldt, Sask. and the strength of local interest, organization and drive created a success story that continues to unfold upon an international playing field.

In writing a book like this, I could have researched indefinitely and still not get all the names of all the people who have contributed to the history and growth of the sport in Kamloops. I apologize to those who I have missed and some the events which failed to surface; yet for all of the possible omissions and flaws, it is a part of Kamloops' history that warrants recall and should not be forgotten.

Hopefully, it will rekindle some fond memories for fans, the slap of camaraderie among old teammates, the elation of victory and the drama and excitement of moments locked in the recesses of Kamloops' hockey's collective consciousness.

I give you 100 years (almost) of hockey history in Kamloops from 1884 to 1981.

Wind & Ice

Shrouded in mist, it hangs above the valley floor like some giant's whitened tongue; silent and harmless now.

It recalls its advance over mountains and valleys in days gone by. Heedless of time, it waits still to unleash its unrelenting power upon the world.

In broad and broken plains that stretch beyond the horizon, it sits upon the world. A vast expanse of white solitude dazzling in the sun. Its ebb and flow is measured in inches and years.

At its edges, slivers crash to the sea and float like teeth upon the northern ocean currents. Their bite capable of ripping out the bottom of the world's largest vessels.

Ice. Ever upon the world. Unrelenting and methodical power that most loves winter when it can tease man with a mere sampling of its unlimited strength.

Yet even at its greatest it is mocked by the dancing winds that whirl about it. Winds that find its deepest nooks and crannies with an ease and freedom the cumbersome mass can never enjoy. Twisting, speeding, whistling and howling, the winds pull at the monster's flesh and send snow devils whipping about.

Wind and ice. To most of Canada, they are a part of our lives and, in all of the country, have shaped our culture. There are some things truly Canadian. Things as true in the Maritimes as in the Yukon, in French-speaking as in English-speaking Canada, in the country as in the cities and for the old as well as the young. One of these is hockey.

It is not a sport; it is THE sport. It warms our blood and puts us on the edge of our seats. To others, it may be a game but, to us, it is the wind which plays with power and freedom upon the frozen lakes, pond, rivers and rinks across a nation. It is a language we all speak. It is a unity that is undeniable.

In a world of commercialism, change and passing fads, it has remained. If the times grew hard and the many teams around the world faded before difficult economic realities, it would remain here. Here, in the country of its birth.

Growing up, I, like most of my friends, envied those heroes who battled for supremacy on the frozen sheets of ice in the hallowed halls of Maple Leaf Gardens or the Montreal Forum. When we donned skates, we became the wind. To grab the puck and race headlong towards the opposing team's net with the breeze tossing our hair and our bodies tingling with the thrill of it all, there was no time. We became the dancing devils that swirled above a frozen world. To deke out the last defenceman and go one-on-one against the crouching goalie. To see him make the first move and to swing around him with a backhander. The puck hitting the twine lifting us with a surge of excitement to leap and dance as if we had just won the Stanley Cup. We would for a moment be Wayne Gretzky or Frank Mahovlich or Aurel Joliat or any number of famous players both past and present.

It was no different for those older or younger. It was only the names and times that changed.

Hockey may have had its birth in Eastern Canada, but it did not take long for the Sons of the West to take up the game. Wherever winter laid its icy breath upon the land, the wind would long to dance.

Along the shores of the Thompson River, beneath the shadow of Mt. Paul, the Canadian game came alive. Like thousands of other communities dotted throughout the land, the dance began and we shared the joy of it all with our countrymen. Amid the sagebrush and the mountains, the game took root and Kamloops began a journey that eventually turned the eyes of the hockey world upon it.

This is Kamloops' story of Wind & Ice.

1

In the Beginning — A Winter's Promise

There is much we will never know about the beginnings of hockey in Kamloops. Much can only be guessed at through whatever voices still call out to us from the past. Of these, the Inland Sentinel, Kamloops' first newspaper, shouts the loudest.

When this newspaper moved to Kamloops from Yale and started its first publication on July 3, 1884, Kamloops was on the verge of dramatic changes. Fewer than 500 souls called it home, of which the vast majority were males, and the economy was ready to burst open with the arrival of rail lines from the East. The small Hudson's Bay Co. fur trade post was about to join the rest of the world.

Scant news relating to hockey found its way into the newspaper in the early years.

The first teaser was an item on Nov. 22, 1887, under the gossip section, "Local News Nuggets."

"On Tuesday, a local Chinaman turned on the water tap in front of E.H. Jones Bookstore and could not turn it off again until the street was flooded. A miniature rink at that point is the result."

It was Kamloops' first recorded rink!

In the following months and years, the newspaper made passing mention of skating at the pond on the reserve, on the river and on a number of rinks that came and went with the fickle hand of nature. Ice carnivals, curling and the desire to keep people off the forever dangerous river were most often the driving forces behind the early outdoor rinks. The first duly recorded man-made ice surface in 1888 lasted only a month before mild weather did it in.

Despite the annual efforts at establishing a more-than passing rink, no mention of hockey escaped from the pages of the Sentinel until Dec. 3, 1897.

"Nicola Lake has a first class team. They are looking forward to a match with the Kamloops boys," rang the Inland Sentinel.

Kamloops' answer was silence.

Again on Dec. 10, 1897 the paper read:

"Nicola team now in first class condition after their many practices. Expectations of a game against Kamloops."

No voices were raised in reply.

Yet, before the season had ended, there came the suggestion Kamloopsians were, indeed, playing the game, albeit quietly. The Feb. 11, 1898 edition proclaimed the Nicola team had to suspend their practices due to poor ice conditions but still expected to play Kamloops before the end of the season. Kamloops had issued a challenge of its own this time. Gauntlets had been thrown down but none picked up.

December 1898 brought more challenges from Nicola and, on Dec. 23 the Sentinel called upon all those interested in forming a hockey club to meet at the hockey rink Dec. 24 at 3 p.m. Again the match did not become a reality.

So it continued as the century drew to a close. The plucky little village of Nicola challenging Kamloops to the initial contest and Kamloops responding in silence or with unmet challenges of its own.

On Nov. 10, 1900, the frustration was summarized in the Sentinel when a challenge match was offered by Revelstoke.

"The members of the Revelstoke Hockey Club are desirous of arranging matches with several outside teams to be played at Revelstoke during the winter. Revelstoke's new rink is almost completed and it has been placed at the disposal of the hockey club for these matches..... Unfortunately, Kamloops has no hockey club to take part in the proposed tournament. It is a pity too as there are many good players in town. A club should be formed."

On Dec. 3, 1901, the Sentinel noted Ernest Fletcher was getting his rink in shape and there was talk of forming a hockey team. Indeed, there was and Nicola finally got its answer.

2

First Foes & the Nicola Boys________1902-25

The Nicola Boys - Kamloops' first rivals on ice. (c. KMA 6183)

The little village of Nicola is no more. Its few remaining buildings now part of a ranch spread along the old highway between Merritt and Kamloops. Yet, it too had its day in the sun and, during that time, it became the first recorded opposition Kamloops faced on an ice surface.

On Jan. 24, 1902, the Inland Sentinel recorded:

"Our hockey enthusiasts have accepted a challenge to play the Nicola Boys at Nicola Lake on Tuesday next (Jan. 28, 1902). They intend on leaving here on Sunday. The Kamloops team are all game sports and will give the Nicola Boys a warm time."

This first team was composed of J.C. Holmes, Angus Nelson, K. Bayntun, E. Unwin, W. Jarvis and B. Prior (captain).

On Sunday, it met at Costley's stables at 7 a.m. and set off on the wagon trip south to the shores of Nicola Lake. History was loath to give up the secrets of that first game. Perhaps Nicola lost and the details were not recorded or Kamloops lost and the Sentinel did not wish to print the bad news. Whatever the reason the outcome remains hidden.

The thrill of competition was enough, however, to spark a rematch in Kamloops scheduled for Feb. 4, 1902 at Fletcher's rink at 3 p.m.. Large numbers of spectators at 25 cents admission were expected to grace the sidelines.

The game date dawned inclement with the threat of snowfall but the game went ahead undeterred. The two teams took to the ice somewhere in the vicinity of the present day flagpole in Riverside Park. The lineups read:

Kamloops: goal-T. Dennings, point-H.A. Adams, cover point-H. A. Cornwall, forwards-Angus Nelson (captain), K. Bayntun, J.C. Holmes, B.G. Prior

Nicola - Rev. Cropp, E. Godlich, Riley, W. Murray, J. Murray, A.R. Carlington and J.H. Duncan.

The night before the game, in the manner befitting the sportsmanship of the times, the Kamloops team hosted the Nicola side at Ms. Harling's Boarding House and extended an invitation to the upcoming masquerade ball. Then it was on to the game.

Despite the weather, it was recorded the Kamloops team *"were in good shape and kept the puck hovering about the Nicola flags"*. These were the days of posts instead of nets, seven-man teams (the extra player being known as the rover), no substitutions and penalties for the goalie going down to make a save.

With Kamloops pouring on the pressure, *"the Nicola team fell back to a block game, their only ambition seemed to be keeping the score down."* Although Nicola came on a bit in the second half (as opposed to three periods), Kamloops more than met the challenge. Nelson, Holmes and Prior were singled out for some *"fine bits of combination play"* while Bayntun, the rover, also caught the reporter's eye.

When the wind finally settled down, Kamloops had won its first ever home game by a convincing score of 8-1.

That first victory had the town in a flap. There was hopeful talk the eastern sport would catch on here and a league could be formed amongst the surrounding towns. Prospects of challenging Revelstoke and Ashcroft were lauded but none became a reality that season.

It was Vernon, Kamloops future arch foe, which came calling next during the 1902-03 season. Nicola was not forgotten and, before that community faded into the mists of time, it would face off again against Kamloops and earn the right to be called Kamloops' first hockey rival.

The trip to Vernon by train proved much easier than the wagon trip to Nicola but the foe more formidable. Angus Nelson, S.W. Dean, K. Bayntun, Clifford Blair, H. Adams, H. Cornwall and A. Winters carried the Kamloops colours that fell 7-0 to a potent Vernon squad playing its first ever home game against an outside team, on Jan. 19, 1903.

The politeness of the event, as with Nicola, was evident. The game was a gentlemanly one throughout and no accident of any consequence marred the pleasure of the match.
Afterwards, dinner was served at the Coldstream Hotel *"where a couple of hours passed in a very pleasant manner, songs and speeches enlivening the evening."* It is hard to imagine such a scene between their hockey descendants.

In keeping with the times, Kamloops then invited Vernon for a match on Kamloops ice. On Feb. 18, 1903, the Kamloops seven of Clifford Blair (goal), S.W. Dean (cover point), A. Greatrix (point), G.R. Mason (rover), Angus Nelson (right wing), H. Cornwall (centre) and K. Bayntun (left wing) faced the Okanagan visitors.

The match was much more competitive. At the-25 minute mark of the first half, Crowell put Vernon up 1-0. By the 10-minute mark of the second half, they went ahead 2-0. Then Mason, on a pass from Nelson, got the home side on the board. Vernon responded to go up 3-1, but Nelson came back with Kamloops second goal to close the gap. It ended that way with some measure of respect regained.

There was a suggestion the civility of the game had taken a bad turn. The Sentinel recorded:

"One of the Vernon players was somewhat inclined to play roughly whenever he came near the puck or a player but after the home team caught on to his tactics they gave a Roland for an Oliver every time."

There were no more challenge matches that season nor any in the following season. Fans had to content themselves with competition between teams such as the CPR, Kamloops College and the town team. The names of Fred Irwin, Parsons and the Munn brothers made their way onto local squads and Angus Nelson continued as what might be considered Kamloops first star player.

The town team, which included Nelson, J. Lapointe, the Munn brothers and G. Barber, ventured to Vernon in the 1904-05 season and were edged 7-6. Despite optimism about play against Revelstoke, Vernon and Nicola for the 1905-06 season it did not come to pass.

It was not until the 1907-08 season that Kamloops again took to the ice against outside competition. Again it was Nicola and this time there was a trophy up for grabs. It was recorded in the Nicola Herald that on Feb. 12,. 1908, the first challenge match for the Haddad Trophy was played at the Nicola rink between Nicola and the Kamloops Athletic Association.

In the style of the times, it was recorded the game started with the visitors (Kamloops) displaying "neat" three-man combinations and the home team providing "spectacular" rushes. After 20 minutes, the home side got on the board with a goal by C. Curtis. Not to be outdone, with less than two minutes remaining in the half, Angus Nelson fooled both Neal and Murray to tie the game.

The second half was more combative. The Nicola forwards pressed only to be stymied by the goaltending of William Brennan. Heavy checking resulted in Thomas Munn becoming the *"unfortunate recipient of a stiff check"* which "placed" him out of the play, however he "pluckily" resumed play afterwards. With time winding down, it looked like overtime was a sure bet.

Then Lapointe of Kamloops had his centring pass intercepted by Nicola's Charlton who banged home the winning goal and gave Nicola the Haddad Trophy. The Kamloops team, which also included T. Somes (captain) and Fred Irwin had just failed to bring home Kamloops' first hockey trophy. It was many years before such an opportunity came again.

The Nicola team favoured Kamloops with a return match. Only 40 spectators saw Kamloops drop another 2-1 game.

The following season local fans contented themselves with house league play with teams drawn from the CPR, the banks, the high school and one with the unusual title of "Orphans." The season also saw the first reference to women's hockey but, thereafter, the newspaper went silent on the subject. Kamloops did not even get an invite to the Haddad Challenge in Nicola.

Women's hockey seldom made the papers but had its roots in the early years as well. A women's hockey game in the 1920s. (c. KMA #9327)

When the 1909-10 season rolled around, Nicola once again threw down the gauntlet. Absent from the list of tryouts for the Kamloops team was Angus Nelson, but he was not done with the hockey scene yet. This time a number of fans were accompanying the squad on the road trip that was to include games in both Nicola and Merritt.

Kamloops had three holdovers from that last contest against

Nicola as did Nicola.

Kamloops	Position	Nicola
William Brennan*	goal	Doc Curtin*
Robb	point	Dancey
Joseph McKinnon	cover point	Charlton*
Hockin	rover	Thomas
Bauman	right wing	F. Riley
Fred Irwin*	centre	Richardson
Thomas Munn*	left wing	E. Riley
		(Howse)

The two teams took to the ice at 3 p.m. on a Friday in Nicola. The play held pretty even throughout the first half until shortly before it ended. Thomas Munn took a pass in front of the net and beat "Old Warhorse" Doc Curtin to give the visitors a 1-0 lead.

The second half was more competitive with Irwin starring for Kamloops and Dancey for Nicola. Dancey showed his stuff by going the length of the ice and then beating Brennan with a shot between the skates. Kamloops went back on the attack with Robb being thwarted a number of times before Irwin beat Curtin to restore the lead. Nicola stormed back and pressed Kamloops but, when the final whistle blew, the lead stood up and Kamloops had stolen a 2-1 victory, its first recorded road win.

That night the Nicola team hosted Kamloops at a dinner. No one knew Nicola and Kamloops would never cross sticks again. The town faded from hockey and existence but not before earning the right to be Kamloops' first hockey rivals. The Nicola Valley had a new foe awaiting.

Once again a victory had fans and organizers talking about expanded play. When a meeting was held at the Leland Hotel to reorganize local hockey, they had the greatest turnout ever. Even Mayor Robinson let his name stand as honorary president Team manager Joseph McKinnon spoke about play against Revelstoke, Nicola and Ashcroft. The Sentinel crowed about boards and lighting for the rink. Reality was quite different, however.

For the next three seasons, outside competition was absent. Hockey fans took in games between city teams with the names such as Harlington's Boarding House, Bankers, Batchelors, Outlaws and the Broadway Speed Artists. The city became more involved as it provided water and light through the volunteer services of the Rocky Mountain Rangers. Angus Nelson lent his services as a referee. The scene remained vibrant.

When town teams ventured out again in the 1913-14 season they met with some rude awakenings. A team under Fred Irwin travelled to Salmon Arm and in a rough game were throttled 16-0. The Sentinel complained:

"No deaths resulted but minor injuries were numerous and survivors each and all declared the game to have been the roughest within their experience."

First mention was made of the problems local teams had with their foes benefiting from better ice conditions and more practice time. The point was driven home the same season when the local Fire Brigade team was waxed 10-0 in Ashcroft.

Kamloops did not venture outside again for two seasons.

The following season saw the emergence of a rather unique league and a controversy. The religious community organized senior and junior leagues under the banners of the Roman Catholics, Presbyterians, Methodists and Anglicans. Controversy arose when the YMCA, which was operating the rink, opposed having it open on the Sabbath while the city council voted 5-4 for a more secular schedule.

The 1916-17 season was generally quiet save for mention of a game between Kamloops and a Chase team that had developed quite a reputation around Shuswap Lake. Kamloops took the first game in what was to be a brief but intense rivalry between the two communities.

The 1917-18 season finally offered a little more for the starved fans.

On Dec. 14, 1917, the paper announced a junior hockey league had been formed and was to play at the Riverside rink.

President William Brennan oversaw the Cyclones, Athletics and Wanderers while Angus Nelson provided the reffing. The Dalgleish family burst on the scene with Sinclair leading the way.

He starred in that first season, winning the scoring title and leading his Wanderers to the league title and the newly awarded Brennan Trophy.

On Jan. 26, 1918, a team from Chase came calling and were turned back 5-1. Ted Buse, Richard Palmer and Sinclair Dalgleish starred in a game where, had it not been for Chase goalie Joliffe, the score would have been much higher. Sportsmanship still prevailed and a collection was taken up to help cover the expenses of the Chase team.

The team was not so fortunate when it journeyed to Merritt and was thumped 6-1 in its first contest against the new foe in the Nicola Valley.

1918-19 brought more of the same. Again there were three junior teams, though, the Wanderers changed their name twice, once to the Dreadnoughts and then to the Monarchs. Two more Dalgleishs entered play. Sinclair did not play that season and, in his absence' Richard Palmer walked away

The Brennan Cup - The first recorded hockey championship cup ever played for in Kamloops. (c. KMA)

with the scoring title, potting 36 goals compared to nine from his nearest rival.

When an all star junior team travelled to Ashcroft, it had three Dalgleishs and two Palmers so it was not surprising they scored all the goals in a 4-3 Kamloops victory.

The 1919 Brennan Cup winning Athletics.
Back row (left to right - C. Faulkner, ? , Hugh Vicars, Alex Swanson,
Middle Row - Barry McCall, Billy Brennan, Stuart Lynes,
Front Row - Allan Milton, Rick Palmer, Alf Bruce. (c. KMA #6183)

1919-20 proved the most exciting and busiest season to date.

The newspaper crowed about sports success in general and proclaimed there would be both a senior and a junior league that year. The seniors would ice the Thistles, Monarchs, Bankers and High School while the juniors had the Wanderers, Athletics and Hornets.

The Sentinel took the liberty of jesting in its coverage of one game.

"On Thursday the Bankers will appear in the open and for once the general public will view their work at close hand. The

Monarchs are expected to make a run on the Banks as they are affected by the high cost of living as much as their humblest of subjects."

Another account of the junior season opener between the Hornets and the Wanderers had the writer claiming the Wanderers had a good excuse for being shutout 6-0. They claimed they had sympathy for the goal judge who had just been vaccinated and they did not wish to force him to raise his arm and cause himself pain. They expected his arm would be fully recovered by the next game.

One of the most interesting incidents of the season arose out of heated competition with Chase. It clearly showed sportsmanship was not always the norm in the early days.

On Jan. 27, 1920, the paper reported the Chase team was coming here for a return match after a Kamloops' pickup team had favoured them with a game. The paper complained they were beaten in a bloody match played on a sheet of the ice the size of a drawing room. The paper railed Kamloops would *"take the visitors to camp as they did Ashcroft"* (Kamloops had won that game 6-2).

The Jan. 30, 1920 headline ran *"Kamloops even up with Chase - game forfeit four minutes before time by visitors who were outclassed."*

It appears the Chase team had come along with a number of its fans. Some of them were so confident of a win they staked money on the outcome, up to $500 the rumour went. It eventually became apparent the boys from Chase were not going to win when, with four minutes left, Kamloops was up 3-1. At that point, so the story goes, one of the Chase fans jumped onto the ice and started such a disturbance the game had to be cancelled. Chase fans, who had put money on the game, then claimed they did not have to pay because the game had not been finished.

The fans and the newspaper ranted against the Chase team and its fans. The former were accused of brutal and violent hockey. One account had the Kamloops' goalie taking a shot between the eyes and lying dazed in front of the net. The Chase team was accused of continuing to pummel away at him despite his obvious condition. Their fans were accused of being poor sports and not being able to control their mouths.

Thereafter, games against Chase took on special meaning.

During the 1920-21 season, an overall sports touring team from the Kamloops Junior Brotherhood travelled to Vancouver for a gymnastics tournament (which they won) and, in the course of their visit, played an exhibition hockey game against King George High School. It marked the first time a Kamloops hockey team played on artificial ice. With this new experience and the lack of any practice, it wasn't surprising they were defeated 7-2. The team did, however, score the last two goals of the game and were confident if they had practice time, they could beat King George.

A similar problem arose when Kamloops visited Salmon Arm and went down 8-2. Only their 4-2 win in Ashcroft with the antics of their fans, especially "Shindy" with his bugle, urging them on, gave any solace. Discontent with ice conditions was increasing.

"A local rink is something that has been lacking in Kamloops and it is hoped that next winter will see this city in a position to accommodate all and sundry who wish to tackle our local team."

The item in the Sentinel was prophetic but unrealized in the short term.

The 1921-22 season offered something old and something new. New was Kamloops joining the Mainline Hockey League along with Ashcroft, Chase and Salmon Arm. Old was the Haddad Trophy which was to be the reward for the league championship.

The season started with a 2-2 tie in Ashcroft, despite two overtime periods, followed by a 5-2 loss to hated Chase. Their third game did not look promising as they went up against Salmon Arm. Even the paper was not optimistic.

"Salmon Arm Coming Here with Great Team"

"Hockey Visitors Wonderful Bunch"

"Salmon Arm will be the Favourites"

"They Usually Take our Boys to Town"

The paper lamented Salmon Arm played as a team whereas Kamloops was split up amongst various teams in the city league. It also urged the "railbirds" to provide a little less criticism and a little more support.

Whatever the reason, the Kamloops boys came out on fire. By the time they were done Salmon Arm had lost 5-0. Richard Palmer and Sinclair Dalgleish each potted two goals. Optimism about winning the league prevailed but reality set in afterwards. The victory over Salmon Arm served as the highlight of the first and only season in the league. Hated Chase captured the league and the Haddad Trophy.

The senior team took time that season for an exhibition series against a visiting Lac La Hache team reputed to be the best in the Interior and defeated only once in the past ten years. Even Chase had only managed a tie with the boys from the Cariboo. The squad came out in their new purple-and-white uniforms to clash against the chocolate-and-white of Lac la Hache.

In the first, Richard Palmer got Kamloops on the board with a power play goal while MacDougall , the goalie, was serving time for going to his knees to make a save. After Percy Ogden tied the score, Ted Buse put Kamloops up 2-1 to end the period. In the second, Lee Weatherby put the home side up 3-1. Thoughts of an upset appeared doomed when the visitors stormed back in the third to tie the game up. Their last goal came with Kamloops two men short and put the teams into overtime.

Two minutes into overtime "chubby" little centre Sinclair Dalgleish, on a pass from Ted Buse, *"Flipped the biscuit into MacDougall s birdcage."* Kamloops had the upset.

The win was not diminished by Lac La Hache winning the next two games by scores of 5-2 and 4-3. The season-ending 3-2 win over Merritt in which Richard Palmer scored the game winning goal on a solo rush capped off the campaign.

In the city's senior league, the Wanderers, Bankers and Beavers fought it out for the Frost Cup while the juniors still contested the Brennan Cup.

The busy season ended with a combined season-ending banquet with local curlers at which plans were revealed for the development of an indoor arena. The Stockbreeders Association was also in need of a facility and the local paper took up the cause claiming even smaller communities had better facilities than Kamloops. The seed was planted but it did not start growing for a while yet.

The 1922-23 season saw both senior and junior leagues providing the bulk of the hockey entertainment. The seniors iced the Monarchs, Tigers and Miltons . The juniors iced the Whirlwinds, Blue Birds, Swallows and Invincibles. The Swallows won the league and the Brennan Cup, while the Invincibles proved anything but as they went 0-5.

Angus Nelson took a rep team to Chase where it went down 5-1 in a game where they took a 1-0 lead into the third. The 1-1 tie in the return match did little to compensate for losing to their arch foe. They closed out the season with losses to Ashcroft and Lac la Hache and a win over Tappen.

The 1923-24 season had a little more spark to it as the rivalry between Chase and Kamloops heated up and one of the local writers enjoyed adding a little flavour to his articles.

On Jan. 24, 1924, the paper headlined *"Chase Peeved but Why?"*

Allegedly, Chase puck chasers had left a note at the newspaper office complaining about the lack of a response to their challenge of Kamloops. They asked if Kamloops even had a team or a manager that year. They even claimed they would be giving Kamloops an advantage because Beaver Murray was not playing for them that year.

Harry Dalgleish responded by claiming no challenge had ever reached them. He added challenging teams should realize Kamloops occasionally likes to have teams visit rather than always having Kamloops go to their "burgs." He was quoted as saying, *"We can see no reason why Kamloops should be the goat all the time."*

The end result was Kamloops travelled to Chase and beat them 1-0 on their own ice. The paper rubbed it in with a claim *"Had the condition of the ice been better the reply would have been more emphatic."*

Although there was little else from the rep level to enthral the fans an article from the Sentinel's "From the Sidelines" revealed there were those anxious to prod the team spirit. The piece by Bert Fiddes ran:

"We would not encourage ragging in any game but Kamloops today is lamentably weak in organized sport. Kamloops has no 'Yell' or 'Yell Leader'. Organized yells are to sport what community singing is to service clubs. Let Kamloops get the yell fever. Let us encourage hockey, basketball, baseball and football teams this way. It develops a healthy 'Kamloops Spirit'."

The article went on to encourage people to donate more at games when the money box came around. It added the old trick of dropping a copper in and hitting the box so it sounds like more was put in was easily detected.

The city league embraced the Brownies, Native Sons and the first coming of a team named the Elks. Six Dalgleishs, including Clair, Sinclair, Harry, Dave, Bruce and Bert, graced the ice.

Something of the old sportsmanship had slipped away over the years and was apparent in one newspaper account.

"A little excitement was caused by a tiff between Bert Dalgleish and Lee Weatherby and Mr. Umps which resulted in poor Bert being banished. Naughty, naughty Bert - you mustn't speak back to Mr. Umps."

"This period (the third) was also enlivened by an impromptu exhibition of the noble art between Gisborne and Weatherby. There must be some fighting blood in Weatherby . He seems to get in to all the scraps. Wonder if he is Irish?"

At season's end, the cry again went up for a covered rink.

1924-25 saw Kamloops squads beat Chase twice, Ashcroft and Clinton while dropping games to Ashcroft and Merritt. The senior league remained unchanged while the juniors won the award for the most unusual names. The Hefties beat out the Wanderers, Irish and Zephrys for league bragging rights.

The 1925 Kamloops Hockey Team. Left to right - Sinclair Dalgleish, Bert Smith, Lee Weatherby, Teddy Buse, Cliff MacDonald Dalton Walker, Rich Palmer, Eddie Docker and Bert Peacock. (c. KMA #5151)

In the spring of 1925, Kamloops had reached a population of 5,000. Demands for a multipurpose facility could not be ignored by city council. On March 6, 1925, the paper reported the city had agreed to build an arena for both the annual bull sale and hockey, between the railway and the river. This rather unique combination of users was more than explained by the fact the Stock Breeders Association was covering 36 per cent of construction costs.

By September, word was tenders were soon to be called. Funding had come in at $4,700 from the July 1 celebrations, $2,500 from the Stockbreeders and $1,000 from the Wool Growers. The Ministry of Agriculture was to provide a, yet unknown but substantial, sum.

Fred Irwin was elected president of the hockey association and ambitious plans were laid for the season. Plans for a regular rep team and invitations to professional teams to visit their new arena were brought forward. Instead, it turned out to be the season that never was.

On Dec. 18, 1925, the paper outlined the skating rules of the new arena (which was still not completed) as well as some significant details. The city was guaranteed 20 per cent of receipts and any surplus over expenses. The Kamloops Skating Club was to administer the arena. Seasons tickets were $3 for men, $2 for women and $1.50 for children. The hockey club was putting in dressing rooms and stoves. Games against outside teams were to get priority.

Of particular note was a stipulation:

"It is distinctly understood that children will not be allowed on the ice at night with the grown ups, as their place is at home doing schoolwork."

On Dec. 30, 1925, the paper was reporting *"Construction of City's Fine $14,000 Bull Sale Arena Nearly Finished."*

The new building was in the east end of Kamloops, had a seating capacity of 1,600 and was to be known simply as the arena. The wooden structure with shingle siding on city block 102 had inside measurements of 165 feet by 70 feet and was topped by a mineral surface roof which included slate. The roof was thus resistant to flying embers from passing trains. Contractors, MacBeth and Miller, who had begun work on the building in November, provided a structure which allowed for an abundance of natural light and had night lighting from 14 500Kw lamps with reflectors. In winter, the ice hockey association was to administer the facility.

On Jan. 8, 1926, the paper boasted that the new arena *"Didn't Cost the City a Cent."*

Alderman Shaw proclaimed it had been completed at under $11,000 after the city had been able to generate $12,280 for construction costs.

So, Kamloops had its first arena. What a year to have one of the mildest winters on record. In January, the paper was contending residents were out lawn bowling.

After hockey fans had been avidly awaiting the dropping of a puck to christen the new building, it was to be something else that dropped. The bull sale got to enjoy the privilege of opening the facility. Hockey had to wait for a new season.

Interior of the Old Arena (c. KMA #6706)

Twenty-four years after Angus Nelson had been with the team that played Kamloops' first recorded home game Kamloops had an indoor arena. He had seen the sport struggle with poor ice and varying degrees of public support and interest over the years. He had continued his involvement through managing and refereeing after his playing days were over. Would he see the new facility bring the dawn of a new day for Kamloops' hockey?

3

New Beginnings But Old Story______1926-1946

"Skaters in Hundreds - Delighted with First Arena Ice"

Dec. 17, 1926
Kamlops Sentinel

The Bull Sale Arena under construction. (c. KMA #7801)

On Dec. 15, 1926, the new arena opened to skaters under the auspices of the city and the local hockey association with Stan McNab's hotdog and coffee stand proving to be the most popular spot in the facility. The paper boasted nowhere outside of the Coast was there an expanse of ice like this. Despite the mild weather, the ice was holding up well.

Hockey did not have long to wait before its turn came.

On Jan. 8, 1927, the purple-and-white of Kamloops faced off against the red-and-white of Merritt. It was appropriate none other than Angus Nelson should have the honour of reffing the first match in an indoor arena in Kamloops. Kamloops trotted out two new stars in Bert Wolfe and Buster Todd before a sizable but disappointing crowd. It was the first chance to see a Kamloops team fly the city's colours in two years. It was a thriller.

In the first, Buster Todd had the honour of scoring the first two goals in the arena but, before the period ended, Merritt got one back. In the second, Frank Gagne' (brother of NHL star Art Gagne), on an assist from Todd, had the home side up 3-1. Again Merritt bounced back before the end of the second, only this time they tied it all up. The fans got their moneys worth in the third.

Merritt was holding on despite pressure coming from Sinclair Dalgleish and Eddie Docker until Buster Todd stole the puck from a mixup in the Kamloops end, skated the length of the ice and scored. Elated fans were soon moaning as Todd's hat trick was followed shortly after by Merritt's tying goal with only a few minutes left in the game.

Despite carrying the play through two overtime periods, Kamloops had to settle for a tie. What a night for the new arena and new star-Buster Todd.

A confident Kamloops squad followed up the tie with a 6-4 win over Salmon Arm, a 6-3 waxing of Clinton and a 5-1 thumping of Armstrong before they faced former local Ted "Red" Buse and his visiting Kelowna team. The bubble burst with a 7-6 loss despite a two-goal contribution from oldtimer Fred Irwin.

Still, it was a self-assured team that squared off against Merritt in the two-game, total-point playdown for the Mainline Region. Down 4-0 in Game 1 in Merritt, the boys came back to make a game of it before bowing out 6-4. Game 2 at the arena saw Merritt jump into a 3-0 lead and hopes were fading. Bert Wolfe looked to make the game respectable when he scored to make it 3-1. In less than a minute, it was 3-2 and, when Lee Weatherby's 20-foot shot found the back of the net, the barn was in an uproar. It did not end there as Kamloops pressed and went ahead by a goal. One more goal and the series would be tied. Alas, when the next goal came, it was for Merritt and with the 4-4 tie, Kamloops lost the total point series 10-8. Still, what a come-back!

Though short, the 1927-28 season was not without its moments.

A city league that offered some continuity, in form if not in names, got off the ground with four teams. The Commodore Café', Golden Gate Restaurant, Kamloops' Motors and Fred Irwin's battled it out in the shortened season, brought on by the mild weather.

The city team started off with a bang by crushing visiting Salmon Arm 10-4, thanks largely to the work of the Wolfe/Dalgleish/Craig line. Wolfe potted four goals and two assists, Sinclair Dalgleish one goal and one assist and Jim Craig four goals. Their loss free season again ended at the hands of Kelowna and their season before the red-and-white of Merritt.

The 1928-29 season saw more of the same as Kamloops fought an uphill battle against Merritt, though, they held their own against other squads. A 3-3 tie at the arena was followed by a 5-2 loss in Merritt as the Merritt "jinx" continued. Finally, in their third meeting, Johnny Craig became the hero as he scored two goals and got one assist in a 5-3 victory at the arena. Still, it was the Merritt skaters who escaped the Mainline Region only to be eliminated by powerhouse Vernon, defending Coy Cup Champions.

The Golden Gate Restaurant team of 1933. (KMA c. #189)

Disturbing rumblings were beginning around the use of the arena by the hockey team as early as December 1928. Favourable terms given to the hockey club were criticized as unfair to other organizations.

In January 1929, more complaints arose. Council was told hockey fans were damaging the arena by knocking 2x4 studs against the walls and seats in the course of expressing their emotions. Alderman Johnstone, contending the hockey association was not able to control these "Stud Thuds" as was their responsibility, called for the cancellation of the lease. It was finally resolved the matter should be brought to the attention of the police commissioner, but it was apparent hockey had some enemies on city council.

The 1929-30 season not only had the Great Depression but hockey fans had Alderman Johnstone proclaiming the club would not be getting a renewed lease on the arena.

Little happened on the ice that year between Kamloops and surrounding communities and even less during the following season.

When word came at the start of the 1931-32 season that the hockey club would not be renewing the lease at the arena, hockey prospects looked bleak. The club requested and received help from the city in setting up an outdoor rink at the foot of First Avenue in present day Riverside Park. It came to be known as Riverside Gardens.

The hockey association had felt badly treated when they were accused of not cleaning up the arena at the end of the previous season. They argued they were asked to leave the sawdust down for the bull sale and were not informed they were expected to clean it up after the sale was over.

The season was relatively quiet though city teams won two of the three intercommunity games they played. The most pleasing victory was a 9-4 smashing of old rival Chase, before a fair sized crowd, in which Bert Wolfe notched a hat trick.

Riverside Gardens was again the main venue for hockey during the 1932-33 season. The hard times of the Depression led to admission prices for skating being lowered as attempts were made to keep the price affordable and to encourage children to stay off the river. To this was added a new clubhouse and lighting.

In January, notice was received the Golden Gate hockey team of the city league had applied to enter the playoffs for the Provincial Junior Championship. They, along with teams from Nelson, Rossland, Princeton, Trail and Vancouver, challenged for provincial honours.

Ed Anderson, Corbin, Coghlan, Howard Portman, Bill Luback, Stan Moffatt, Jackson, Tymich, Peter Luback, Murray Querns (goal) and Don Fraser faced off against a bigger older and more experienced Princeton squad at Riverside Gardens on Feb. 15, 1933. From the start, Kamloops was in tough.

For five minutes, Kamloops held Princeton off the scoresheet but afterwards the visitors went up 3-0 before Ed Anderson responded with a Kamloops' marker. In the second, Kamloops held their opponents scoreless for 16 minutes before giving up another three goals to be down 6-1 entering the third. The third was not a minute old before Princeton was up 7-1. Rather than lay down, Kamloops stepped up its game. Peter Luback on an assist from his brother, Bill, got their second goal while Ed Anderson, clearly the Kamloops' star, made numerous rushes despite being closely checked by Princeton. Howard Portman was the rock on defence although his enthusiasm netted him three penalties. He had the honour of setting up Eddy Anderson for Kamloops' third goal and finishing the scoring in the game. Final: Princeton 7, Kamloops 3. Kamloops was eliminated.

Though disappointed at the loss, the local fans consoled themselves their squad had played well in the last 10 minutes and they were a young team with promise for the future.

The other big game of the year was the senior team beating Ashcroft 6-3 in Kamloops to salvage what would otherwise have been a winless season. The paper read:

"It has been years since a record crowd attended a hockey match and cheered, booed, shouted and gave vent to their feelings and wagered side bets............on the outcome of the game."

Hockey fans of Kamloops had another source of excitement that season as the paper began to carry articles on the exploits of the community's first bona fide star.

On Jan. 18, 1933, the paper extolled the skills of Arthur Gagne' of the Edmonton Eskimoes as he potted five goals in a nine-goal onslaught that buried the Saskatoon Crescents in the professional Western Canada Hockey League. Arthur had moved his family to Kamloops in 1929 while still toiling at hockey's greatest heights.

In the course of his six seasons in the NHL, he played for the Montreal Canadiens, Boston, Detroit and Ottawa. For three of those seasons, he skated on a line with Hockey Hall of Famers Howie Morenz and Auriel Joliat and was a resident amongst the league's top scorers. Before and after his NHL days, he played in the Western Canada pro leagues, primarily with the Edmonton Eskimoes. There, he played right wing for another Hall of Famer in the person of Duke Keats.

That team, coached by Kenny MacKenzie, was good enough in 1923 to win their league and reach the Stanley Cup finals before losing to the Ottawa Senators.

His presence was eventually felt in Kamloops' hockey circles as was that of coach MacKenzie.

The 1933-34 season was again centred upon Riverside Gardens which now boasted dimensions of 200 feet by 85 feet. The town team had a 1 and 2 record in their short intercommunity play with local fans having to content themselves largely with city league play.

Fans again had Arthur Gagne's exploits to cheer on as the paper praised his two goal and four assist performance in Edmonton's win over the Vancouver Lions. Fans were told to be on the lookout for him in the summer when he could be seen playing tennis at the local courts.

1934-35 saw the town team struggle to a 1-1-1 season with a win and tie against Clinton and a loss to Merritt. 1935-36 was much the same though the 3-3-1 season reflected the longer, colder winter and the chance for more play. It marked the first time that a Kamloops' team took to the ice against a team from Alberta. The Calgary CPR Flyers were seen as a solid team that already had won two games on their tour. When they came back against the locals to win 5-4 after being down 4-2, it looked as if game two of the series would give them a sweep. Indeed, in that game, Calgary was up 2-1 before a heads-up play by Kamloops Robert White turned the tide.

Art Gagne. The Flying Frenchman, Kamloops' first professional star. (c. Keith Gagne)

Calgary was pressing the play when White called to a Calgary player to pass him the puck. Without thinking the player did just that and White took off with Eddie Anderson who beat the Calgary goalie to tie the game up. After that, it was all Kamloops as they swamped the visitors 5-2. Icing up the skates on that squad was Joe Hall, the son of Joe Hall, the Hockey Hall of Famer with the Montreal Canadiens.

1936-37 saw only one foray against outside teams as 49-year-old Fred Irwin led a team to Merritt. Their adventure saw them fighting the elements as they had to dig vehicles out of snow drifts and push them onto the road as well as get shut out 3-0 in the Nicola Valley.

In 1937-38 the hockey association was once again leasing out the arena under terms which saw the city get 10 per cent of the revenue after $75 profit by the club, in lieu of rent. In turn, the association agreed to take out the ice after the season and to indemnify the city for any damages.

It must have been frustrating as local fans read about the

opening of Vernon's new artificial ice rink in January 1938. Almost 100 Kamloopsians journeyed to the opening of the 3,800-seat arena that had been erected for $50,000. Vernon would reap benefits from that arena which would keep other communities on their heels for years to come.

The drowning deaths, in the same month, of two young people who had been out skating on the South Thompson again brought home the need for safer, off-river skating facilities. In response, free skating on the city's two outdoor rinks was suggested.. Cries for a an artificial ice rink were raised but the looming war squashed any prospects.

On the ice, the presence of retired pro hockey star Arthur Gagne' led to hopes his hockey savy would see local squads improve their performance. In fact, they did worse than they had for many years as they went 1-6 on the season largely due to poor ice and a lack of practice time.

The 1938-39 season saw Kamloops parading young players at more levels than ever as squads represented the community at senior, junior and midget. The midgets provided the greatest thrill of the season.

Benefiting from the coaching of Arthur Gagne, the squad journeyed to Merritt to take on the reigning provincial midget champs who had not lost a game in three years. The Cromie Cup holders were handed a 7-3 drubbing by Kamloops in their own backyard. That Kamloops team had Bill McDermid in goal with Keith Gagne' (Arthur's son), Stewart Peterson, Earl Klinck, T. Leslie, Jim Baird (who got four goals and one assist), Billie Peterson (one goal), George "Lefty" Marriot (two goals), Walter Wasykow, George Signoretta, William Boyd and Melville Querns.

Arthur Gagne' was not just busy on the ice as he became one of the leaders in pushing for an artificial ice rink. Appearing in January before the Rotarians, he pointed to viable rinks in Trail, Vernon, Nelson and Kimberley as examples of what could be done. He laid out plans for a joint curling and skating rink housing 2,000 fans that could come in at between $49,000 to $57,000 and be managed for $6,310 per year. Small figures by today's standards but still big money during the latter days of the Depression. The Second World War put an end to such thoughts.

The 1939-40 season saw the start of the war and lean times on the hockey front. The senior team ventured out twice against Merritt and went 1-1. In the first game, played at the arena, Jim Burtnick scored all three Kamloops goals in a 3-2 victory. The game was marred more by the sloppy ice conditions than the play as the 400 fans got to enjoy the spectacle of players getting showers every time they went to the ice. Merritt came back on home ice to even the series with a 4-3 overtime victory. The juniors did not fare as well as they went down to defeat twice to their Merritt rivals.

1940-41 saw permission to use the indoor arena withheld. The military had made alterations to the building and the city did not want to make any changes as they hoped the military would continue to use it. A later assessment revealed the building was structurally unsound and could not be used as a skating facility in any event. It was now a far cry from the excitement it had drawn at its opening only 15 years before.

Hockey all but disappeared from the sports pages during the war years although the odd mention of games in the city leagues provided proof it was still alive and well. The lull was followed by the promise of the great changes.

With the start of the 1945-46 winter season, talk about an artificial ice arena moved from if it was going to be built to when. Plans for the funding of Memorial Arena hit the pages with lotteries and car draws.

On the actual hockey front, local interest boomed under E.H. Martin as the minor hockey association president and Arthur Gagne' as the field coach. Three outdoor rinks were to be constructed at the exhibition grounds with the city providing free light and water. Dryland training was well underway by mid-December and hopes were that local rep teams would be sporting the purple-and-white of Kamloops before the end of the year.

There were now intermediate, junior, midget, juvenile and bantam squads carrying the city's colours. Under Arthur Gagne' as the association coach, there was Ted Jardine leading the intermediates, Ernie Butterworth overseeing up the juniors, E.H. Martin guiding the juveniles, Len Scott the midgets and Jimmy Green the bantams.

The juveniles did the best going 4-1 on the season before being rudely thrown from the playdowns by a Vernon team benefiting from artificial ice. They lost 12-2. Their lineup included one Jim Ashby, father of future NHLer Don Ashby.

The intermediates garnered only one win out of three tries but it was a memorable one for reasons other than the play. Their 7-4 win over arch rival Merritt was played under the watchful eye of goal judge Angus Nelson. The old star, who had carried Kamloops' colours for those first historic games 44 years earlier, appeared for the last time in the sports pages. He was soon to follow the faded village of Nicola into the annals of history.

The 1946-47 season spelled the end of the era that had seen the beginnings of hockey along the banks of the Thompson River. Riverside Gardens was erected for the last time and, to meet the growing demands for ice time, another rink went up at the exhibition grounds.

By the time competition with outside teams got off the ground in January, the playoffs were quickly approaching. Once more it was the juveniles who gave the best showing. With Jim Ashby again in their lineup, they took out Clinton and Revelstoke to advance against the Vernon Lions. They were decimated 19-0 by a team that had the advantage in conditioning and practice that could only be gained by having artificial ice.

The season ending quote in the paper was prophetic:

"Perhaps there will be another year when Kamloops has an indoor rink here?"

More than 40 years had passed since those first tentative steps were taken in an era of good sportsmanship. Steps that pitted local heroes against the stars of now faded Nicola as well as Merritt, Ashcroft, Clinton, Chase and, most notably, the powerhouse Vernon. Sometimes there was as much adventure getting to the other communities as playing the games. The adversities of outdoor play fell upon players and spectators alike and often influenced the flow of the game. Rinks varied in size and quality and competitions, though few in number, carried the intensity of anticipation and natural community rivalries. Over the years, sportsmanship declined in the face of intensified and more frequent competition with different communities gaining advantages due to better natural ice conditions or the benefits of artificial ice

Angus Nelson had seen it all but he did not live to see the greatest change yet. Not long before artificial ice became a reality, Angus was back in town for the last time. With a new day dawning for Kamloops' hockey, when players were no longer at the mercy of the inconsistent weather, the venerable veteran faced his greatest test. He breathed his last at Royal Inland Hospital. Both he and an era came to an end.

The same season, far away on the Prairies, forces were put in motion that eventually rippled upon the shores of the Thompson. Bill Slater obtained the job of arena manager in Humboldt, Sask. and convinced the town fathers to endorse a junior hockey team for play in the Saskatchewan Junior Hockey League. The team took the name Humboldt Indians after the old senior hockey league team that had taken their name from their sponsor, McCall Frontenac Oil Company, whose symbol was the Red Indian. Most of their original players hailed from Regina and Moose Jaw, with some locals. One of those players was Dick Warwick who Kamloops fans would come to love and hate in the years ahead.

It was the beginning of one of the greatest, one might even argue the greatest, junior hockey franchises in the world.

The first edition of the team that was to eventually become the Kamloops Blazers — 1946-47 Humboldt Indians. (c. Humboldt Museum & Gallery)

4

Turning Over a New Leaf__________1947-48

"10 DAYS BETWEEN KAMLOOPS AND ARTIFICIAL ICE "

The headline rang from the Sentinel on Nov. 19, 1947, proclaiming the impending opening of Kamloops' first artificial ice rink on Nov. 29. Mayor Fred W. Scott opened the rink housed in the old Bull Sale arena, which checkered history as the focal point of hockey was about to have one last swing.

Hockey plans ran apace as Kamloops' new senior team, the Hub City Leafs, joined the new intermediate Mainline Hockey League along with the Salmon Arm Tigers, Vernon Legionnaires and Kelowna Aces. The goal was the Coy Cup, emblematic of provincial intermediate hockey supremacy. The president of the new league was Kamloops' own Arthur Gagne' of NHL fame.

Cliff Mills who skated for the Hub City Leafs and the Elks. His star rose and tragically fell during the heyday of the Seniors. (c. KMA # 5479)

The Leafs boasted players whose hockey skills were mostly learned on the Prairies although their roster did include stick boy Larry Candido, a local lad who would etch his name into Kamloops' hockey history. Their trainer was Johnny Cassidy who was with the 1937 Coy Cup champions from Merritt. He was joined by Frank Sharp in goal, Johnny Brkich, Grant MacLeod, Bob Affleck (who along with Ernie Hughes coached the team), Clancey Ulveland (part of the Ulveland hockey clan that peppered the local hockey scene), Eugene Hakansen, Frank Bobrowich, Bill Schall, Ralph Snider, Raymond LeClerc, Cliff Mills, Al Swaine, Len Scott, Jack Shero (brother of New York Ranger Fred Shero) Tom McGrath and manager Art Huston. They were later joined by Bob Donald, Guy Ludgate, Doug MacKay, Gordon Sunden and Al MacDougall.

Mayor Fred Scott dropped the puck to officially start the first game for the Hub City Leafs against the Tigers from Salmon Arm on Kamloops' first artificial ice rink. League president Arthur Gagne' was one of the 900 fans in attendance and his son, Keith, announced the game over the radio. It was a game to remember or forget depending on which bench you sat on. Salmon Arm fell before an onslaught that saw them down 6-0 by the end of the first and, after 60 shots at the final whistle whipped 19-6. They had managed 24 shots but were so clearly outclassed they dropped out of the league leaving only Kelowna and Vernon to vie with Kamloops.

The Kelowna Aces next took on the Leafs in front of 1,250 fans and fared no better as they were stoned 11-2. Bobrowich burned them for five goals.

Then came Vernon and a reality check.

In Vernon, the Leafs were humbled 10-3 and the return match in Kamloops saw the Legionnaires take away a 6-4 victory. The rivalry was on.

Throughout the remainder of the 16 game season, Vernon and Kamloops battled it out with Kelowna offering little more than practice sessions for the top squads. Vernon took the lion's share of the games but Kamloops was not to be outdone as it posted wins of 7-4 and 8-3 to go along with their season ending 3-0 victory over the Legionnaires. Vernon finished first with 25 points, Kamloops second at 20 and Kelowna last at 3.

The best-of-three semifinal between Kamloops and Kelowna was a mismatch as the Leafs humbled the Aces by scores of 25-1 and 17-5. However, the real test was ahead.

Vernon's 4-3 home ice victory to start the series was not secured until the 17-minute mark of the third; it was hardly a convincing win. When Kamloops took Game 2 4-1 back home, it looked like an possible upset in the making. The Legionnaires quickly stopped any such thoughts as they took out the Leafs in Vernon 10-3 in Game 3. The Leafs never recovered.

The Leafs could take some solace in the exploits of Al Swaine who won the scoring title with 32 goals and 49 points in 16 games.

As that first season neared the end, president Gagne' proclaimed it would only get better. He noted Vernon was in a class of its own largely due the advantage it had from having artificial ice for more than 10 years; however, Kamloops had shown strong signs of improvement since it had recently obtained artificial ice. Kelowna would improve too as soon as it had a similar advantage. His words were to ring true and did so quickly.

Before Vernon could walk away with the league championship, it had to contend with another challenger from the shores of the Thompson, the Kamloops' Aces.

The Aces had won the city league championship and thus earned the right to start a playoff series with the ultimate aim of challenging the winner of the Mainline League. After being surprised at home by the Clinton Bluebirds 5-4, they journeyed to Clinton where they won 6-4 to take the two game total point series. Next came the Lumby Flying Frenchmen, the undefeated Okangan Senior B Champs. In Game 1, Rocky Ulveland was the star as the Aces stunned Lumby 10-4. Game 2 saw the Aces remove any doubt as to superiority when to they took out the Frenchmen 7-3.

Then came Vernon.

Inter-city competition was no longer the sporting show of 1902 with good will being demonstrated by all concerned. It was downright nasty. Fans and players got into fights, police threatened charges against visiting teams and, on occasion, were drawn into on-ice melees. Civic officials condemned the behaviour and the newspapers for fanning the flames by focusing on the violence. Some humour did escape as attested to by one game where the referee, appropriately named Sparrow, complained about the Kamloops fans resorting to bird calls when they disapproved of his performance.

Poor sportsmanship remained to end, however, as the clearly superior Legionnaires denied the Aces the right to use three Leafs as replacements for the unavailable M. Desjardin, Jack McNeil and Gordon Marriot. Instead, they were allowed to suit up two juniors, Maurice Clark and Harold Ulveland. It was a slaughter. Vernon was up 22-0 before Kamloops got one back. Goalie S. Beamish stayed in the nets until knocked out by a puck when the score was 19-0. In the end, the battered Aces went down 28-2.

The Aces and the Leafs began a tradition that year which saw the senior team go up against the second act in town. The first game ended, as expected, with a 17-5 Leaf victory.

Minor league hockey remained very much in evidence, but both the midgets and the juniors faced the same fate as the seniors when they ran up against the squads from Vernon. However the midgets had one field day of their own in a 21-2 thumping of Revelstoke.

A notable item revealing itself in the rosters of the minor league teams was the increased presence of Japanese Canadian players. The names Takanaka, Yoshido, Kobayashi, Kashino and Yamada graced the rosters and the score sheets. The pattern would leave a strong impression upon the hockey scene for years to come.

While play went on, plans for the new Memorial Arena were hardening. It was to be twice as big as the old arena and have seating for 2,500. Cost was estimated at $185,000.

Off on the Prairies, the Humboldt Indians were lacing up for their second season. Donning the pads was a homegrown product who was destined raise the rafters with his play and eventually take his place in the Hockey Hall of Fame. Glenn Hall skated with his home-town Indians for two years before he began his climb to hockey's greatest heights and the title of Mr. Goalie.

5

Championship at Last ______________ 1948-49

The second year of the Mainline Hockey League paralleled the first with Vernon and Kamloops thrashing it out for bragging rights.

What did change were team names as the Leafs became the Elks, the Legionnaires the Canadians and the Aces called themselves the Packers. To the changes was added a controversy which served only to amplify the already intense rivalries.

It was also the season that brought Kamloops its first ever provincial championship.

The Elks — Kamloops' Senior A squad that quested for the Allan Cup. (c. Riverside Coliseum Wall of Fame)

The Elks were still playing out of the old arena and had many of last year's squad suiting up again. Guy Ludgate, Grant MacLeod, Gordon Sunden, Eugene Hakansen, Frank Bobrowich, Clancey Ulveland, Frank Sharp, Bob Donald, Cliff Mills, Earl Hughes, Bill Schall, Al MacDougall and manager Art Huston were joined by Ross MacKay, Frank and Alex Kulay, Johnny Ursaki (playing coach), Wilf "Cookie" Cook, Rod Hull, Jack Beecher, Peter Schall, Bill Gannon, Walter Malahoff (goal) and former Humboldt Indian Jimmy Van Buskirk. During the course of the season, Huston stepped down and had his place taken by

Bob Affleck.

The season began and ended with Vernon. The Canadians took the opening game 3-2, but then the teams played virtually even up the rest of the year to finish 1-2 again. A more competitive Kelowna made the season a bit more entertaining.

Controversy erupted near the end of the season when the battle for first was still very much alive. Kamloops had obtained the services of Andre Fredette from Montreal in the latter part of December and were comfortable he was eligible to play. Later, the league executive decided Fredette was not, in fact, eligible and Kamloops was both fined and penalized . The penalty was the stripping of two wins and the awarding of those points to Vernon and Kelowna respectively. It didn't help that the league president who handed down the decision was Mayor Becker of Vernon. The decision virtually gave Vernon first place and a bye into the finals.

At the end of the 32 game season,Vernon was first with 40 points followed by Kamloops with 31 and Kelowna with 27. Without the penalty, Kamloops would have had 35 points to Vernon's 36 and the closing games of the season may well have been a bit more combative if the Elks still had a chance at first. It would not be the only season where controversy erupted. In fact, such situations seemed to continuously plague the league.

Season's end had Cliff Mills taking the scoring championship and two future Elks following close behind. Kenny Stewart of Kelowna and Buzz Mellor would later bring their act to Kamloops. The controversial Fredette had played only two games and had no points.

The league all-stars had Cliff Mills and Ursaki with the second string including Malahoff in net and Jack Kirk, a later season addition, and Cook out front.

A late acquisition by the team was a name familiar to NHL fans and his addition was to bring to the sagebrush city its greatest successes at the senior level.

Paul Thompson, the new coach, was anything but a routine acquisition. He had starred with the 1926 Calgary Canadians junior team which won the Memorial Cup and then went on to win the Stanley Cup with the New York Rangers in 1928 and Chicago Blackhawks in both 1934 and 1938. He finished second in team playoff scoring in both Chicago wins and twice made the all stars .

After retiring, he then took over the coaching reins in Chicago and in 1944 guided them to the Stanley Cup final. Leaving the NHL, he coached the amateur Vancouver Canucks of the Pacific Coast League to the league championship and the United States Amateur Championship. His list of successes were to continue in Kamloops.

Paul Thompson brought accomplishments of three Stanley Cups, one Memorial Cup, two NHL all star selections and more to the the Kamloops Elks.Under his coaching they reached their highest level and took the Savage Cup in 1950.
(c. KMA #5482)

Although Kelowna put up a better fight than the previous year, it still went out two straight in the best-of-three by scores of 12-2 and 6-4.

The Elks stormed out of the gate in Game 1 in Vernon and took the home side 5-2 in front of 1,800 fans. Not to be outdone, Vernon returned the favour with a 4-1 win in Kamloops before 1,237 fans. The return trip to Vernon had the Elks suffering the effects of a 3 1/2-hour train delay, yet it still took an empty net goal at 19:57 of the third for the Canadians to steal a 4-2 victory. Back in Kamloops, the Elks put on a show for their fans with an 8-4 drubbing of Vernon to force a fifth and deciding game.

It was a letdown when the Elks fell 8-1 to be eliminated, though the paper claimed the score did not indicate the play. The "what ifs" were bandied about. Without the Fredette penalty,would Kamloops have finished first and, if they had had home ice advantage, would they have taken the Canadians? Still, it was an improvement and the rivalries could only serve to heighten interest in the league.

The Intermediate B squad, which took the name Merchants, came under the guidance of Bill Gannon and advanced past Clinton and Salmon Arm before succumbing to the Lumby Flying Frenchman. It looked good at first when the Merchants beat Lumby in Game 1 of the two-game, total point-series by a score of 9-6 but, on home ice, the Frenchmen were dominant and skated away with a 9-3 series-clinching victory. Some of the players had skated with the Elks and thus began a pattern that would prevail throughout the days of the senior leagues. One player in particular, Don Campbell, was not through with hockey championships that season.

While the players were pounding away on the ice hockey interest was being verified by dollars. The Civic arena took in $10,570 against expenditures of $8,200 and, with all expenses accounted for, netted a $250 profit. Five hundred and two of the 700 available seasons tickets were sold with attendance averaging 1,000 per game and gates of $680.

The minor leagues still saw Vernon dominating as witnessed by the Kamloops juveniles falling 8-0 and the midgets 14-4 in league playdowns.

However the season was not over yet. Kamloops High School sent its reps, the Ramblers, to Kelowna for the Provincial High School Championship in March 1949. There, they contested for the Department of Physical Education and Recreation Trophy emblematic of hockey supremacy amongst British Columbia's 52 high schools. Kelowna was listed as the favourite and not surprisingly made the final.

The Kamloops High School Ramblers — Kamloops' first Provincial Champions. Back Row: (l-r) Ed Gary, Reg Norberg, Noel Paget, Tony Freeman, Jim Palmer, Stan Kato, Dickie Lee. Front Row: John Brkich, Jack Kirwan, Larry Candido, Nick "Zeke" Brkich, Bob Saklofsky, Jerry Brookall (Mgr.), Don Cambell (coach) (c. Larry Candido)

The local team composed of Jack Kirwan, Noel Paget,

Stan Kato, Bob Wyman, Johnny Brkich, Nick "Zeke" Brkich, Eddie Garay, Tony Freeman, Jim "Squirt" Ross, Dick Lee, Julian Palmer, Reg Norberg and "Mr. Zero" Larry Candido (the former Hub City Leaf stickboy) in net was managed by fellow student Gerry Goodal and coached by Kamloops' Merchant player Don Campbell.

Candido had been given the nickname Mr. Zero after the team had blanked Bralorne in the opening game 4-0 and then shutout Trapp Tech of Vancouver 3-0 in the semifinal to advance against Kelowna in the final. They were facing the favoured Owls before 1,500 fans in Kelowna's new War Memorial Arena.

When Kelowna got the first goal, on a deflection off of Brkich, there was joking on the Kelowna bench that Larry was not Mr. Zero anymore. When they went up 2-0 at the end of the first, it looked like the odds makers were right. With the second period drawing to a close, the Owls were up 3-1 and looked to be taking their lead to the dressing room. In a sudden turn of events, however, the Ramblers netted two quick goals to knot the score They came out inspired and were rewarded with a goal and a 4-3 lead. At the 15-minute mark, they extended it to 5-3. Kelowna pressed and managed to score to make it 5-4, but Candido's heroics held the fort and the Ramblers took the game and the championship. Kamloops had its first ever provincial hockey championship.

Years later, Candido recalled how close the game was. Kelowna had actually scored two other goals but one was called back on an offside and the other went in after the whistle had gone. The win seemed ironic to him as he had been billeted with Stan Burns, one of the Kelowna players.

Few Kamloops fans had made the trip, but the significance was not lost on the city's fathers as they were there, led by the mayor, to greet the conquering heroes on their return home.

The Ramblers could wear their red, black and white team jackets with the pride of knowing they were the first team ever to bring a provincial trophy to the sagebrush city. Two of them, Kato and Lee, were not done yet.

Larry Candido — "Mr. Zero". (c. Larry Candido)

6

Savage Season ____________ 1949-50

The 1949-50 season started and ended like no other.

It began with the opening of the new Memorial Arena. In its beginning, it was one of the best arenas in the province and drew attention to Kamloops in much the same way Riverside Coliseum would many years later. It first drew the attention of Kenny Mackenzie and his New Westminster Royals of the professional Pacific Coast Hockey League. Mackenzie brought his Royals to Kamloops for their training camp and had the honour of seeing them and the Seattle Ironmen play the first hockey game in the new facility.

Memorial Arena 1949 — At last a level playing field.
(c. KMA #1798)

More than 1,500 fans took in the game which ended in a thrilling 4-4 tie when Seattle came back to score with only five seconds remaining. The Royals, with a number of players who became familiar with Kamloops fans either as players or opponents, established a working agreement that began a series of hockey connections between Kamloops and the Royal City that persisted for many years.

Playing for the Royals were Earl Betker in goal, Ken Ullyot, Don Slater, Willie Schmidt and Dick Warwick, all of whom sooner or later left their mark in Kamloops. In the case of Warwick, he would, in turn, be hated and loved. Even the legendary MacKenzie would bring his spark to Kamloops before his hockey days were over.

After the Ironmen and Royals had their moments, the main tenants took over. The Elks and their foes were not only playing in a new arena, but they were also playing at a higher level as the Okanagan Mainline Senior A Hockey League threw its hat into Senior A competition and the quest for the Allan Cup. The three Interior teams were joined by two coastal teams, the Nanaimo Clippers and the Kerrisdale Monarchs.

Holdovers Kirk, Ursaki, Malahoff, MacDougall, Mills, Ludgate, Swaine, Sunden and Gwynne Lovett were joined by Earl Betker, Don Johnson, Art Thomson, Ken Terry, Bob Irvine from Vernon, Walter McIntyre, Billy Hryciuk, Buzz Mellor from Vernon, Steve Witiuk and Don Campbell (not to be confused with the Don Campbell of last season's Merchants). Paul Thompson was behind the bench for his first full season and Cy Young handled GM duties.

Competition was fierce that year with the two teams from the coast and a much improved Kelowna squad. Each team took turns capturing and holding first place until on Feb. 22, 1950, the Sentinel flashed the headline "Elks Win the league."

More than 2,000 fans were on hand to see Kamloops take the title with a 4-1 win over Kelowna and get a bye into the final for the Interior. Vernon had to take on Kelowna this time but the result was not in doubt. Vernon and Kamloops were to slug it out for the third year in a row.

In Game 1 at Kamloops, history appeared to be repeating itself as Vernon was up 2-0 at the end of the first. The 2,623 fans had little to cheer about. The second period changed all that as the Elks came back to tie it at 9:58 and then pot another at 17:00 to take a 3-2 lead into the dressing room. The third was all Kamloops and they skated away with a 4-2 series opening win.

Some 2,800 Vernon fans turned up for Game 2. Unaccustomed to losing to Kamloops in the playoffs, they saw their Canadians fall 5-3 on home ice and face possible elimination in three straight going back to Kamloops.

Game 3 was worth the price of admission and more. Some 2,500 Kamloops faithful hoped to see their boys eliminate the arch rival which had pretty much had the run of the hockey scene for a number of years. At the end of the first, the teams were deadlocked at one and, at the end of two, Kamloops held on to a narrow 4-3 lead. The third had Kamloops go up 5-3, but Vernon closed again to within one. Kamloops went ahead 6-4 only to see the Canadians come back again to make it 6-5. At 17:10, Vernon took the air out of the sails with the tying goal. The teams played on in what was, in effect, sudden death. Overtime looked a certainty but it was not to be. At 19:57 former Canadian Buzz Mellor drove a stake into the hearts of Vernon with the game-winning goal. The Elks had their revenge and with their fans revelled in the moment.

Unlike previous years, the Interior champion had to beat out a team from the Coast before it could claim the Willoughby Cup and advance any further. That foe was to be Nanaimo and the series began with controversy.

Nanaimo claimed it was unfair all games were to be played in the Interior although Kelowna was hosting the Nanaimo home games and that was hardly friendly territory for the Elks. It did not start well for Kamloops.

In Game 1 former Humboldt Indian and league scoring leader Dick Warwick led the Clippers to a 5-2 victory to snap the Elks' playoff unbeaten string. In regular season play, Kamloops had taken the series 4-2 but the playoffs were a new season. Game 2 was set for Kelowna.

Billy Hryciuk stole the show with five goals in an 8-5 Elks' victory. Again in Kelowna for Game 3, it was goalie Betker's time to shine as the Elks came out ahead 5-2 to put Nanaimo on the brink of elimination. Game 4 went in Kamloops.

This time there was no doubt. At the end of one, it was 2-1 Elks. At the end of two, the score read 4-2 and, with the final whistle, the Elks took the Willoughby Cup with a 6-2 home-ice victory. Sixteen teams were left in the hunt for the Allan Cup and Kamloops was one of them. Their next test was the toughest yet.

To take the Savage Cup, symbolic of the Provincial Senior A Championship, they had to get past the legendary Trail Smoke Eaters and they would have to do it in Trail's new $500,000 state-of-the art arena.

Rested and waiting, the Smoke Eaters took out a train weary Elks squad 7-4 in Game 1. Looking at a must-win situation in Game 2 the Elks held on to win 4-3 and even the series. The Smoke Eaters were set back on their heels in the third game when the Elks came out even stronger to take it 7-4 and put Trail on the verge of elimination in their own backyard.

Game 4 was described as a knock-down-drag-'em-out battle before 3,700 fans in which the reffing was loose. The Elks garnered a 2-0 lead at the end of the first but saw it turn into a 3-2 deficit early in the second frame. Regaining their composure, the Kamloops squad surged ahead to end the period up 5-3. The third saw only one goal and that went to Kamloops as it took the game 6-3, the series and the Savage Cup. The Mellor, Campbell, Hryciuk line had dominated with seven points while the Kirk/ Johnston tandem had starred defensively. Kamloops was the British Columbia Champ.

The fans were waiting in Kamloops for the greatest hockey celebration yet seen. A motorcade was organized to pick up the team in Spences Bridge rather than have it wait for the connecting train to bring it to town.

The champs were transferred into open cars at the Royal Canadian Navy ammunition depot, then outside of town, and paraded through through the city streets led by a B.C. Police escort. The Elks band and banner-bearing Jaycees accompanied them with M.C. "Cranny" Cranston of the Elks and GM Cy Young sitting on the hood of a car holding the handsome Savage Cup. It seemed like every politician and city VIP got into the parade as it wound its way slowly through town cheered on by hundreds of fans. There were now only five teams left in the Allan Cup hunt and Kamloops was still alive.

Games 1 and 2 of the first inter-provincial series Kamloops had ever played were to be held in Kamloops. The Calgary Stampeders had won the right to face the Elks after they put out the Edmonton Flyers four games to two. Although heavily favoured, they were facing a highly energized Kamloops squad on its own turf.

The Stampeders were stunned in Game 1 as the Elks stormed out of the gate to upset them and the experts with a convincing 6-1 victory. The elation was short-lived when Calgary came back to take Game 2 5-2 and leave Kamloops with the daunting task of having to win the series on Calgary ice. The remaining games of the best of seven series were to be in Alberta even if they went the full seven. Still, Kamloops had pulled it out against Trail so it was possible.

Despite playing well in Game 3 the Elks went down 5-3. Even more frustrating was Game 4 when they outplayed Calgary but still lost 3-2. They were on the verge of seeing their Allan Cup dream end. In the end, it did as they had nothing left for Game 5 and bowed out after a 6-3 loss. Three of the players who had helped eliminate them would soon be suiting up in Elks colours. Johnny Milliard, Jack Taggart and Gunnar Carlson would be cheered when they next played at Memorial.

The defeated Elks were greeted as winners by the Kamloops fans and honours rained down on them at a gala dinner and dance. The success of the team in the their first year at the Senior A level and the opening of Kamloops' new arena put other hockey news in the shadow. Yet, it was there and the local talent was improving.

The Provincial Senior A Champions — the Kamloops Elks 1949-50. (c. KMA #5475)
Left to Right: Back Row: Cliff Mills, Merrick Cranston, Paul Thompson, C.Y. Young, Ellard Hebb, Centre Row: Ken Terry, Don Clarke, Don Campbell, Bill Hryciuk, Don Johnson, Al McDougall, Johnny Hryciuk, Jack Kirk, Bottom Row: Jack Forsey, Al Swaine, Art Thompson, Walt Malahoff, Earl Betker, Johnny Ursaki, Steve Witiuk, Tommy Love.

The intermediate competition abandoned by the Elks was taken up by the Falcons and another local squad that went by the name Stampeders. In their sole match against each other, the Falcons prevailed 6-3. Although they got past Kelowna in Round 1, the Falcons were again sent packing by the Lumby Flying Frenchmen.

The high school Ramblers with a 4-0 win over Rutland and a 9-0 shellacking of Trapp Tech looked set to repeat as provincial champions. This time, however, the Kelowna Owls took them out in a close semifinal by a score of 8-7 and then went on to win the province.

Minor league teams were clearly showing improvements.

The Juveniles beat out Vernon 11-10 in a two-game, total-point series to win the Vernon Lions Club Cup before bowing out to a superior Vancouver team. The Juniors advanced past Nelson before being stopped by Nanaimo and the bantams reached the Okanagan final against victorious Kelowna.

It would not be long before Kamloops minor hockey began turning eyes in the province.

The 1949-50 season had been the best yet and it added fuel to an already hot hockey fire.

7

After the Party's Over ______________ 1950-51

When Paul Thompson reassembled the maroon and white of the Elks for the 1950-51 season, he was minus a few stars who were tempted elsewhere.

The Calgary Stampeders had been so impressed with the Mellor-Campbell-Hryciuk line they took it lock stock and barrel along with Don Clark on defence. Thompson added Kenny Stewart (from Kelowna) who had played briefly under him when he coached the Chicago Blackhawks and later grabbed Buddy Evans from Kelowna, too. Both players were destined to leave a lasting impression on Kamloops hockey. Coming along from Calgary was Gunnar Carlson and from the Edmonton Flyers Bernie Bathgate.

It proved to be a season of hopes and disappointments.

The new interlocking schedule gave the fans a chance to see the Trail Smoke Eaters, Kimberley Dynamiters, Nelson Maple Leafs and Spokane Flyers of the Western International Hockey League.

The other players lacing up for the beginning of the year were Lorne Lussier (goal), Frank Kulay, who was later traded to Kelowna for Buddy Evans, Don Johnston, Ken Terry, Mike Fischler, Rod Booth, Frank Willock, Neil Winchester, Finlay "Moose"McNaughton (a former Humboldt Indian) and Johnny Ursaki along with trainer Ellard Hebb and general manager Cy Young.

A February team photo of the Savage Cup champs added Al Swaine, a returned Buzz Mellor, Peter Wywrot, Ivan Wilson and another ex-Humboldt Indian Bud Andrews.

The first home game of the season was full of the fanfare that went with being reigning champions. Some 2,493 fans crowded Memorial Arena for the opening match against Vernon and enjoyed seeing Thompson receive a plaque recognizing the Elks run of the previous season and nabbing of both the Willoughby and Savage Cups. Mayor Moffat, after a brief speech extolling the values of "friendly rivalry," dropped the puck. A perfect evening was topped off with a 7-2 victory.

All season long Nanaimo, Kamloops and Kelowna fought it out for first place while Kerrisdale and Vernon struggled below .500. Things got even better for the Elks when Don Campbell rejoined the team and Harvey Stein was added to the roster. Yet, at the end of the season, it was Nanaimo, with future Elk Andy Clovechok in the lineup, that stole the title. Kamloops had to play a round robin against Kelowna and Vernon with the two surviving teams going head to head in a best-of-three semifinal. Surprisingly, it was Vernon and not Kelowna that joined Kamloops in the semi.

The Elks had taken the Canadians in 12 of 16 games that season and outscored them 89 to 65, so it was not unrealistic to see them as heavy favourites to advance. Keith Gagne', writing for the Sentinel, had cautioned early in the season Vernon was a team to watch out for, but it was difficult to see how a team so far behind them in the standings could pose a threat. Yet, when Vernon rolled over Kamloops 7-3 in Vernon and took the series in two straight it left both Kamloops and Kelowna scratching their heads. Ursaki had reason to smile, however, as Kamloops had released him part way through the season and he was picked up Vernon.

In interlocking play, Kamloops felled Nelson, Trail and Spokane in their first tilts. The loss to Kimberley was rather galling as former Elk Bill Hryciuk potted two goals and an assist against his old squad.

At season's end five Elks adorned the all-star teams, including Stein (the league scoring leader) and Johnston on the first team and Lussier, Fischler and Peter Wywrot on the second. Veteran Stewart finished fifth in team scoring with 21 goals and 31 assists but his greatest contribution to Kamloops' hockey was yet to come..

The Senior B team that year simply went by the name Stars and, with numerous former Elks and Leafs in its lineup, marched past the Vernon Coldstream Cruisers by scores of 13-6 and 18-5 in the first round of the playoffs. Cliff Mills was a one-man wrecking crew as he scored 10 goals. Despite their subsequent elimination at the hands of Trail, the victory over Vernon helped somewhat in redeeming some lost civic pride.

Little solace was offered with minor hockey as the bantams advanced the farthest before being eliminated in the Okanagan final by Kelowna.

So, after the party, local hockey enthusiasts suffered a hangover whose only cure was an improved 1951-52 season.

Kenny Stewart — On ice stardom was to be eclipsed by his coaching success. (c. Kenny Stewart)

8

No Need to be Coy________________1951-52

Optimism prevailed for the Elks as the 1951-52 season rolled around.

Rejoining the team was former scoring star Billy Hryciuk along with former Calgary Stampeders Johnny Milliard and Jack Taggart. To this mix came 28-year-old Andy Clovechok from last year's Willoughby Cup champion Nanaimo Clippers. Buddy Evans, Don Campbell, Harvey Stein and Don Andrews were back.

Kamloops star Johnny Milliard as a member of the Portland Buckaroos. (c. Gloria Milliard)

The team even came close to nabbing future minor league pro star Guyle Fielder who had come to camp from the Lethbridge Native Sons. Kenny MacKenzie, in town for his New West Royals' training camp, spotted the budding star and whisked him away to the pros.

The power of the Elks was confirmed in their first two games as Lorne Lussier shutout Kelowna 4-0 in Game 1 and Clovechok got his first hat trick of the season in the next game, a 4-2 win in Kelowna. United with Bernie Bathgate, who he had played with in both Edmonton and Vancouver, and Milliard, Clovechok was part of one of the greatest lines to ever play in the old league or, indeed, Kamloops. Together, they terrorized the circuit and set a record unlikely to ever be touched anywhere. By mid-November, after an 11-1 victory over Kerrisdale Monarchs in front of 2,193 home fans, in which Stein scored three goals in 39 seconds, the Elks were 12 points up on their nearest rivals.

Buddy Evans — A cornerstone in Kamloops' hockey success. (c. Buddy Evans)

Andy Clovechok with Allan Cup taken by his Edmonton Flyers. (c. Andy Clovechok)

During one of their few losses that year, 5-4 to Trail, a face from the past emerged in the stands. William Brennan, who had guarded the Kamloops' net during its earliest years and whose name graced the first trophy played for in Kamloops, the Brennan Cup, had not been to a hockey game since 1937. Kamloops had lost that game to Merritt which led Brennan to suggest perhaps he should stay away for another 14 years.

The early optimism was well-founded as on Feb. 4, 1952, the sports headlines read "Elks Clinch League Title with Win Over Canadians." Their 8-3 victory over Vernon had nailed down their conquest of a league which had grown to incorporate Dick Warwick's Penticton Vees.

At season's end, Clovechok had five hat tricks, Bathgate three and Milliard a four-goal game. More remarkably all three had tied for the league scoring lead with 79 points. Up to that, date such a feat had never been accomplished and it is unlikely it has been since. The dominance of the Elks was further demonstrated by Hryciuk finishing fourth, Stein sixth and Gunnar

Carlson eighth. Bathgate, Milliard and coach Paul Thompson landed on the first all-star team, while Clovechok, Lussier and defenceman Taggart filled out the second squad.

They took first with 72 points, followed by Vernon at 54 and third place Kelowna, which did not even achieve a .500 season.

Buoyed by their season dominance over the league and Kelowna, which they had beaten six times out of 10 meetings and outscored 41-32, the Elks were further encouraged with their Game 1 3-0 win in the league finals. Each member of the top line got a goal. It seemed like nothing, even a Kelowna team that had squeezed past Vernon, was going to stop their advance this year. But it did.

The Milliard, Bathgate and Clovechok line. All three tied for the league scoring lead with 79 points each. (c. Andy Clovechok/Inland Sentinel)

In one of the biggest disappointments in Kamloops' hockey history, the wheels came off the track. The Packers thumped the Elks 7-2 in the second game and then squeaked out a 4-3 victory at Memorial Arena to take the series lead. Game 4 in Kelowna ended it all with Kamloops being eliminated by a 5-0. A team that had aspirations of an Allan Cup challenge was knocked off in what was easily the biggest upset of the year in Senior A hockey.

Years later, reflecting on that series, Clovechok said he felt it was Kamloops' dependence on the big line that hurt it. Kelowna's ability to shut it down was the difference. Yet, he would some day have his revenge on Kelowna.

Again a great season had come to a crashing halt. The difference this year was fans would find joy from an unexpected source.

The Besette Loggers took the city league and earned the right to carry the city's colours in the quest for the Coy Cup, albeit with a lineup drawn from the city's best players. Campbell was initially selected to coach the team.

The Coy Cup had originally been a tournament cup played for in Victoria. Donated by Colonel Coy of the 50th Gordon Highlanders, it became symbolic of the Provincial Intermediate Hockey Championship in the 1919-20 season. Despite a number of efforts, Kamloops had never even made it to the cup finals. Other Interior towns, such as Merritt, Enderby and especially Vernon, had the privilege of sipping from the mug. This year, Kamloops felt it had a shot.

In exhibition play, the Kamloops team's only two losses had come at the hands of the Prince George Lumbermen. They had defeated Vernon, Clinton and Revelstoke and were pitted against Clinton to start the playoffs.

Familiar faces dotted the lineup. Johnny Ursaki, Walter Malahoff, Cliff Mills, Bob Irvine, Grant MacLeod, Al MacDougall and Ernie Hughes were all former Elks or Leafs. Other locals joining the team included Freddie and Archie Gaber, Ron Evensen, Stan Kato, Tosh Takenaka, Joe Paquette, Ernie Langlois, Kenny Dore, Dean Desireau, Leo Delbuchia, Dickie Lee, Nick O'Brien, Pat Dohm and Ken Berry.

Not surprisingly, Clinton offered little resistance and fell two straight by scores of 13-4 and 14-6. Vernon was expected to be a tougher test, but Mills' five goals in an 11-4 opening-game romp suggested otherwise. Vernon did come back to tie Game 2 9-9, but was eliminated on total points. The Vancouver PNE Indians were next on the list and Kamloops added veteran Kenny Stewart to the mix.

The Indians went the same way as the others, falling in two straight by scores of 11-2 and 8-6 at Memorial. Kamloops was in the Coy Cup final for the first time. It was not be their last nor was it the last time they faced a team from British Columbia's hockey hotbed of Trail in the final. Although it had to play the entire series in Kamloops, Trail was the same team that had won the Western Canada Intermediate Championship the year before.

In Game 1, Trail was leading 4-1 early in the third when the Loggers began to make their comeback. The home crowd was in an uproar as the Loggers stormed back to tie the match and then go ahead 5-4. The barn was hopping until Trail settled it down by tying the score with less than three minutes left. Game 1 had to be settled in overtime. Still the crowd was not denied when at 8:04 of the first overtime Irvine, on a pass from Mills and Berry, gave Kamloops the 6-5 win.

Game 2 was no easier. In the first period, Al Swaine put Kamloops up at the six minute mark but four minutes later Trail knotted the score. Within 26 seconds, Swaine gave Kamloops the lead back and they took it to the dressing room.

The second started well as Stewart set up Irvine and then Mills for a 4-1 lead. Trail persisted and, by the end of the second, the comfortable lead dwindled to 4-3.

Again Kamloops pulled ahead in the third when Ursaki and Swaine set up Dore for the 5-3 marker. Three minutes later Trail climbed to within one and, then within a few seconds, tied the game up. And so they battled until 14:05 when Mills took a shot from the blueline that beat the Trail goalie. Trail stormed the Kamloops' net trying to find the tying goal but Malahoff denied them and, at the final whistle, Kamloops had won the Coy Cup.

Kamloops First Intermediate A Provincial Champs. The Coy Cup winning Besette Loggers 1951-52. Front: Dickie Lee, Tosh Takanaka, Johnny Ursaki, Al Swain, Cliff Mills, Bob Irvine, Dean Desireau, Kenny Doire, J. Paquette, Stan Berry, Stan Kato, Grant MacLeod, Ernie Hughes, Al McDougall, Kenny Stewart, Leo Delbuchia, Walt Malahoff. At back: Sam Corea, Sandy Sandford, Doc Christie, Mike Murphy, Foss Besette. (c. Riverside Coliseum Wall of Fame.)

Nine former Leafs or Elks shared in the moment of bringing Kamloops its third provincial hockey championship, of some form, in four years. In their midst, the former high school Ramblers Kato and Lee experienced the added joy of being on two of them.

The road led on to the Canmore Legionnaires, the quest for the Edmonton Journal Trophy and a chance to reach the national final.

The visiting Canmore team disappointed the 1,100 fans at Memorial by taking Game 1 7-4 and then added insult to injury by taking Game 2 7-5. In a best-of-five series, it looked like it was game over for the provincial champs. Perhaps Canmore was too sure of itself for the Loggers put on their best show in an 8-3 win and then showed it was no fluke by taking Game 4 8-6. The team looking to bow out in three had now forced a fifth and deciding game in Canmore.

Some 1,900 Canmore fans roared their approval when their boys jumped out into a 3-0 lead by 7:28 of the first. Stewart silenced the crowd as his two goals closed the gap. At the end of one, Canmore was ahead 4-2. In the second, Canmore got the only marker. At 4:23 of the third, Irvine brought back memories of the comeback against Trail when they were down 4-1. This time it was not to be as Canmore scored next and carried on to eliminate Kamloops with an 8-4 victory.

The Loggers had reason to hold their heads up as they had travelled farther down the playoff road than any Kamloops team before them.

Records are confused on the coaching of the team with reference being made to both Ursaki and Stewart as coaches . Regardless, these two former teammates with the Lethbridge Maple Leafs were major factors in the team's success. Stewart would return to Alberta with more challenges in the not too distant future.

Kamloops was getting used to having provincial trophies.

Off in Humboldt, the Indians had their most successful season to date under new coach Scotty Munro, a name that became synonymous with western junior hockey. The team took the Saskatchewan Junior Hockey League championship with a roster that included an 18-year-old centre by the name of Ernie Vincent MacLean. He would become famous under his nickname "Punch" and be associated with the franchise in three of its incarnations.

9

Look Out Below 1952-53

The Elks were hoping to atone for the disappointments of the last two seasons and all the signs suggested it was not an unrealistic goal.

The Andy Clovechok, Johnny Milliard, Andy Bathgate line was back intact and they were joined by Billy Hryciuk, Buddy Evans, Jack Taggart, Gunnar Carlson, Ken Terry and, later, newcomer Norm Larsen. Budding star Hal Gordon took over in net as Lorne Lussier went to Vernon. Paul Thompson remained behind the bench.

The regular season champs — the Kamloops Elks. The team that could have gone all the way. Back row: (l-r) Andy Clovechok, Ken Terry, Dick Kotanen, Herbie Lunmark, Norm Larsen, Danny Mac Dougall Middle: Cy Young (trainer), Johnny Milliard, Bernie Bathgate, Jack Taggart, Jack Smith, Hal Brown, Paul Thompson Front: Lorne Slater, Bill Hryciuk, Gunnar Carlson, Buddy Evans, Bob "Busher" Jackson, Hal Gordon. (c. Andy Clovechok)

The opening game of the season was in Penticton against last year's cellar-dwelling Vees. This season, they were armed with both Bill and Dick Warwick and surprised the favoured Elks 5-4. The big game, however, was the home opener against the team that put them out last year. Some 2,000 fans at Memorial Arena were not disappointed as the Elks sent Kelowna packing 5-1. The season proved tight as all four teams were competitive.

In November, novelty and tragedy hit the Elks as they donned new home uniforms and then heard popular trainer Ellard Hebb had been seriously injured in a car accident. Cy Young took over his position. Ellard never returned.

At the start of December, the Elks were struggling around .500 and looking up at first. That spot was held by a Penticton team which had added a third Warwick, Grant, former rookie of the year in the NHL with the New York Rangers. Still, by the end of the month, Kamloops had put together a seven-game winning streak to capture first and sit five points up on the Vees.

In January 1953, the Sentinel ran a photo of the 1940-41 Chicago Blackhawks in order to show its influence on the Okanagan Senior A Hockey League. The coach was Paul Thompson and there was Bill Carse (coach of Penticton), Phil Hergesheimer (coach of Kelowna) and Dave "Red" MacKay (coach of Vernon).

By mid-February, the battle was over when a 7-3 victory by Kamloops over Penticton in a penalty-filled game gave them the regular season bragging rights and the new Becker Trophy. The much improved Vees had to settle for third, though, they had the pleasure of taking the season-ending game against the Elks 6-2.

Kamloops finished with a 30-21-3 record and outscored the opposition 246 to 210 in the 54-game season. Gordon had the best goals-against average in the league and five of the top scorers were Elks. Gordon, Dick Kotanen, Paul Thompson and Johnny Milliard made the first string all-stars while Taggart landed on the second. They took this and their second straight regular season pennant against fourth place Vernon while Kelowna and Penticton squared off.

Although they had won 11 of the 18 games against the Canadians they knew from the past two seasons victory in the regular season meant nothing in the playoffs. They took Game 1 convincingly 7-2, but then Lussier came back to stone them 5-0 in Game 2 in his old stomping grounds. They redeemed themselves in the third contest as Evans notched a hat trick, Clovechok garnered three assists and Larsen potted two in a 7-1 rout. Game 4 went to Kamloops 3-1 and Game 5 ended in a 4-4 draw. Vernon had nothing left for Game 6 and was decimated 10-1. The Elks moved on to face Penticton.

The Vees had taken out last year's champs Kelowna. The two teams that had spelled disappointment the last two seasons were gone.

Game 1 at Memorial Arena was tight and going into the final minute was tied 2-2. With less than 10 seconds remaining, it looked like Penticton was going to steal a point but it got worse. With only four seconds left, Dick Warwick shot an arrow into the Elks' heart and the Vees won 3-2.

Game 2 in Penticton was no help either as Ivan McLelland backstopped his team to a 6-3 victory.

Back in Kamloops, the Elks finally pulled it together to take a 4-2 victory and then returned to Penticton to take one point with a 2-2 tie.

Home ice brought another win, 5-2, for Kamloops but Game 6 on the road went to Penticton. Game 7 was in Kamloops. A tie was no good for the Elks. They needed a win to stay alive.

At the start of the third, Kamloops was holding on to a 2-0 lead. Penticton got one back but, with less than a minute remaining, Kamloops was holding on to its one-goal lead. The fans were thinking Game 8 but at 19:22, as he had done in Game 1, Warwick broke their hearts. On assists from brothers, Bill and Grant, he tied the game. It stayed 2-2 and, with the one point, Penticton took the Willoughby Cup. Winning in dramatic fashion became the trade mark of the Vees and the brothers Warwick.

For the third season in a row, the Elks had excelled in the regular season only to be dropped on their ears in the playoffs. Still, they had plenty of company that year as the Vees made it all the way to the Allan Cup finals. Though they lost, they were to return and go beyond Canada in their future exploits.

On a more sinister note, problems were beginning to crop up around the arena as the team's executives and the Memorial Arena Commission began quarrelling over deficits. It was the first crack in what was to prove a weakening dike.

The Besette Loggers were again the toast of intermediate play and went 9-1 in exhibition play. Kenny Stewart was still lacing them up on the squad as the playdowns started against the Penticton/Summerland team. It proved no contest as the Loggers prevailed 9-4 and 9-1 to advance to the Provincial final for the second straight year. Again the foe was Trail.

All games were set for Trail, which was bad enough, but a 12-5 thrashing in Game 1 left little room for optimism. Though they played better in Game 2 they still lost 6-5 and were put on the verge of elimination. After managing to get a 2-0 lead in Game 3 Kamloops saw the walls slowly crumble as they fell 4-2 and went golfing. Trail was to prove a thorn in the side of Kamloops' hockey teams for many years to come.

The minor leagues were giving local fans reason for optimism for the future. Young stars, such as Melvin Recchi, in net for a 4-0 victory over the Vernon peewees in February 1953, suggested local hockey pride was not in danger.

The bantam team went the farthest as it captured the Ted Martin Trophy emblematic of the Okanagan championship. In net for that team was a young lad named Don Wilkie who was destined to see his star rise even higher in the years ahead.

The Kamloops' minor hockey system was improving under the tutelage of an involved sports community. Two names stood out above the others in the persons of Don Reid and Hec MacKenzie as these two became hockey mentors whose praises were sung by many a player, parent and fan.

With the start of each new season, the dedicated fan had plenty of opportunity to get his fill of hockey and see local players leaving an impression.

10

Make that Two Cups Please__________1953-54

For four years, the start of each new season had been filled with a sense of promise with old stars returning and new prospects joining the Elks' fold.

The year, 1953-54 saw Hal Gordon return along with the Andy Clovechok line, Jack Taggart, Billy Hryciuk and Buddy Evans plus new players Nick Pyevach, John Young, Fred Creighton and Jim Fleming. Ken Terry and Ken Booth filled out the roster for the opening game.

However, a major piece of the puzzle was missing. Paul Thompson had stepped down from coaching and his position was taken over by playing coach Paul Ullyot. The success of the Elks had been anchored as much in Thompson as it had in any of the stars.

Doubts were confirmed when the Elks struggled out of the gate losing their first three games. Ullyot picked up Marlowe MacDonald and Chuck Henderson and hoped Game 4 would produce some improvement. The visitors were to be the Kimberley Dynamiters, from the WIHL, which had on its roster some familiar names in the persons of Earl Betker in goal, Norm Larsen and Don Campbell. Ullyot got his wish as the Elks finally put a win on the board at 8-5.

One game doesn't end a slide and with Christmas approaching Kamloops was struggling in and out of the basement. Ullyot grabbed Don Slater from the New Westminster Royals and hoped for improvement in the new year. Surprisingly, the Elks were saving their best performances for the powerhouse Penticton Vees.

Matters got worse as Bernie Bathgate, dissatisfied with his own play, left the team. Then Pyevach was released. Despite trades and additions, the end of 1953 saw the Elks with their worst record since the team began. Bill Swarbrick, Mark Keaton and, later, Fred Denny joined the squad.

Redemption seemed to come with the new year as the Elks took seven of their first eight games. Hryciuk, Clovechok, Milliard, Evans, Fleming and Henderson all got hot at the same time. Team confidence went up against the Vees in a two-game series with the added incentive of facing their old team mate Bathgate, who had returned with the foe. Alas, Penticton took both games and rubbed it in with Bathgate netting two goals and three assists in a 6-2 Vees win at Memorial Arena.

Season's end had Kamloops holding third ahead of the Vernon team that had gone from first to last in a dramatic tailspin. Kamloops lined up against Kelowna in the semis. The playoffs did not help spirits as the once proud Elks bowed out four games to two. Kelowna fell, in turn, to a Vees team destined to win the Allan Cup that year and go on to represent Canada at the World Hockey Championships the following season.

Kamloops' worst season had few saving graces apart from defensive stalwart Taggart landing on the second all-star team. Troubles did not end there as financial concerns were becoming more apparent. The Nov. 20, 1953 Sentinel noted the fan club, known as the Elks' Aiders, were taking on the job of raising $2,300 to obtain players.

Kenny Stewart was back as a player/coach with the intermediate squad that continued to boast a smattering of ex-Elks. Coming up against Vernon in the playdowns, the Loggers lost Game 1 8-7 but protested on the grounds that Vernon had used an ineligible player, Sarge Sammartino. They followed it up with an 8-1 win which, when coupled with their successful protest, gave them the series. Few teams challenged that year so, with their win over Vernon, they advanced to the Coy Cup final. Waiting for them was their usual foe, Trail.

Despite playing all the games at Memorial Arena, the Loggers bowed out three games to none with one game tied. If senior hockey offered little for the fans that year, minor hockey did.

The bantams again challenged for the Okanagan Championship and the Ted Martin Trophy. In Game 1 in Kamloops, they took Vernon 5-2 and then hung on in Vernon for a 3-2 loss which gave them the series on total points.

The biggest story was the midgets whose roster included Everett Millar and Don Wilkie in goal, Gordon Tansley, Hugh Fossett, Dave Gillespie, Bud Schollen, Bob Gannon, Al Raymond, Bruce Harrison, Gulchern Singh, Doug Smith, Wayne Olsen, Jerry Stenson, Norio Sakaki, Dick Sawada, Tom Miyahara and Ronnie Baker. George Morton coached and Cece Williamson was general manager.

They had to start the playoffs on unfriendly ice in Kelowna but they still put away last year's provincial champs 6-1. Taking momentum back to Kamloops, they put away their foes 7-1.

Then came Trail. Game 1 was close but Kamloops held on for a 5-4 win. Their follow-up 7-3 victory dropped Trail from the race.

The midgets next journeyed to Kerrisdale and, in a hard fought contest lost Game 1 4-3. They couldn't afford to lose another game. Bob Gannon's hat trick in Game 2 was not enough as Kerrisdale stormed back to tie the game. Bud Schollen came to the rescue with an unassisted goal which gave the boys a 5-4 victory and a chance in Game 3.

It was no contest. The line of Singh, Stenson and Raymond broke out for the first time in the series and, with a 6-2 victory, the midgets took home the Cromie Cup as provincial champs. A frustrated Kerrisdale team skated off the ice without shaking hands and no formal presentation of the cup was held.

This was made up for when the squad returned home. There, waiting for them, were the dignitaries of the city and sports agencies as well as hundreds of local fans. The Sentinel beamed on March 22, 1954 with the headline "Heroes Welcome for our Champions" accompanying a photo of the winning team.

If the fortunes of the seniors were waning, juniors were waxing. The future looked promising.

11

Season of Change ________________ 1954-55

Not unsurprisingly the disappointing 1953-54 season led to changes.

Ullyot was gone as coach, being replaced by former Kelowna Packer (and former Chicago Black Hawk) Phil Hergesheimer. Returning were Gunnar Carlson, Billy Hryciuk, Johnny Milliard, Don Slater, Jack Taggart, Buddy Evans, Andy Clovechok and Ken Terry. New faces included Norm Knippleberg, Andy Defelice, Fred Creighton, Doug Stevenson (goalie), Sandy Hucul, crowd favourite Joe Con, Leo Lucchini, Joe Connors, Bill McCully, Mick Gilday, App Dorohoy, "Boomer" Rodzinyak (goalie), Gordie Kerr, Howie Amundrud and Dave Duke. PaulThompson was still around as honourary president and Hal Gordon had moved off to Vernon.

The community also had the excitement of hosting the New York Rangers training camp and got to see Alan Stanley, Harry Howell, Andy Bathgate, Johnny Bower, Camile Henry, Larry Popein and Dean Prentice.

The Elks campaign started off against the Allan Cup champion Penticton Vees, scheduled to head off to the Worlds to represent Canada. Although they dropped the opening game in Penticton, they came back to take their opener against these same Vees by a score of 7-3.

As the season progressed, it became apparent Vernon and Penticton were going to fight it out for first while Kamloops and Kelowna vied for third. The Elks captured that spot with 49 points over Kelowna's 44 and rightfully expected to have home ice in the first round. They were then informed that, despite their better season, it was to be Kelowna with home ice advantage. Because Penticton was going off to play internationally, Vernon got the bye.

An irate Elks squad got home ice back in a hurry as they took Game 1 in Kelowna 4-3. Back in Kamloops in Game 2, Milliard potted a hat trick as the Elks' 7-1 victory put them within a game of the final. In Game 3 Milliard starred with Rodzinyak in taking the game and the series 3-0. A rested Vernon Canadians team, backstopped by former Elk Gordon, was waiting.

A tired Elks squad dropped Game 1 5-3 in Vernon and then lost a heartbreaker 2-1 at home. Despite outplaying Vernon in their own arena in Game 3 they lost 5-3 and faced the prospect of being swept. Back home with an inspired crowd behind them, they managed a tie but that was the best they could manage as they bowed out in Game 5 3-1.

The season was not without its successes as Hryciuk finished second in scoring behind Grant Warwick and Milliard managed eighth. Rodzinyak had the most shutouts (two) and Kerr, acquired late in the season, was the only league player to average a point a game. Stalwart defenceman, Jack Taggart, joined the Penticton Vees overseas and brought back a gold medal to Kamloops.

Financial problems were increasingly plaguing the team and the league with declining attendance, increased costs and taxes taking the bulk of the blame. The season started with the team holding a $293.10 deficit which was praised as being better than any of the other teams. Still, it was financial problems that were pointed to in November as the reason for releasing Clovechok, Evans and Terry. In December of 1954, local businessmen lined up behind the Elks to help combat the deficit but the hole in the dike was doomed to get worse.

The Senior B team, the Millionaires, played in the Okanagan Mainline Hockey League along with the Vernon Monarchs, Penticton Combines and Kelowna. Once again many former Elks dotted their lineup, in particular Evans and Terry, who ended up leading the league in scoring. At seasons end, Kamloops stood one point back of first place Vernon with Penticton and Kelowna well back.

In the playdowns, Penticton forfeited the series after being bombed 18-1 in Game 1. Four players got hat tricks and Clovechok netted six points in total.

In the league final, Vernon charged out of the gate to take the Millionaires 10-2 in Vernon in Game 1 but the Elks bounced back on home ice to take Game 2 12-4. Only 350 fans were there to take in the victory at Memorial Arena.

The third game, in Vernon, went into overtime before Al MacDougall netted the winner for Kamloops and gave the Elks the chance to eliminate Vernon on Kamloops' ice. What had started as a possible series blowout by Vernon ended with Kamloops' taking Game 4 11-1 on the strength of Gordie Kusumoto's hat trick and Gord Tansley starring in net. The Millionaires were the Okanagan Mainline League champions.

The Victoria Navy team was the only remaining obstacle to another appearance in the Coy Cup final, and, to make matters worse for the sailors, the entire series was to be played in Kamloops. After Kamloops took Game 1 6-3, they came back and whitewashed the Navy 9-0 in Game 2. Evans, Stan Berry and Al Swaine were the big guns that sank the fleet.

Their opponents in the final would once again be their nemesis, Trail. Making it tougher was the fact the entire series was to be played in Trail.

Trail took Game 1 4-3, but the Millionaires stormed back in Game 2 to pull out an 8-6 win. The series went to a third and deciding game. Once again the boys from Trail prevailed. This time by a score of 7-3 to take home the silverware. Had there been a bridesmaid trophy, Kamloops would have won it hands down. It was their fifth cup appearance in a row and the fourth loss; all of which had come at the hands of Trail.

At the minor league level, the midgets were again the dominant squad. Powering past Vernon they met Kelowna for the Interior Championship and the Vernon Kinsmen Trophy. Led by Wally Wozniak and Al Raymond, they took Kelowna 10-3 in the series opener at Memorial and then won 5-3 back in Kelowna. One trophy in hand, they marched into the provincial finals with a two-game, total-point victory over Kerrisdale. They took the coastal squad 6-1 in Game 1 and then lost 6-4 in Game 2. The provincial final saw them face off against Trail and be forced to play the entire series on Trail ice. They fell 8-3 and 5-3 and relinquished the Cromie Cup to the Kootenays.

In other hockey news, the paper carried an item "Local Lad Cracks Prairie Junior Ranks". It spoke of Don Wilkie, the 15-year-old goalie who starred for the provincial midget champs last year and who was now on the roster of the Moose Jaw Canucks. The item claimed Wilkie "is believed to be the first home bred boy to make it to top flight hockey."

At the same time, another Kamloops' favourite, Freddie Gaber, was starring for Medicine Hat in the same league. Gaber was a Prairie boy who had played minor hockey in Kamloops but had not come up through the local minor hockey ranks.

Still on the Prairies, the Humboldt Junior Indians had walked away with the Saskatchewan Junior Hockey League Championship after beating out Flin Flon in the final. Changes were hanging over the head of the franchise as it looked forward to the 1955-56 season.

12

Hard Times 1955-56

The Elks' 1955-56 season again started with a new player/coach but this time there were no illusions about being a favourite. From the beginning, the Elks where deemed to be a dark horse.

Their new coach was Kevin "Crusher" Conway who had last season gone to the World Championship with the Vees and brought back gold. He was joined from the Vees by Don Moog (father of Andy Moog) and Eddie Kassen while all-star defenceman Jack Taggart went the other way. Returnees included Bill Swarbrick, Johnny Milliard, Billy Hryciuk, Don Slater, Joe Connors, Fred Creighton and, later, Buddy Evans. Newcomers included former Humboldt Indian Howie Hornby, who lined up with Milliard and Hryciuk; Freddie Gaber, the local lad who played last season with Medicine Hat; Bob Leek, George Ferguson, Gaff Torner and two more former Humboldt Indians Art Asleson and Ron Larsen. Later in the season, Don Busch, from the Seattle pro team, joined the squad.

Seeming to defy the odds makers, the Elks stormed out of the gate winning their first five games before the wheels started coming off. Despite great seasons by Hryciuk, who finished second in scoring, and Milliard, the season could not be salvaged. Ex-Elks were sprinkled about the league and in the Western International Hockey League and, more often than not, they came back to haunt their old teammates. Even when the Elks went up against the local Senior B team in their traditional exhibition game, they suffered the embarrassment of a 6-4 loss. The only consolation was Conway, Ferguson and Hryciuk made the second all star team.

At season's end, Kamloops was dead last, 30 points behind their playoff opponent, first-place Vernon Canadians. Their regular season record of 2-13-1 did not give reason for optimism nor did their opening game loss by 7-2 in Vernon.

The series proved to be rough with coach Conway threatening to pull his team off the ice if the ref did not control the play. In one case, fans got into the act and charges were laid against a spectator for causing a disturbanc. In Game 2, the Elks clawed out a 5-4 win in a game that deteriorated into a brawl.

The third and fourth games went to Vernon by scores of 6-3 and 5-3. Whatever hopes were left were dashed in Game 5 at Memorial Arena when the Elks went down 6-2 and were eliminated.

The changes went deeper next season.

The financial crisis deepened, too. In December, the league representatives met and acknowledged costs had to be cut or the league disbanded. Mistrust between teams persisted and Kamloops later made claims both Penticton and Vernon were not abiding by salary agreements. In an effort to survive, the players took a 25 per cent salary cut in January. The team moaned it needed 2,000 fans per game to deal with its $5,130 deficit. It had originally budgeted for an average attendance of 1,600 but was only averaging 1,100. Despite the clear problems, claims of the imminent death of the league were, as yet, untrue, albeit it was gasping for air.

The Senior B team found a new sponsor, Balco Forest Products, and a new coach in oldtimer Busher Jackson. When the playdowns started, none other than Kenny Stewart was back in the lineup. In Game 1 against Summerland, he scored the winning goal as the Balcos took the contest 7-6. Five hundred fans turned up to watch the Balcos take Game 2 at Memorial Arena 9-2 and to advance against the Nanaimo Clippers.

The hotly contested series saw Kamloops lose Game 1 6-5 despite a hat trick by Don Jakes. Game 2 went to Nanaimo 2-1, though, the squad protested the game on the basis of the poor playing conditions. Their protest was not upheld and Kamloops failed to send a team to the provincial finals for the first time in five years.

Local minor hockey saw the bantams capture the Interior for the third time in four years, while the juveniles got by Vancouver by scores of 10-4 and 9-2 to make the finals against Trail. The Trail jinx held.

As spring began its serene call, the senior league was experiencing increasing problems with attendance and management of costs. At the same time, minor league hockey was beginning to sprout its wings.

Back in Saskatchewan, the Junior Indians finished its first season as the Humboldt/Melfort Indians. In an effort to survive, the franchise took the unusual step of having the team shared by two communities. Despite success on the ice, the experiment would only last another season and the franchise would make the move which eventually set it on the road to national attention.

13

What's in a Name ______________________ 1956-57

The 1956-57 season brought more changes for the Elks than anyone had expected. Not only did the coach change but so did the ownership and the name.

Kenny MacKenzie's association with hockey went back to the pioneering history of the sport in the West. As a coach, he had taken the Edmonton Eskimos to the Stanley Cup finals in 1923 having on board the Flying Frenchman himself, Arthur Gagne'. Gagne' had made his home in Kamloops after finishing a pro career that had seen him playing alongside Aurel Joliat and Howie Morenz on the Montreal Canadians and had played a part in the development of local hockey in Kamloops. Mackenzie had gone from Edmonton to the New Westminster Royals of the professional Pacific Coast League and had made a name for himself in that community as well before buying the Elks.

He was not unfamiliar with Kamloops either because his Royals had, for a number of years, held their training camps at Memorial Arena. In fact, his Royals had the honour of playing the first hockey game in the facility in an exhibition match against the Seattle Ironmen in 1949. Mackenzie was not one to make his entry quietly and his introduction to Kamloops proved no exception.

To say MacKenzie was colourful would be a bit of an understatement. He was an individual always capable of getting the pot stirred and people involved, even if they were not always happy with what he was doing. With Mackenzie at the helm the team was never at a loss for publicity.

Bob Dawes accompanied Mackenzie from New Westminster and replaced outgoing Kevin Conway as player coach. Other new players included Jim Shirley in goal, Peter Whyte, Mark Marquess, Gerry Prince, Peter Semko, Jim MacKenzie, Lloyd Hinchberger, Gerry Kernaghan, Puddicombe, Meldrum , McDougal and Larry Berg; another former Humboldt Indian.

To this mix was added Fred Sasaskamoose, a full blooded Cree from Debden, Sask. who had made it all the way to the NHL with the Chicago Black Hawks. Though he only survived for 14 games, he became the first First Nations player to ever reach that level. In Kamloops he became the fan favourite with more than a few claiming that he was the first person they ever saw use the slapshot.

Returnees included Buddy Evans, Johnny Milliard (named team captain), Billy Hryciuk, Don Slater, Howie Hornsby and Don Moog. Local products Gordie Kusumoto, Tony Spelay and Frank Basaraba also had the opportunity for some ice time with the big club.

Change didn't stop there as Mackenzie had a contest for the renaming of the team. The names rolled in and included the Kamaroons, Loggers, Cow Pokes, Punchers and, hearkening to the teams' history, Hub City Leafs. In the end, he settled upon Chiefs.

The new chiefs with their new Chief soon let it be known they would not be anyone's doormat that season. By late December, they were in second place and challenging for first. Then at the end of a solid 6-0 triumph over Kelowna, came a sour note recalling the earliest days of the league.

Sasaskamoose had proven a crowd favourite at a time when attendance was crucial to the league's survival. He brought in the fans as attested to by the 2,200 who saw him pace the Chiefs to a 5-2 win over Vernon just prior to Kelowna's filing of an official protest over his eligibility. It was shades of the Andre Fredette case all over again. Mackenzie vowed revenge against Kelowna for their protest of his use of ex pros and promised to keep using Sasaskamoose despite their protest. It was a mistake.

Mackenzie's use of Saskamoose cost the team points; in particular, they had to give up two points they had taken from front running Vernon. Sasaskamoose was forced to sit out the rest of the season and feelings ran hard against Kelowna. The Chiefs fell 10 points back of Vernon in the battle for first.

At season's end, the Chiefs captured second. Their last game being a penalty-ladened 6-3 victory over first place Vernon at Memorial Arena. Finishing on a positive note by securing a plus .500 season and winning their last 13 games on home ice, they had reason for optimism going into the playoffs. Milliard, Evans and Hryciuk finished in the Top 10 scorers and Jim Shirley was the best goalie with a 3.75 average and three shutouts. They were also to have the pleasure of going up against Kelowna in the first round.

In Game 1 the Chiefs went into Kelowna's own backyard and, before 1,900 fans, put it to the Packers 7-0 with the Milliard, Hryciuk, Evans line grabbing five goals. Game 2 finished tied at two and the Chiefs squeezed out a 5-4 victory in Game 3 for a commanding lead. Though they lost 6-5 in Game 4 their 6-3 Game 5 win put them within one victory of moving on.

Injuries had cost the Chiefs and, in Game 6, Kelowna took advantage with a 5-1 victory that tightened the series up.

However the Chiefs were not to be denied as Game 7 saw Hryciuk net two goals and Dawes pot one as the squad, behind the MVP goaltending of Shirley, put away the Packers. They had their revenge. Now, the understaffed and tired team had to take on Vernon.

Playing with only 12 players to Vernon's 15, the Chiefs dropped Game 1 in Vernon 5-3. After managing a 3-3 tie in Game 2 they were again downed in Vernon; this time 5-4. Game 4 was played before 2,611 fans at Memorial who were hoping for a comeback against the Hal Gordon led Vernonites. It was not to be as the Canadians pushed the Chiefs a game closer to elimination. Going into Game 5 in Vernon down three games to none and without stars Milliard or Slater, the end was predictable. Vernon captured the Willoughby Cup with a 6-0 victory.

Despite the loss, the Chiefs had brought back a measure of respectability with their strong season. Shirley came away with the Bob Johnston Trophy as the league MVP while Hyrciuk made the first team all-stars. The second team had Dawes as player coach and Milliard.

Mackenzie was vowing an Allan Cup contender next year.

By November, the Senior B Balcos announced their intention of pursuing the Coy Cup under manager Sam Corea and coach Kenny Stewart.

Without a league to play in, the team had to content itself with exhibition matches until the playdowns arrived. Those began in February against the Penticton-Summerland Macs and saw the Balcos skate away with a 5-2 victory in the opening game before 1,200 Kamloops' fans. On home ice, the Macs proved much tougher and were up 3-0 before the Balcos started to get untracked. But untracked they did get as two goals by Busher Jackson and singles by Kusumoto, Al Swaine and Bud Schollen gave them the victory and the right to move on against Nanaimo.

This series proved no contest as Balcos downed the visiting Clippers in two games by scores of 10-2 and 7-2 to get revenge for the previous year's elimination. Then came the second controversy of the season.

For once they were not scheduled to go up against Trail

in the provincial Coy Cup final as Kimberley had won the Kootenays that year. Balcos was scheduled to travel to the Columbia Valley to play the entire series on the road. They baulked and claimed it was not fair for them to travel again as they had had to travel to Nanaimo last year and to Trail the year before. Kimberley was awarded the Coy Cup by default and Kamloops was further penalized by being prohibited from contesting the cup next season.

The minor hockey scene saw Schollen, Bob Gannon and Tansley getting ice time with junior teams on the Prairies. On a less positive note, though, was the departure in February 1957 of Hec MacKenzie, who was credited with having been a prime mover of minor hockey and sport in general since coming to Kamloops in 1938.

Kamloops iced a junior team to compete for the Mowat Cup for the first time in 10 years. In reaching the finals, they disposed of Kelowna and Vernon in round-robin elimination play by decisive scores of 10-6 (Vernon), 14-8 (Kelowna) and 11-7 (Kelowna). Their foe in the final was like a bad dream—Trail. Though they dropped the final in two straight games by scores of 4-3 and 7-3, they showed well in their first trip back to the juniors in 10 years. They did not wait another 10 years.

The juveniles also showed promise by winning the Okanagan in grand comeback fashion. After losing Game 1 10-6 in Kelowna, they bounced back to take the two-game, total-point series 18-17 on home ice by virtue of a 12-7 victory. Even the peewees got into the act, taking the Okanagan by defeating Penticton in the final.

Names cropping up on the peewee rosters, that were soon to become known to local fans, were Terry and Eric Shishido, Ricky McShane, Eddie Begg, Ron Hay, Glen Edwards and Peter Sternig.

Midget rosters ran the names of Vic Minamede; the bantams had Murray Owens and Jim Letcher and the juniors had Al Raymond, Melvin Recchi, Kusumoto, Bruce Harrison, Ron Stiles, Schollen and Lyle Sandyke.

From top to bottom, Kamloops was a hockey town.

14

Warwicks 1957-58

Never at a loss for words, Kenny MacKenzie started out the season with bombs and bouquets.

After chastising the league for scheduling the Chiefs with too many games against the Penticton Vees, he turned around and threw laurels at his adopted home town. *"I think they are going to have to bury me in this part of the country. I never want to leave it."*

The serious business at hand, though, was the rebuilding of a team which had raised expectations from the year before, Fred Sasaskamoose was back, legally this time, as was last season's MVP Jim Shirley. Others included Billy Hryciuk, Lloyd Hinchberger, Gerry Kernaghan, Buddy Evans, Johnny Milliard, Gerry Prince, Bob Dawes and Don Slater. Ron Leopold and Alf Cadman were scheduled to come to camp from Calgary. They later regained Mark Marquess from Spokane. Don Busch, the Brandon-born local player, was lured away from the Seattle Americans to join the squad. The biggest news though was the signing of Dick and Bill Warwick. Even better news came late in the season.

For years the Warwicks had been a thorn in side of the franchise, now they were heroes. Bill and Dick were now Chiefs. Dick, who had been on the first Humboldt Indian team, had contested against the franchise from its inception and, with his two brothers in Penticton, became one of the premier brother acts in Canadian hockey history.

After being jolted 8-2 in Penticton in their opening game against a team that still sported ex-Elks Jack Taggart, Bernie Bathgate and Kevin Conway, they rebounded. In their season home opener, they flattened the Vees 10-3 before 1,800 fans with Hryciuk netting four goals. In their second game, they stormed out against old teammate Hal Gordon and on hat tricks by Sasaskamoose and Leopold stunned Vernon 10-2.

In mid-November, the news got even better when word came Grant Warwick was joining his brothers. By that time, the scoring stats saw Hryciuk leading the league with Milliard third and Buddy Evans sixth. Later that month, Grant tallied two goals and one assist in a Chiefs 4-3 victory over Penticton.

Before the month was over, the biggest crowd of the season, 2,441 fans, saw the Chiefs beat Kelowna Packers 4-3 to gain a share of first place. Dawes celebrated his 33rd birthday by going the length of the ice to score the game winner at 19:56. The goal went along with three assists.

Despite the excitement attendance was hovering perilously close to the break even-point. With a required average of 1,900, the 1,934 being achieved was uncomfortably close. The Chiefs and Kelowna battled to the very end for the regular season championship and the Becker Trophy, but it was to be Kelowna that grabbed the laurels at season's end. The first-place struggle and the presence of such crowd-pleasers as the Warwicks and Sasaskamoose help put fans in the seats as did the scoring prowess of the Pony line comprised of Hryciuk, Evans and Milliard.

It was a season of excitement and promise that had not been seen for a number of years along the Thompson. From the play on the ice to the measured barbs sent out by colourful owner MacKenzie, fans could not help but be interested.

In late January, both MacKenzie and Sasaskamoose were feted with a special evening. For the owner, it was the awarding of the haggis on Robbie Burns night, while Sasakamoose was made an Honorary chief of the Kamloops' Indian Band by counsellor Gus Gottfriedson. Resplendent in headgear, crafted by Andy Paul, and christened with the title Chief Thunderstick Freddie was honoured by 200 First Nations child dancers adorned in their regalia. The evening ended on the same note as Prince scored three goals in a 4-0 victory over Kelowna that put them into first place.

MacKenzie's resourcefulness was put into play again when coach Dawes stepped down. Instead of merely naming a captain, he let the fans decide who would be best in the job. Not surprisingly they chose Grant Warwick.

Season's end saw Hryciuk picked to the first all star team and the second graced with Shirley, Dawes and Leopold.

Round 1 of the playoffs had the Chiefs up against last year's champs, Vernon. A chance for some revenge? Vernon managed to grab a 2-2 tie in the first game at Kamloops but the Chiefs came back in Game 2 at Vernon and took it 4-2. The third game, at Memorial, was everything the 3,200 fans could ask for as their squad dominated in a 7-3 victory. It looked like the Chiefs were going to roll over the Canadians, but Vernon had other thoughts and came back to take the next two games. Kamloops again took the series lead only to see Vernon win again to force an eighth and deciding game at Memorial.

Some 2,800 fans were on hand to watch a nail biter as the Chiefs finally eliminated the Canadians on the strength of a 4-3 victory. It could hardly have been closer. No sooner had the cheering died down than MacKenzie's controversial nature clashed with veteran Grant Warwick. After the dispute, Grant left the team and spent time with his brother, Bill, who was in hospital with a serious head injury. It was not a good time to be without Grant's leadership as the Chiefs went up against Kelowna for the Willoughby Trophy.

Cadman got Kamloops' only marker in the 3-1 opening game loss in Kelowna. Game 2 at Memorial Arena saw the Chiefs manage a 2-2 tie in front of 2,200 fans. Grant returned to the fold in Game 3 in Kelowna and the Chiefs, led by two goals by Leopold, pulled out a 4-2 win to knot the series. Grant was soon buoyed by the news Bill was out of the hospital 12 days after hemorrhaging from a blow from a stick in a game against Vernon on Feb. 26, 1958.

Despite a pair of goals from Evans in Game 4, the Chiefs fell 6-4 heading back to Kelowna. Game 5 proved to be a back breaker. Down 4-3, Sasaskamoose performed heroics to tie the game at the 19:46 mark of the third and force overtime, but there was no gas left in the tank and Kelowna took it in overtime. Facing elimination in Game 6, the Chiefs got up from the mat on the strength of three goals by Leopold, two by Prince and singles to Hryciuk, Dick Warwick and Cadman to elate 2,300 fans with an 8-4 victory.

It was the last gasp, however, as Kelowna took the trophy in Game 9 on the strength of a 3-0 victory and one of the most exciting seasons in recent memory came to an end. There was never to be another season like it as dark clouds were gathering on the horizon.

Years later, Dick Warwick spoke in praise of the 1957-58 Chiefs as a team that could have gone all the way to the Allan Cup.

In minor league play, the Kamloops Midget Braves walked over the Revelstoke Legionnaires in the first playoff round by scores of 9-5 and 22-2 and then took the Okanagan Championship with 9-5 and 4-2 victories over Kelowna. This gave the Braves, backstopped by Jim Letcher, the opportunity to play Trail.

It was getting ridiculous; there had to be something in the water. Once again, despite playing all the games at Memorial Arena, Kamloops fell before Trail by scores of 9-6 and 8-5.

The bantams, whose roster included such future notables as Terry Shishido, Don Newman, Murray Owens and Bert Marshall, took out Kelowna in two straight by scores of 9-4 and 7-4 to claim the Okanagan Championship and the J .R. Robinson Trophy. It was the fourth time in six years.

The promise of minor league hockey was rising even as the Sun was beginning to cast shadows on the senior league.

A new team skated out in the Saskatchewan Junior Hockey League that season. Scotty Munro (with his Boston Bruin connections) moved his Indians to Estevan and joined forces with former Indian Ernie MacLean. A new home, new arena and a new name. The Estevan Bruins eventually brought the success of the franchise to the national scene and the triumvirate of MacLean, Bill Shinske and Munro began carving out the success story that still reverberates to this day. What had begun as a solid and successful franchise in Humboldt was to reach new heights in Estevan and a Kamloops' hockey product was to be a major part of that success.

15

More of the Same ____________________ 1958-59

Kenny Mackenzie was still at the helm when the 1958-59 season began; however, the Warwicks had moved on.

Optimism remained, though, as many of the team's stalwarts returned. Billy Hryciuk (replacing Bob Dawes as player coach), Johnny Milliard, Buddy Evans, Gerry Prince, Alf Cadman and Fred Sasaskamoose led the way and were joined by Jim Kuntz in goal, tough guy Ted Lebodia, Don Busch, Gord and Marvin Tansley, Ron Duperreault, Gus Braumberger, Joe Morneau, Gordie Kusumoto, Cliff Lennhart, Rudy Balon, Mike Cardash, Cliff Bristow, Gord Matheson, Harvey Hamilton, Bill Poiriere, Ken Harris, George Hunchuk, Gord Hudson, Twardorski, Bob Gannon, Larry Berg and Freddie Gaber at varying times through the season. Even Bob Dawes found his way back to the team.

At one perilous point in the season, it looked like the team and the league may fold and local players increasingly filled in for those who began abandoning what looked like a sinking ship. Melvin Recchi had a chance to star in a 5-4 victory over the Vees and even legendary Kenny Stewart suited up.

At the end of December, it looked like it might all be over. Attendance was down by 50 per cent and only seven regular players remained. Colourful Kenny let the franchise go to a number of local businessmen who resuscitated the team, called on the players to come back and for the fans to show their support.

And come back they did. Evans returned to score a hat trick in the revamped Chiefs 9-0 victory over Penticton. Kuntz returned to hold the Vees to a 5-5 tie. The return of Sasaskamoose was celebrated by dropping 500 free tickets from a helicopter and a 5-3 victory over Kelowna. Everyone pitched in. On Jan. 12, 1959, the Sentinel proudly reported 2,500 fans had turned out for the last game at Memorial Arena.

Hryciuk and Evans came to the fore night after night as the revitalized Chiefs climbed back to respectability. Hryciuk rewrote the records books by scoring 118 points and drew out the fans to a special night honouring the 33-year-old-vet. To top it off, he took the league MVP award for the second time in his career. Close behind him in scoring was Prince with 100 points.

At season's end, the Chiefs had regained enough stature they felt they had a chance of advancing past the powerhouse Canadians. Vernon took Game 1 in Vernon 8-3 but Kamloops returned the favour with a 7-1 victory at Memorial Arena in front of 1,500 fans. Game 3 in Vernon saw the Chiefs battle back from a 4-1 deficit to come within a goal. Back on Kamloops ice, the Chiefs again evened the series with a 4-1 win. Returning to Vernon, they lost a nail-biter 7-6. Facing elimination on home ice, the team got goals from Evans, Hryciuk, Bristow and Lebodia to force a seventh and deciding game in Vernon, where they had not won a game all season.

League scoring champ and record setter — Elks Billy Hryciuk with 118 points in the 1958-59 season. (c. KMA #5490)

The storybook finish was not to be as Stecyk scored a hat trick for Vernon and led them to a 5-2 victory over the Chiefs. The book on Senior A hockey was slowly beginning to close but there were still a couple chapters left.

The Senior B team was once again back and in the hunt for the Coy Cup. Taking on the name Rockets, they had the benefit of sponsorship by the Central Hotel. As the playdowns rolled around, some familiar names made their way into the lineup including ageless Stewart. Their first obstacle was the Okanagan All Stars in a best- of-three which they took two straight by scores of 9-4 and 6-4.

Then they came face to face with another Trail team; this one with the ominous Smoke Eaters name. At least all three games were in Kamloops.

Only 300 fans turned up for Game 1 to see the Rockets take it 6-3. In Game 2, Kamloops entered the third period up 3-2.

That lead held until 17:57 when Bob Irvine put the Rockets up with what proved to be the winner. Trail got one back but that was all. Even if they did nothing else, they could glory in finally getting past a team from the Smelter City.

The Vancouver Pilseners stopped the Rockets in the final and once again Kamloops had to settle for the Bridesmaid Award.

It was up to the minor leaguers to bring home glory and some cups again that season.

At the start of the season, the Sentinel announced 20-year- old Gordon Tansley was off to the Montreal Canadians training camp. He was hailed as the first recorded Kamloops' product to ever try out with an NHL squad. Though he did not stay, his very invitation was a source of pride and he acknowledged the influence of Don Reid and Hec MacKenzie in his development.

On the ice the peewees, led by Butch Senkpiel, won the Okanagan Championship over Summerland convincingly.

The bantams took the Okanagan Championship and the Robertson trophy for the fifth time in seven years by decisive scores of 8-2 and 7-2 over Penticton. Their lineup included Peter Sternig in net, Terry Shishido, Bill Steinke, Ricky Telford, Ricky McShane, Don Anthony, Will Moffatt, George Meridew, Clair Long, Butch Senkpiel, David Clark, Eric Shishido and Ken Takeuchi. Many of those names were very soon to be grabbing headlines at a higher level.

In Vancouver, a former star with the Elks was fighting for his life in the hospital. Cliff Mills, who played five years with the Elks and was a former Senior B scoring champ, was facing his greatest challenge yet.

16

The Beginning of the End__________1959-60

The 1959-60 Chiefs saw the return of Buddy Evans, Billy Hryciuk, Larry Berg, Ted Lebodia, Ken Kuntz, Alf Cadman and Cliff Bristow along with locals Fred Gaber, Gordon Tansley, Bob Gannon and Gordon Matheson. Import goalies Don Hamilton and John Panagrot later joined the team and locals Melvin Recchi, Don Busch and Ron "Shorty" Stiles also got in some ice time.

Crowds were down dramatically around the league; often not exceeding a thousand, even for weekend games. All the while registration of minor league hockey players continued to increase and more locals were gaining the attention of major junior teams and even NHL scouts.

Goalie Mel Recchi. The first in the family to make his mark on the ice. (c. Mel Recchi)

Gaber started out on a tear scoring two goals in an 11-2 win over Penticton and following it up with four goals in an 8-7 triumph over the Packers. Veteran Evans showed little sign of slowing down and, by the end of January, was leading the league in scoring.

At seasons end Kamloops secured third spot behind Vernon and Kelowna with a respectable 22-23-2 record. Penticton Vees had tumbled and managed only five wins all year. Evans finished second in scoring and Hryciuk third.

They had the daunting task of going up against Vernon in the first round. The Canadians had lost only nine games all season, though, three of them had come at the hands of the Chiefs.

Game 1 in Vernon was disheartening as the Chiefs were decimated 13-0. Panagrot guarded the pipes in the next game played before only 500 fans at Memorial Arena and led the Chiefs to a 6-3 victory to tie the series. The promise of the second game ended there as Vernon proceeded to take the remaining three games to eliminate the Chiefs in Round 1.

The curtain fell on a season of poor attendance, financial losses and a quiet demise. As the last of the fans emptied out of the arena, there was no certainty the Chiefs or even the league would be around next year. Was an era coming to an end?

In Vancouver, Cliff Mills had died.

Senior B play took on a different look as Kamloops and Merritt, with its new arena, shared a team; known as the Central Caribous. Play was in the Pacific Coast Amateur League along with Powell River Regals, Chilliwack Volvos, New Westminster Carlings and Nanaimo Clippers. They played an imbalanced schedule which saw road games worth four points and home games worth three. Of the 16 home games five were played in Merritt.

Former Elks and Chiefs star Johnny Milliard joined the squad.

At season's end, the Caribous outstripped all the others. Fan attendance in Kamloops was disappointing, ranging from 400 to 600, while the team was embraced by Merritt and was capable of drawing out 900.

During a “friendly” exhibition match between the Chiefs and the Caribous in Merritt, 1,200 fans became more intensely involved than usual. Fighting and stick swinging characterized the game and the fans got into it with chants of "Go Home Chiefs." Their vocal support was not enough for the Caribous as they fell to the Chiefs 8-1.

Another eventful game that season had the Japanese national team in town for a game against the Caribous. Although the Caribous clearly dominated and won 6-1, the fans demonstrated a warm spot for the Japanese squad. The game also provided an opportunity for Kamloops to ice the all Japanese Canadian line of Gordie Kusumoto, Vic Minamede and Norio Sakaki. The Sentinel went on to note the depth of Japanese Canadian hockey talent in Kamloops by pointing out up-and-coming players such as midgets Kats and Mike Kitamura along with Terry and Eric Shishido, bantams Ken Takeuchi, Ricky Nishizaki, Tick Kariya, Eddie Sakaki and Coke Koyangi as well as peewee Rick Sakaki.

The Caribous entered the playoffs with every reason to be optimistic and their victory over a team from Williams Lake did nothing to dispel it. Their best-of-three semifinal series, played in totality in Nanaimo, saw them come out on the short end and hang up their skates for the season. The Coy Cup eluded them yet again.

Minor hockey provided more than its fair share of excitement.

The juvenile rep team advanced farther than ever before. After losing Game 1 of the Okanagan final to Kelowna, they bounced back to take the series and move on to Quesnel where they battled Smithers for the Mainline Northern Juvenile Championship. Wiping Smithers out 11-2 and 9-3, they then skated past Kerrisdale by scores of 9-4 and 7-4 to capture the Kamloops Lumber Trophy. Cranbrook and the provincial title was next. They took Game 1 right in Cranbrook 10-3 but that was where the bubble burst as the Kootenay squad took the next two games and the province.

The bantams decimated Revelstoke and Williams Lake to reach the Okanagan final against Kelowna. They had won the trophy five out of the last seven years and did not disappoint as they regrouped after a 6-3 loss in Game 1 to take game two 11-3 and the total point series 14 -9.

The midget Braves easily eliminated Vernon and squared off against Kelowna for the Okanagan Championship. Don Reid's team carried stars Murray Owens and Bill Schall who turned up big time in game one in Kelowna. Schall picked up 5 goals and Owens 4 in a 14-3 bombing. Starring on defence was future NHLer Bert Marshall. Kelowna fell by the wayside as did their next opponent, Nelson, by scores of 13-3 and 9-2. Kamloops had the W.J. Moffatt Trophy as Interior Champs and were headed to the Provincial final.

Even with home ice advantage New Westminster proved ill equipped to stop the Braves who took the Provincial Midget title and the Cromie Cup after their 11-3 second game victory. The trophy that they had last won in 1954 was welcomed along with the team by 200 fans upon their arrival in town and at a reception at Memorial Arena. This season competition did not end with the Provincials.

The Commodore Café put up the Commodore Cup for a challenge match against the Alberta champs; the Edmonton midget Canadians. Kamloops had twice before gone up against Alberta in playoff action and had twice tasted defeat. Third time lucky?

The first game of the series saw Kamloops jump out to a 4-1 lead and sit back as the Canadians chipped away to finally tie the game in the final few minutes of the third. Murray Owens and Skip Holmes contributed singles while Schall potted two. Kamloops' fans were ecstatic when Schall appeared to score his third goal of the game and the game winner with time expiring on the clock. Initially, the officials let the goal stand and declared Kamloops the winner 5-4 but, after consultation it was disallowed as coming after the buzzer. The 4-4 tie stood. It all came down to one game.

1,600 fans were on hand for the deciding game at Memorial. Schall again dazzled the crowd with a hat trick while another Brave, and future Estevan Bruin, Don Newman, added a further two goals. Will Moffatt added two of his own and capped the exciting contest.

The game took much the same form as Game 1. The teams were tied 1-1 at the end of the first, but Kamloops climbed into a 5-2 lead by the end of the second and appeared to have the game in hand. Edmonton, as in Game 1, came charging back and, in the dying seconds of the third, were pressing for the tying marker. Moffatt had given Kamloops its seventh tally at 12:23 and, when the buzzer sounded, it stood up as the winner in a 7-6 victory.

Braves captain Owens was awarded the Commodore Trophy. Although he had not scored, he had set up five goals. The Braves became the first Kamloops' team to take a championship from a Prairie club. Ironically, especially for Marshall, that team was from Edmonton.

Farther out on the Prairies, the Estevan Bruins were adding players with solid NHL careers in their futures. That year Dallas Smith, the Boston Bruin of tomorrow, graced their lineup. He was one of many to come.

17

The Last Hurrah________________1960-61

Ever since the 1947-48 season, Kamloops fans had their senior team to cheer on and, since the opening of Memorial Arena, they had hopes of one day challenging for the Allan Cup. There would be only one more venture at that highest level of senior hockey. The 1960-61 season was the last gasp.

The Chiefs started the season under player ownership as the Kamloops Cooperative Players Association and turned to fund- raising to keep the team alive. New rules required teams carry at least three players produced from their local minor hockey leagues. Where once this may have represented a liability, it was certainly not the case anymore.

The league actually expanded that season as the Merritt Grand Luckies, under the guidance of Walter Malahoff, joined the league and iced a number of players from the Kamloops area in order to fill out their roster.

Willie Schmidt, formerly of Penticton, was the new coach and iced a team, including Noel Hunt, former Humboldt Indian John Yanchuk, Rod Gagnon, Larry Berg, Andy MacDougall, Vic Minamede, Don Busch, Ross Jardine, Ted Lebodia, Gordie Kusumoto, Ron Stiles, Murray Owens, Walter Hryciw and the line of Bob Gannon, Freddie Gaber and Rex Turple, that was to tear up the league. Buddy Evans was gone to Penticton and even Billy Hryciuk had moved on.

After taking Merritt 3-1 at Memorial Arena in their opener before 800 fans, they dropped the return match in the Nicola Valley 9-3 before 708 Merritt faithful. A drubbing 10-3 in their next game, against Vernon, brought concern but no dramatic changes. Lebodia left for the pros and Gord Matheson returned. Things got better.

Schmidt formed the "Short" line of Kusumoto, Stiles and Berg which netted 11 goals in five games. Evans came back to haunt his former teammates before 1,400 fans in Penticton one night as he garnered a hat trick. All five Kamloops goals were scored by the "Production Line" of Gannon, Gaber and Turple.

By early November, the Grand Luckies, wallowing in last

place and being embarrassed by other teams, opted out and switched to Senior B play.

Attendance was generally down, but in one game against the visiting Trail Smoke Eaters team that was to go to the World Championships, 1,797 fans turned out to see their Chiefs in a respectable 6-5 loss.

Dec. 1, 1960 brought the news the Vees were folding as they could no longer find and maintain jobs for their players. The only good part was that Evans returned to the fold where he had plied his trade for the past eight seasons. Within six days, matters got worse as Kelowna Packers folded, leaving only Kamloops and Vernon. In possibly the last game for both Vernon and Kamloops, the Chiefs dropped a 6-3 decision in Vernon.

Just when it looked like it was all over, however, Penticton and Kelowna announced they had collectively formed a team, appropriately named the Combines, and were ready to resume play with a new league schedule.

In the revised schedule, Vernon took first while Kamloops, despite the heroics of the Production Line, fell to last place. The Feb. 6, 1961 Sentinel reported only 550 fans turned up for what proved to be the last regular season game at Memorial for the Senior A Chiefs. Recalling the heady days of the past and perhaps realizing an era was passing, Kamloops showed its best stuff in defeating the powerful Canadians 8-5. They squared off against the Combines in the playoffs.

They were slammed 12-4 in Game 1 and it looked like they were going to go out with a whimper. This thought was dispelled when they took Game 2 6-2 at Memorial Arena before 600 fans. Game 3 went to the Combines 9-3 in Kelowna, but the Chiefs again bounced back in the homer series 4-3 in front of 800 fans. Drubbed 9-4 in Kelowna, they returned to Memorial Arena knowing it could be the last game for the team if they could not pull it out.

Turple, Gannon and Kusumoto starred that night when there were more ghosts than fans in the stands. An era came to an end with an 8-3 Chiefs victory that forced a seventh and deciding game in Kelowna.

Facing the same prospect as Kamloops the previous game, the Combines played to their ghosts and took Game 7 by a score of 6-3. With that loss, Senior A hockey on the Thompson died. For 12 years, it had been the big act in town but its time had passed.

They had left good memories for those who had watched them and shared in their triumphs and failures. The "Production Line" had brought back some memories of the Bathgate/Andy Clovechok/Johnny Milliard combination of years before by finishing 1, 2, 3 in scoring; albeit not tied. Gaber surpassed Bill Hryciuk's season record 118 points by garnering 130 while Turple came in at 94 and Gannon at 89. Gaber and Turple landed on the first all-star team while goalie John Panagrot and coach Schmidt landed on the second.

Befitting the times, Kamloops did not ice a Senior B team.

Junior hockey took on a new dimension in British Columbia when the Provincial Amateur Hockey Association decided to enter play at the major junior level and vie for the Memorial Cup. Until that time, fans had to content themselves with players going off to major junior teams in the Prairies.

At the start of the season, 17-year-old Glenn Madsen, who had played with the juvenile Falcons the previous year, was off to the training camp of the Estevan Bruins. He joined three other Kamloops' locals on the Prairies, one of whom, Jim Letcher, ended up being traded to Estevan by the Regina Pats.

When Kamloops first enjoyed the benefits of artificial ice and began serious competition against outside teams, it was the skill and experience of players from the outside that came to dominate play. Now, locally developed players increasingly drew the attention of fans and scouts alike. It wasn't that the imported players had disappeared; far from it. Many had made Kamloops their home and shared their love and knowledge of the game with youngsters in the minor hockey leagues. During the 1960-61 midget season alone, Andy Clovechok, Johnny Milliard and George Ferguson, all former Senior A players were coaching city league teams.

In early January 1961, major junior hockey made its first appearance in the uniforms of the Kamloops Central Rockets. Don Brown was the manager and a familiar face worked the bench. The Grey Ghost, Kenny Stewart, had the honour of guiding the first junior team.

The squad played a series of exhibition games against teams from Kelowna, Vernon and Penticton and eventually formed part of the Okanagan All Stars that vied for provincial honours and the right to represent B.C. on the road to the Memorial Cup. Unlike junior teams of today, the squad was composed of local players and gave a genuine indication of the strength of the local minor hockey system.

The first roster included Vic Minamede, Skip Holmes, Don Newman, Bill Donaldson, Barrie Hunt, Darrel Eckhart, Ron Recchi (uncle of future star Mark Recchi), Tom Endean, Dick Hart, Waverly Conan, Glen Madsen (who had returned from Estevan), Bill Bowles, Buck Crawford, Vic Endean and Glenn Richards. In goal were Brian Wallace and Bob Bradley.

Some 535 fans took in the team's first game at Memorial Arena. When they went up against the New Westminster Royals later in the month, they were facing a team that had been together for three years. In front of 900 appreciative fans, the Rockets, backstopped by Wallace, took the visitors 5-3 to go 4-1 in their short inaugural season.

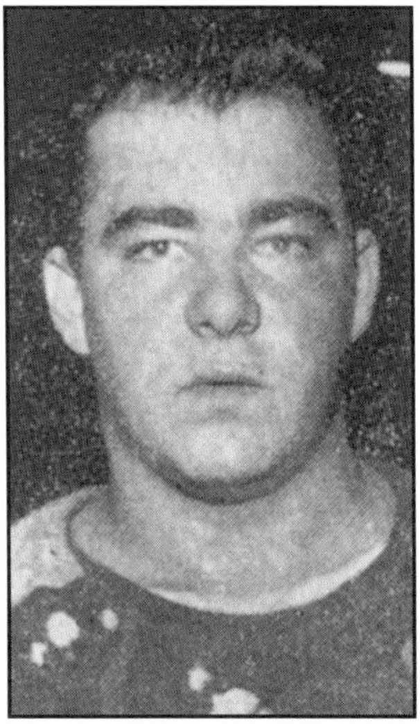

The second Recchi, Ron, stellar defenceman on the junior Rockets. (c. Ron Recchi)

Stewart was selected to coach the Okanagan All Stars which fell to the Rossland/Trail squad. That team went on to represent B.C. and faced the powerful Edmonton Oil Kings which was on its way to its second straight Memorial Cup appearance. It was no contest as Edmonton won four games to none..

In minor play, the midget Braves, under coach Don Reid, demolished Prince George Loggers and then rolled over Penticton to advance to the provincial semis against New Westminster. The Royal City fell and the Braves took the Moffatt Trophy as Interior champs. They were in the finals and faced Trail for the Cromie Cup, in Trail.

They stunned the Kootenay squad 8-4 in Game 1. Another win and they would be provincial champs for the second year in a row.

Kamloops, on goals by Barry Paterson, Will Moffatt and George Meridew, took a 3-1 lead into the dressing room at the end of the first. They maintained their two-goal edge going into the third at 4-2. Trail did not roll over and came back to tie the score at 4-4. Kamloops settled down and at 16:05 Dale Sandyke, on a pass from Moffatt, put the Braves up by one. Trail pressed and at 19:45 pulled their goaltender. Two seconds later the puck was in the net. Fortunately, it was off of the stick of Terry Shishido into an empty net as Kamloops took the game 6-4 and the series in two straight.

Once again the Commodore Cup was put up for a challenge match between Alberta and B.C.. The Edmonton Canadians Athletics came to town and this time skated away with the silverware in two straight.

The Jardine-sponsored bantams, in one of their most successful seasons to date, brought home the Northern Trophy under the guidance of coach Doug Cousins and manager Frank Bell. There skated on the squad a young lad who was soon to become very recognizable. His name was Jimmy Harrison.

The juvenile Falcons, who got as far as the semis before being knocked out by Trail, did not fare quite so well as they had last year; however, on the team was another player destined for stardom at the highest level, Bert Marshall.

As disappointing as the senior hockey situation turned out, what with the demise of Senior A hockey and the Chiefs elimination in the playoffs, the prospects for junior hockey could not help but generate excitement. Not only were local teams doing well but individual players were beginning to make their way into higher and higher calibre play.

The fading star of the seniors was being overtaken by the rising sun of the juniors.

Off in Estevan, the team photo revealed Kamloops' own Jim Letcher in net.

18

The Rockets Take Off _____________ 1961-62

The start of the 1961-62 season was different than any other.

The Senior A league had died and, with it, any dreams of an Allan Cup. Although senior hockey remained at the Senior B or Intermediate A level, junior hockey, with its ultimate prizes of the Mowat Cup and Memorial Cup, supplanted it.

The first tentative steps of the year before were solidified with the beginning of the Okanagan Mainline Junior Hockey League featuring the Kamloops Central Rockets, the Vernon Junior Canadians, the Kelowna Buckaroos and the Penticton Junior Vees. The league winner was destined to go up against the Kootenay champs for the right to contest against Alberta.

The Kamloops team was sponsored by Ernie Davies of the Central Hotel and kept Kenny Stewart and Don Brown in their old positions. Mike Shabaga was assistant coach. The imbalance in playing against Prairie teams was immediately evident as Skip Holmes, Don Newman, Will Moffatt, Murray Owens and Bill Schall were all suiting up for Prairie teams that were, in fact, competing with Kamloops in the quest for the Memorial Cup. Meanwhile, Kamloops was relying entirely upon local products.

As the junior season neared, the roster shaped up with the return of six veterans and a host of rookies. Bill Donaldson, George Meridew and Barrie Hunt formed the first line, followed by Jackie James, Glenn "Cowboy" Richards and Larry Bedard on the second line, and Glenn Madsen, Vic Minamede and Bob Nishamura. Defence had Terry Shishido, Ron "The Fireplug" Recchi, Bill Steinke and Buck Crawford. Peter Sternig guarded the pipes and was later joined by Brian Patterson.

The Rockets blasted out of the gate taking their home opener 12-0 over Penticton before 300 fans. James had eight points and Madsen four goals. Vernon fared no better. Then in Kelowna before 735 fans, they learned the season would not be a walk, the Buckaroos handed them their first defeat at 5-4.

When they met again, in Kamloops, the Rockets squared

the season series at 1-1 before 900 fans with a 7-3 victory. They came right back to take the next game 6-1 and move into a first-place tie with Kelowna.

The battle for first led to an intensity that spilled over in their next game. The Buckaroos were well ahead when Kamloops began its comeback and the rivalry reached a flash point at 19:37 of the third when fighting broke out that eventually involved the fans. Game officials finally had to call game which ended 7-5 for Kelowna. One Kelowna player was suspended for two years for cross checking a referee. Kamloops was still in first.

The rivalry with Kelowna was bringing out bigger crowds but, by late January, the suspense was over. Kamloops secured first place and the Elks Trophy by virtue of an 8-0 whitewash of Penticton. The same team that had to face Kamloops in the first round.

The series started off with an upset loss to the Junior Vees in front of 1,200 fans. Kamloops took Game 2 at home 4-1 and then delighted 1,300 fans with a 5-0 win in Game 3. The Rockets put the Vees away in Game 4 to move on against Kelowna,

1,500 fans turned up at Memorial for the opening game of the final and saw Crawford score three and set up two in an 8-3 shellacking of their strongest rival. Showing it was no fluke, the Rockets went into Kelowna and won 6-1. They were set to win the best of five on home ice.

Kelowna showed heart in the face of possible elimination. Down 6-4 in the third and before an unfriendly 1,400 fans, they clawed back to tie the game at 16:35 and forced overtime. In OT, at the 1:30 minute mark, Kelowna got control of the puck with Sternig out of the net but could not get a shot away. It remained for Crawford to be the hero when he fired a shot from his side of the blueline, at 8:32, to score on Don Kennedy who had kept Kelowna in the game. The league was theirs.

The foes in the next round came with an ominous ring. They were the Trail Junior Smoke Eaters. Teams from Trail were not Kamloops' favourite opposition. More often than not, Trail had been the roadblock to many a Kamloops team's aspirations for provincial championships. This time, they stood between Kamloops and its first opportunity to win the junior provincial title and go on for the Memorial Cup.

Trail had been successful in overcoming the Okanagan All Stars the year before and going up against a team drawn solely from the Kamloops area would seem to be an easier task even if the best-of-three series was being played in Kamloops. The 1,800 fans who crowded into the hockey shrine had no idea what to expect. History was not on Kamloops' side but that night history had to take a seat in the back row as the Rockets throttled the visitors 8-3.

More than 2,000 fans gathered for Game 2 and the opportunity to see history made. The bigger and heavier Trail squad got the first goal but then the teams jockeyed back and forth until the third. Kamloops had taken a 4-2 lead but Trail had bounced back to tie. For six minutes after the tying goal, the teams kept the fans on their hands. Then, with less than two minutes remaining, Nishimura on assists from Madsen and Minamede raised a backhander into the Trail net to give the Rockets the lead. In desperation, Trail pulled their goalie but the move backfired as Donaldson picked up a loose puck and raced down the ice to score and put the game out of reach. The final read 6-4 and the Kamloops' Rockets were provincial junior champions and holders of the Mowatt Cup.

Provincial Junior Champs and winners of the Mowatt Cup in their first year — the Kamloops Rockets.
Back Row: (l-r) Bill Cochrane, Bill Donaldson, Brian Patterson, Glen Madsen, Jack James, Brian Stoodley. Middle Row: Glen Richards, Vic Minamide, Terry Shishido, Barry Hunt, Larry Bedard, Bob Nishamura, Bill Steinke, Front Row: Ernie Davies, Leroy Hart, Don Brown, Buck Crawford, Ken Stewart (coach) Peter Sternig, Jim Stewart.
(c. Riverside ColiseumWall of Fame)

The previous season the Trail juniors had gone down four straight to the Edmonton Oil Kings, being outscored 32-7. The Rockets were facing the same Edmonton team and Sentinel writer Wally Cross suggested the odds were stacked against them by commenting even if they were to lose against Edmonton the season should be seen as a major success.

Kamloops was required to pick up six players from other British Columbia junior teams to bolster their squad but that paled by comparison to the geographic draw that the Detroit Red Wing sponsored Oil Kings relied upon. Sonny Hebst (Kelowna), Fred Thomas, Phil Larder, Bob Gruber, Seiko Ouchi (Vernon) and goaltender Dale Harder (Vernon) suited up in Kamloops' colours for the journey to Edmonton.

Despite playing on unfriendly ice, the Rockets were in Game 1 at the end of the first being down only 1-0 and 2-0 at the end of the second. Only 1,346 fans were on hand to see Edmonton unleash 26 shots in the third to take the game going away at 6-0. Kamloops only managed three shots. On the opposite side of the ice skated, a name still associated with success and Edmonton to this day. Glen Sather's Oil Kings were already a well -known team which was on its way to its third straight Memorial Cup appearance. It was, in fact, the franchise with which Kamloops battles to this day, only it now plays out of Portland.

Harder was again in net for Game 2 which saw the Oil Kings fire 45 shots and skate away with a decisive 10-1 victory. Kamloops was in danger of going out in three straight without even having the ability to claim a close game. The one saving grace was Game 3 was to be at Memorial Arena.

Some 3,100 fans crammed into the barn with hope springing eternal. The odds were stacked against their boys but this was the road to the Memorial Cup and no Kamloops team had been on it before. Stewart put Sternig in net and he stopped 12 shots in the first to keep the score deadlocked at 0-0. In the second, the play was closer and Kamloops was only outshot 8-7. Alas one of those shots found the net at 17:20. Still, going into the third, the Rockets were far from out of it. The Oil Kings poured it on outshooting the Rockets 11-3 but Sternig was solid in net until the 12:10 mark when Edmonton netted a second goal. Kamloops allowed no more but they were not able to get any past Gray in the Oil Kings goal either. The Rockets' season ended with the 2-0 loss.

Players, fans and media alike drew consolation from the Rockets' gutsy performance. One writer commented at times it was hard to distinguish between the $45,000 Detroit Red Wing-sponsored team and the $5,000 upstart B.C. Junior Champs. Junior hockey had come to town with a bang and it was not about to let up soon.

At the senior level, the Chiefs dropped down to the B level and arranged to play some of their games out of Merritt in order to accommodate the new act in Kamloops. They joined the Pacific Coast International League along with Chilliwack Steel Heads, Powell River Regals, Vancouver Luckies and Seattle. Almost all their home games ended up being in Merritt and the squad managed to finish in second.

In the playdowns, the Chiefs went up against the Summerland/Penticton Macs which sported a few former Elks and Chiefs on its roster. Don Moog, Jack Taggart and Kevin Conway were all part of a Macs team that quickly put Kamloops on the golf course on the road to grabbing the Coy Cup. They made it all the way to the national final with pickups from Kamloops to help out in their quest. Don Busch, Bob Gannon, Buddy Evans and Freddie Gaber fortified the squad.

Andy Clovechok's Juvenile Legionnaires. Provincial finalists — with future NHLer Bert Marshall in the lineup. Back Row: (l-r) Doug Dawes, Rick McShane, George Meridew, Ken Cooper, Bernie Martin, Robert Davoren, Larry Roberge, Barry Patterson, Melvin Meachem, Andy Clovechok. Front: Bill Gagliardi, Bert Marshall, Glen Esselmont, Brett McGillivray, Bill Graff, Clare Long. (c. Andy Clovechok)

The glories of the past seemed well behind the Chiefs now but things are not always as they seem. Just ask Buddy Evans.

Minor hockey did not add any provincial cups to the growing trophy case but the juvenile Legionnaires, under the guidance of Andy Clovechok and listing Bert Marshall on their roster, reached the provincial final before going down to defeat at the hands of the Trail team.

In Estevan, the team photo added future NHLer Joe Watson. They took the regular season championship in their division but came up short in earning provincial rights to playoff towards the Memorial Cup.

19

Raise a Cup to the Tribe ____________ 1962-63

The 1962-63 season began with all eyes on the Rockets who proved well worth watching; but there were some thrills from an unexpected source.

The Rockets training camp opened with the definite loss of some players and the prospect others might be picked up by Prairie competition or even minor league pro teams. The Sentinel noted that a number of Kamloops players were attending the training camp of the Edmonton Oil Kings. One, in particular, stuck. Jackie James, at 18, was off to the University of Denver, Glen Richards and Bill Steinke to the Seattle Totems, Buck Crawford to Portland and players Bob Nishamura, Bill Donaldson, Vic Minamede and Barry Hunt graduated from junior hockey. With the team still relying on local talent, this was a good year to find out just what depth there was locally.

Hopefuls included Bill Cochran, Barry Patterson, Robby Jamieson, Dale Sandyke, Eddie Begg, Terry Shishido, Ken Rinaldi, Paul Amacher (goal), Larry Bedard, Ricky McShane, Larry Roberge and Ken Rogers. Fortunately Steinke and Richards returned and joined Glen Madsen (team captain), Eric Shishido, George Meridew, Ron Recchi and Roy Hart as returnees.

Any doubts were quickly dispelled as the team roared out of the gate winning 13 and tying 1 before losing a game to their closest rival, Kelowna. Kelowna battled again for first. The Vernon Blades, so renamed after receiving an equipment donation from the professional Los Angeles Blades, and Penticton Vees were also-rans again that season. In one game against the Don Slater coached Vees, Eric Shishido got five points and Eddie Begg six in a 19-1 throttling.

Some controversy arose during the season when Don Brown, the Kamloops GM, complained about Kelowna recruiting a player from Williams Lake contrary to the agreement amongst teams to only use locals.

Despite the great start, it was Kelowna that secured first at season's end. Kamloops, Vernon and Penticton followed in that order. Goalie Jim Letcher was added to the Rockets roster for the playoffs after Hart had carried the bulk of the work during the regular season. Kamloops had no trouble disposing of Penticton and similarly Kelowna put away Vernon to set up a replay of last year's Okanagan final.

Kamloops dropped Game 1 in Kelowna and evened the series after taking Game 2 on home ice. It looked like a homer series until the Rockets waltzed into Kelowna for Game 3 and stole it and home ice advantage 5-3. After taking Game 4 back in Kamloops, the Rockets had the Buckaroos on the verge of elimination. The Bucks staved of the golf season to force a sixth game back at Memorial.

Nearly 2,400 fans poured into Memorial Arena in the hopes of seeing their Rockets advance towards a second Mowatt Cup final. Before the first period ended, two goals by Begg and one by Richards gave Kamloops an insurmountable lead. The two scorers finished the night with a hat trick each as the Rockets took the game 6-2 and eliminated the Buckaroos.

The Rockets journeyed to New Westminster to face the Royals at legendary Queen's Park Arena. A stubborn Royals team grabbed a comeback 4-3 win in Game 1 to put the Rockets on the edge in the best of three. Game 2 saw the two teams tied at 2-2 and heading into OT . The Rockets' opinion of the reffing was not fit to be printed in a game that clearly got out of hand. In the end, the 4-2 score did not favour the Rockets and their season ended.

It left them, however, with a score to settle.

The Senior B team was up and rolling that season in an Interior league that included Kelowna Packers, Vernon Canadians and the Penticton/Summerland Twin City Macs. Mike Shabaga was behind the organizing of the team and Buddy Evans took on the task of player coach.

The Twin City Macs folded before the season got underway leaving the remaining three to duke it out. Kelowna and Kamloops began their season-long battle for supremacy with Kamloops getting a boost in December with word that Grant Warwick was set to join the squad. The battle went down to the wire.

The playoff format had first place getting a bye while second and third battled it out in Round 1. The Chiefs last game of the season was against the Packers which held first by two points. A win by Kamloops would create a tie and a two-game, total-points playoff to determine the league winner. Evans stole the night with three goals in a Chiefs 8-4 victory. The teams were tied.

Game 1 of the two game series went in Kelowna but it didn't deter the Chiefs who stole it 12-8. On home ice, they took Game 2 9-6 to win first place in the reborn Okanagan Intermediate A Hockey League.

Insult was added to injury for the Packers who fell in two straight to a rested Vernon squad. In an effort to match the Chiefs, the Canadians added two Senior A players and travelled to Memorial Arena for the opening game. They made it close but Bob Gannon potted the winner for Kamloops in a 7-6 victory before only 300 fans. Nine hundred turned out in Vernon hoping for a repeat of the upset over Kelowna but were disappointed when the Chiefs easily turned the Canadians aside 10-3. It was all but over and the 5-3 victory in Kamloops secured the league for the Chiefs.

The fact they were the second act in town was obvious from the fan support and their ousting from Memorial in favour of the Rockets' playoff dates. They had to play their next series in Merritt. To make matters worse, they had to go up against the Trail Smoke Eaters.

Again history took a back seat as the Chiefs rolled over the Smokies in two straight to advance to the Coy Cup final against the Powell River Regals. The two had met twice in preseason play and split the series. It looked like anybody's series with the nudge going to Powell River because of home-ice advantage for the whole series. Kamloops was bolstered by Tom Stecyk from Vernon.

In Game 1 the visitors, on two goal performances by Freddie Gaber and Gordie Kusumoto, came from behind to beat the Regals 6-4.

The Regals, with their backs to the wall and playing in front of 1,100 fans, put out their best effort and were rewarded with a 2-0 lead at the end of the first in Game 2. Bill Donaldson brought Kamloops to within one early in the second and then, before the period ended, Kusumoto knotted the score. In the third, Bud Schollen gave Kamloops its first lead but it was short-lived. Schollen came back to give the Chiefs the lead again. Within 38 seconds, the score changed again only this time it was Gaber who notched the point and gave Kamloops its biggest lead of the night. The Regals couldn't hold their two goal lead, could Kamloops? At 17:18 the Regals got one back and in the final minute with their goalie out, were pressing for the equalizer.

At 19:22 of the third, Gaber pickd up the loose puck and had a chance to ice the game and the cup for the Chiefs. He did.

The Chiefs regained for Kamloops the cup that had come to the city 10 years before and, for the second time, was provincial Senior B champions.

The Chiefs now had to face the Alberta champs in their drive for the nationals and the Hardy Cup. The best-of-five was scheduled to be played in its totality in Olds, Alta. against the

1962 - '63 Coy Cup Champions - Kamloops Chiefs

Top Row: (L. to R.) – Bud Evans, Don Busch, Buddy Schollen, Ross Jardine, Don Schollen, Bill Donaldson, Fred Gaber, Gordie Kusomoto. **Front Row:** (L. to R.) – Mel Recchi, Ev Miller, Bobby Gannon, Shorty Stiles, John Panagrot Missing – Bruce Harrison, Buck Cranford.

Coy Cup Champions — Kamloops Chiefs

Olds Elks. The Chiefs bolstered their squad with Brian Roche and Bill Jones of Kelowna.

"Shorty" Stiles netted two goals as Kamloops skated away with a stunning 6-1 victory in Game 1 to grab the early series lead. Olds regrouped to grab a close 4-3 victory in Game 2 and were then forced to overtime before taking Game 3 4-3. There was nothing left in the reserve tank for Game 4 and the Chiefs fell 5-0 to end their quest.

Their season had been the best experienced by a Kamloops' senior club for many years and there was optimism for next year.

Although no provincial trophies came to Kamloops by way of the minor hockey rep teams, two players were getting more than a little interest. The midget Elks sported Jimmy Harrison while the peewees had a young phenom named Randy Rota tearing up the stats sheets. In one game against Salmon Arm, he netted five goals and five assists in an 18-0 shellacking.

The player who had been grabbed out of Kamloops' own backyard to join the powerhouse Edmonton Oil Kings was Bert Marshall. He and his teammates had the pleasure of finally winning the Memorial Cup after reaching the final for the fourth straight time. On the road to the cup, they overcame the Estevan Bruins which had Don Newman, another Kamloops product, in its lineup

Kamloops was spreading its wings beyond the Rockies.

Bert Marshall of the Edmonton Oil Kings. First Kamloops produced player to get his name on the Memorial Cup. (c. Riverside Coliseum Wall of Fame)

20

A Season to Remember ____________ 1963-64

There are seasons fans look back on and say "That was a season to remember." Seasons when even the disappointments carry promise. 1963-64 was just such a season for Kamloops hockey fans. Both the rising Comets and the fading stars shone in the heavens.

The junior season began with the usual questions about departing players and bright-eyed rookies. Kenny Stewart and Don Brown had 11 returnees in Ken Rinaldi, Bill Steinke, Glen Richards, the Shishido brothers, Larry Roberge, Eddie Begg, Ricky McShane, Dale Sandyke, Robbie Jamieson and Leroy Hart in goal. Gone were Jim Letcher, Glen Madsen, Ron Recchi, Larry Bedard and Bill Cochran. The newcomers were Jim Stuart, Ken Rodgers, Harvey Budarick, Lee Simpson in goal, Len Demarchi, Brian Fourt and Jimmy Harrison.

The New Westminster Royals came to town for two exhibition matches and reminded the Rockets of last season's defeat by taking Game 1 10-6. Not to be outdone, the Rockets came back in Game 2, on two goals by Harrison, to win 8-3. Then it was time to get down to business.

McShane got off the mark quickly with a hat trick in an 8-2 season opener against Kelowna. In Game 2, Harrison got the winner in a 2-1 victory over the Vernon Blades. In Game 3, Eric Shishido got two goals and three assists in a 9-3 win over Vernon.

With the team standing at 4-1, they got good news from Regina. Murray Owens was returning to bolster the already strong squad. It was a year of big nights for many players. Roberge had a five-goal night in a 12-2 win over Vernon while Brian Fourt scored four in an 11-5 thrashing of the same Blades. Steinke came up with six points in a 12-6 victory.

Partway through the season, tradition was broken and a hint of changes to come was suggested by the acquisition of an outside player. Paul Levens from Williams Lake was their first import.

There was no question who was going to win the Elks Trophy and Kamloops finished a full 18 points ahead of second-place Kelowna. Vernon was last in the three-team league. The season-ending stats had Roberge winning the league scoring title only two points ahead of teammate Eric Shishido. Budarick was top goalie ahead of teammate Simpson. Kenny Stewart as coach, Simpson as goalie along with Richardson, Eric Shishido and Rinaldi landed on the all-star team. Even when they went up against the Coy Cup Champion Senior B Chiefs, they came out with a 5-5 tie.

The season ending playoffs proved there is never any consistency as the three teams played off in a round robin which gave Kamloops no benefit for having won the regular season. It didn't matter as they went 6-1 in the round robin to skate away with the Davis Trophy which was presented to team captain Glen "Cowboy" Richards.

The next foe was the Trail Junior Smoke Eaters but their 12-3 romp in Game 1 at Memorial Arena led by Owens two goals suggested the old curse was not so strong anymore. Any gloating stopped in Game 2 when the Smokies rebounded for a 6-4 win and sent the series to a third-and-deciding game.

Some 1,800 fans took in the rubber match and kept their nails trimmed in the process. Despite dramatically outshooting the Smokies, the Rockets found themselves down 2-0 by the 11-minute mark of the first. Relief came 35 seconds later when Sandyke finally got Kamloops on the board. Eight minutes later Eric Shishido tied it up and that was how period number 1 ended. The same held true in the second as Trail went up 3-2, but within 15 seconds, Begg had tied it again. Kamloops grabbed its first lead on a second marker by Sandyke but the Kootenay squad tied it before the period ended.

At 1:45 of the third, the air went out of the crowd as Trail once again took the lead. They could breath again when Kamloops tied it up within a minute on a goal by import Levens. The Rockets poured it on and were rewarded when Owens restored their lead at 6-5. Sweaty palms continued until 17:35 when the barn erupted in response to Begg's 7-5 tally.

The Smokies were finished and Kamloops was on its way to the Mowatt Cup final for the third straight year. There was revenge in their hearts.

The Rockets had a score to settle with New Westminster Royals, although they were going to have to start it in the unfriendly confines of Queen's Park. Undeterred they took Game 1 3-1 and then Roberge did the damage himself with two goals in the Rockets 2-0 shutout in Game 2. The Rockets were coming home up two games to none. The run continued as Richards led the team with three goals and one assist in a 10-3 thrashing of the Royals. The Mowatt Cup was within their reach.

New Westminster didn't lay down and die in Game 4 and, at the end of the first period, was only down 3-2. They were still respectable at 5-3 at the end of the second but the third belonged to the Rockets. The Mowatt Cup was theirs when the buzzer sounded and Kamloops took the day 8-3. Once again it was the Edmonton Oil Kings waiting for them.

Kamloops Rockets 1964 — Provincial junior champions for the second time in three years. Riverside Coliseum Wall of Fame
From back: (l-r) Murray Owen, Terry Sheshido, Lee Simpson, Eric Shishido, Art Yuen (trainer), Ken Rodgers, Jim Harrison, Ken Stewart, Don Brown, Rick McShane, Robbie Jamieson, Paul Levens, Ken Rinaldi, Dale Sandyke, Larry Roberge, Brian Fort, Bill Steinke, Eddie Begg, Glen Richards, Harvey Budarick. (c. Riverside Coliseum Wall of Fame)

The Memorial Cup champions were on their way to their fifth straight Memorial Cup appearance and were not yet done with their consecutive streak. The situation facing the Rockets was the same as two years before. The stacked Oil Kings were effectively an all-star team by comparison to the Rockets. The fact it was not a level playing field was clearly evident by the fact Edmonton had reached into Kamloops' own backyard to grab away defenceman Bert Marshall. The Oil Kings dominated the West and, in that season, rolled by the Calgary Buffaloes by scores of 14-3 and 10-3 to take Alberta.

The Rockets added six players from the other British Columbia junior teams and had the benefit of playing the first two games at Memorial. It didn't help.

In Game 1 the Oil Kings walked all over the Rockets 10-1 in front of 2,700 fans. Marshall notched a goal while the line of Glen Sather, Butch Paul and Max Mestenser tallied seven. Game 2 was little better as Marshall garnered two assists in a 7-2 victory before 1,832 resigned fans. Simpson made 43 saves compared to only 27 shots directed against Edmonton. It was nothing compared to what awaited him in Edmonton.

The Oil Kings knew they could lock up the series with a win over B.C. and they did it in the most humbling fashion. Eighty-eight shots were fired on Simpson who managed to stop 69 of them. Edmonton's Russ Kirk only faced nine but the Rockets got five past him with Owens getting three and Richards two. Kamloops was in the game at the start of the second only being down 4-2 but, at the end, the clock showed 13-3. Marshall tallied two in a game witnessed by only 1,563 fans. 19-5 was the final.

Arguably one of the best teams to come out of B.C. had been demolished. Despite the prowess of local talent, there was no way a team drawn solely from a small Interior city could compete against an all-star team that could grab Kamloops' own budding stars. The strength of Kamloops' minor hockey was demonstrated when Prairie teams came scouting the shores of the Thompson and whisked away its brightest prospects. The performance of one of the Rockets had not gone unnoticed in Estevan. Marshall was destined to have another follow his footsteps.

The wars with the Oil Kings franchise go on to this day in the form of the Kamloops Blazers and the Portland Winter Hawks, though, they now play on a level playing field and it is Kamloops that holds the upper hand. Those two franchises were not strangers to each other before their battles came farther west.

When news of the Kamloops' Chiefs hit the paper in November 1963, familiar names dotted the lineup and Buddy Evans was there as playing coach. Without a league to play in, they struggled for the competition necessary to hone their skills. By the time the playdowns started they had managed only five games.

Regulars listed on the team included Freddie Gaber, Bud Schollen, Don Romeike, Ev Miller, Buck Crawford, Ross Jardine, John Panagrot and Melvin Recchi in net, Gordie Kusumoto, Bob

Gannon, Ron "Shorty" Stiles and manager Nick Pyevach.

Word came they were scheduled to play the winner of the Caribou Intermediate Hockey League. The best news was the Coy Cup final was scheduled for Kamloops, March 21-23 and the Interprovincial Intermediate Championship in Kamloops, March 31 to April 7. The prospect of playing for the championship in front of a home crowd was a big incentive. However it did not start well.

In the first game of the two-game, total-point series the Quesnel Kangaroos elated their fans with a 5-3 win. It looked like Kamloops may not even make it by the first round. Regrouping the Chiefs came back to take Game 2 6-2 and advance to meet the Powell River Regals.

The 1963-64 Chiefs — Two straight Coy Cups for the Chiefs.

Going into that final series, the Chiefs carried a tradition of the Interior winning championships more than any other area of B.C. In the 28 years the Coy Cup had been competed for province wide, the Interior took it 20 times and the Coast only eight. Of those 20, the Okanagan had taken it 12 times and Kamloops twice. Kamloops was out to match Vernon's back-to-back Coy Cup championships which occurred twice; once in the '20s and once in the '30s.

The Chiefs bolstered their lineup with Odie Lowe of Vernon, Don Jakes, Don Busch, Glen Madsen and Larry Bedard.

The line of Crawford, Gannon and Gaber owned the first game as the Chiefs walked all over the visitors 8-4. Game 2 was not so easy.

Facing elimination, the Regals went to the attack and were up 2-0 by 9:30 of the first. Busch narrowed the gap on an assist from Kusumoto before the period ended. Fifty seconds into the second Kusumoto tied the score. The score held until 19:05 when Schollen set up Gaber for the go ahead goal that had to demoralize the Regals. In the third, Schollen put them up 4-2. When playing coach Evans put the Chiefs up 5-2 it looked to be all but over. With time winding down and the celebrants getting ready however, Powell River took the wind out of the sails. They scored at 18:07 but Kamloops still had a two-goal lead. Not to worry? A two-goal lead with less than two minutes remaining; they couldn't lose. Then came heart stopping time. The Regals scored again with 35 seconds left.

Powell River pulled its goalie and pressed for the equalizer but there was to be no miracle for the Regals. The buzzer sounded and the Chiefs began celebrating their second straight provincial championship.

Only once had a Kamloops team beaten an Alberta team in interprovincial playoff competition. Don Reid's Cromie Cup champion squad had beaten the Edmonton Canadians for the inaugural Commodore Cup in 1960. The Edmontonians returned the favour the following year. The old Elks had been stopped by Calgary, the Rockets twice by the Oil Kings, the Loggers by Canmore and the Chiefs last year by the Olds Legionnaires. This year, Kamloops was hosting the Alberta - B.C. final and the Red Deer Rustlers were their foes.

Herb Greyeyes from Quesnel joined Odie Lowe and Don Jakes to bolster the squad. The Chiefs lined up with Greyeyes, Gaber and Gannon on one line and the other two formed by Kusumoto, Jakes and Lowe, and Buddy Evans, Schollen and Stiles.

In Game 1 Kamloops' defence held the Rustlers at bay in a hard-fought, 5-4 victory. Ray Hamilton joined the team from Quesnel for Game 2 but it wasn't enough as the Rustlers rebounded for a solid 7-3 win. The Chiefs turned the tables in the third game outshooting Red Deer 42-20 as Evans came up with two goals in a 5-2 triumph. The Chiefs were on the verge of going to the national final against either Maidstone, Sask. or Warroad, Minn. and there were only 800 fans in the stands to cheer them on.

Despite being down to an 11-man roster, the Rustlers were not about to go down without a fight. A pair of goals by Lowe gave the Chiefs an early 2-0 lead but ex-Chief Rex Turple came back against his old buddies with two of his own to knot the score. The Rustlers continued to press the Chiefs, outshooting them 14-6 in the period, but they could not get another past Panagrot.

The second period settled nothing and ended tied at 3-3. In the first rush of the third Bob Gannon fired his second goal of the night to give the Chiefs the lead. Lowe completed his hat trick to put Kamloops up 5-3. When the Rustler's pulled their goalie in a last desperate move, defenceman John Yanchuk drifted a shot over playing coach Ray Yanosik to seal a 6-3 win.

The Chiefs had advanced farther down the playoff road than any Kamloops team before them. The national intermediate final was to be an all western affair as the East did not field any intermediates that year. It was also Kamloops' first international playoff as they went up against the Warroad Lakers at the neutral site of Winnipeg.

The Lakers were a largely American-born team that included three players from the United States national team: Bill and Roger Christian, of Minnesota's famous Christian hockey family, and Sammy Grafstrom.

In Game 1, despite three goals by Greyeyes, the Chiefs fell easily 8-4. In Game 2 a late burst by the Lakers netted a 6-4 win to put the Chiefs on the verge of elimination.

With elimination on the line, the Chiefs roared out to a 2-0 lead by the four-minute mark of Game 3 but, within a further six minutes, the Minnesotans had bounced back to take a 3-2 lead. This time the Chiefs came back at 19:43 of the first the tie the game up.

Momentum did not stay with the Chiefs as Warroad controlled the second and led 7-5 going into the third. The Chiefs didn't fold and pulled to within one. Two minutes later, the Lakers restored their two-goal lead. Again, at 14:36, on a goal by Stiles, Kamloops closed to within one but there were no more goals after that. The Chiefs had to watch as the Warroad Lakers skated off with the Canadian Intermediate A hockey championship.

They returned to Kamloops having missed an opportunity to bring Kamloops its first national title but they had journeyed farther down that road than any team before them and it was years before another Kamloops team was to skate out on the national stage.

Minor league hockey in Kamloops was thriving. It was recorded a record 135 players had registered for league play in just one day.

Though none of the rep teams brought home provincial hardware, they all had more than respectable playoff runs.

The midget Elks sailed by Salmon Arm, Summerland, Vernon and Prince George to come up against the Trail midget all stars in the semi-finals. Of late, history had been kinder to Kamloops in its matches against Trail but, in Game 1 Trail dropped the Elks 8-4. They now had to make up four goals in the two-game, total-point series.

In the second game, Roy Sakaki gave Kamloops a 1-0 lead but Trail tied it before the end of the first. Gerald Janicki, a former Kamloops' player, put Trail up 2-1 in the second but Kenny Begg tied it. Robbie Osborne garnered two to give Kamloops a 4-2 lead and hopes of making up the margin. In the third, Janicki got the only marker and Kamloops, though winners of Game 2, fell 11-8 in total points. The Trail coach praised the Elks who had outshot Trail 54 to 29 despite taking 10 of the 15 penalties. Future Kamloops resident Murray Finlay was in the nets for Trail that game. Not only did he steal the show that night he eventually caught the eye of the Chicago Black Hawks and played a number of years in their professional organization.

On the Prairies, the Oil Kings, which had decimated the Rockets, went up against the Estevan Bruins, the winners of the Saskatchewan - Manitoba final. The Bruins had future NHLer Ross Lonsberry along with Terry Simpson, Fran Huck and Kamloops' own Don Newman in their lineup, but they were no match for the Oil Kings either as they went out 4-1 in the series. The Oil Kings march to the Memorial Cup continued.

Both Estevan and Edmonton were soon to cast their eyes on a Rocket from Kamloops that would light up the Prairie sky.

21

Brave New World ________________ 1964-65

The 1964-65 season began with as much, if not more, promise than other seasons. The Chiefs and the Rockets were provincial champs and the minor league rep teams remained a provincial force to be reckoned with.

Ken Stewart and Don Brown were back but the team lost Murray Owens, Larry Roberge who went to the Nelson Maple Leafs, Lee Simpson to the Moose Jaw Canucks, Glen Richards to to the University of British Columbia, Brian Fourt, Bill Steinke and Paul Levens. Most importantly they lost a budding star in Jimmy Harrison, who was picked up by the Estevan Bruins but also was to have a place in Edmonton Oil Kings fans' hearts. Still, management thought that the Rockets were the team to beat. Eddie and Ken Begg, Eric and Terry Shishido, Dale Sandyke, Robbie Jamieson, George Meridew, Charlie Cook, George Uyeda, Roy Sakaki, Joe Bedard, Wayne Laveay and Brent Campbell (from Merritt) filled out the skaters while Harvey Budarick and Bob Steinke guarded the pipes. Hopes were that Barry Patterson would rejoin the team. Later in the season, Ricky McShane, Ken Rinaldi, Bob Haywood (goal) and Ken Rodgers joined the squad.

They started off quickly winning their first nine games and confirming management's confidence. Eric Shishido was burning up the league and the Begg brothers were having an impact. The Penticton/Summerland Broncos had joined the league, but initially found themselves struggling to remain competitive. Kelowna again proved to be Kamloops' greatest challenge and a late season slump by the Rockets made for a close battle for first place. The late season reacquisition of McShane helped the cause considerably.

The Jan. 24, 1965 Inland Sentinel headlined a photo of team captain Terry Shishido holding up the Elks Trophy and, for the third time in four years, the Rockets were regular season champs. Brother, Eric, had won the scoring title and joined Terry on the all-star squad. Eric finished 24 points ahead of his nearest rival, teammate and league MVP Sandyke. Sandyke joined the all-stars along with Kenny Stewart and Jack Taggart, of the

Penticton Broncos, as coaches.

Given the regular season results, it was not unreasonable to think that Kamloops would roll over the Broncos in the first round. Reality proved different.

The Rockets took game one, on a hat trick by Sandyke, 5-2 and, when Eddie Begg got the 5-4 winner in Game 2, it looked like the series was all but over. A 6-3 win by the Broncos at Memorial was a bit of a shock and the following 7-4 loss in Penticton caused a bit of anxiety. However, the 5-3 loss back in Kamloops, which put the Rockets on the edge of elimination, caused genuine alarm. If they were going to stay alive, they had to win the next game in Penticton. That they did 5-1 and set the stage for a seventh-and-deciding game at Memorial.

Some 2,500 fans passed the turnstiles and watched as the Broncos fired 42 shots on Budarick. However, it was the Rockets who skated away with the 5-3 victory and the series.

The Buckaroos were rested and waiting.

Despite being outshot 71 to 37 in Game 1 at Memorial Arena, Kamloops forced overtime only to lose 4-3 and give up home-ice advantage. Kelowna took advantage of their home ice in Game 2 to win 5-1. Game three back in Kamloops had the Rockets down 3-0 before they staged a comeback. They still lost 5-4 and were on the verge of going out four straight. Kelowna used home ice in devastating fashion as they fired 50 shots on Budarick and crushed the Rockets 10-0. It was shades of the 1951-52 Elks season as the highly favoured Rockets fell to the upstart Buckaroos.

However, there is one thing about such upsets. It sets the stage for revenge.

Meanwhile, the Chiefs had managed to keep it together for another season. Buddy Evans initially agreed to come back as player/coach but left partway through the season to devote more time to minor hockey. Ev Miller took his place.

Without a league, the Chiefs had to settle for exhibition games to qualify for a Coy Cup challenge. In the course of their exhibitions, they took five of eight games played against the Vernon Luckies. They had to feel quite confident in taking on the Luckies in the first round. A Feb. 17, 1965 photo of Miller, Bob Gannon, Bud Schollen, Fred Gaber and John Panagrot holding the Coy Cup was the picture of confidence.

Game 1 in Vernon was tough and close. The Chiefs forced overtime but it was Vernon that netted the 5-4 win. The hopes of evening the series on Kamloops ice were dashed in Game 2 as the Luckies took the contest 4-2 and the series in two straight. Vernon carried on to bring the Coy Cup back to the North Okanagan. For the Chiefs, it was truly the end as they did not return.

Their place would be taken.

Since the 1947-48 season, the Hub City Leaf/Elks/Chiefs franchise had been a local fixture. They brought championships, glory and attention to the city on the Thompson. They had been the instrument to bring in outside players who stayed and helped to build the Kamloops minor hockey system into the imposing and successful system it is today.

In time, a roster that had been largely filled by imported players came to be dominated by those who had learned their skills locally and had often made names for themselves outside of Kamloops. Kenny Stewart, Buddy Evans, Johnny Milliard and Andy Clovechok had etched their impressions upon on the young locals and players such as Bob Gannon, Gaber, Madsen, Kusumoto and others had risen to prominence.

The seniors had provided both entertainment and the nurturing ground for the seeds of hockey that fell along the Thompson. The influence was to be felt so long as the legacy of its many players washed over Kamloops. If you look closely, you can see it still.

The minor hockey system continued to draw more players each year and its success was displayed on ice surfaces both near and far. Peter Sternig was playing goal for the Regina Pats; Owens, Jim Letcher and Buck Crawford were in the Western International Hockey League (where many Kamloops players plied their trade in the years ahead) with the Nelson Maple Leafs; Bert Marshall was still with the Edmonton Oil Kings; Gannon had turned down an invitation to the Toronto Maple Leafs training camp and Harrison was making his presence felt in Estevan. If Angus Nelson had still been alive, he would have marvelled at hockey in Kamloops 62 years after he had donned skates against Nicola at Riverside Park.

By Jan.14, 1965 the midget Elks, under the guidance of Andy Clovechok, had sealed possession of first place in the Okanagan loop after defeating Salmon Arm 14-5 at Memorial Arena. In the first game of the playoff against Vernon, they were rocked 12-7 and put behind the 8-ball in their best-of-three. Eking out a 3-2 victory in Game 2 at Memorial kept them alive and their 5-2 third game triumph secured them the league. A photo of smiling players Grant Evans (son of Buddy), Don Clovechok (son of Andy), Don Steinke, Gerry Janicky and Andy Clovechok in the Feb. 19, 1965 Sentinel said it all. They had made it to the semis against Trail.

History took centre ice as the Elks fell two straight to Trail; however, Andy Clovechok and some of the boys were going to be back in the provincial scene next season but not where you might have expected. There was an old score to be settled.

The bantams, with phenom Randy Rota, had one of their best seasons to date. They skated by Penticton to win the Okanagan before losing two straight in Prince George.

So Kamloops had gone from two Provincial championships to none? Not quite. The Kamloops Braves, with Peter Sasaskamoose in the lineup, won the B.C. Indian Hockey Championship at Salmon Arm going undefeated in the tournament and outscoring the opposition 25 to 10.

Peter Sasaskamoose was leading scorer with six goals and five assists in the four games. The Braves came to dominate First Nations hockey in B.C. so much that they were given the original trophy and a new one was made up.

The depth of Kamloops' hockey had reached the point even disappointing seasons had unmistakable successes and promise.

In Estevan, Ross Lonsberry posed in the team photo along with fellow future NHLer Jimmy Harrison. It is hard to know if Estevan realized yet what they had in the scrappy player from the other side of the mountains. If they didn't, they soon would.

22

North vs. South________________1965-66

The 1965-66 season saw something new emerge on the Kamloops hockey scene that could be viewed as good or bad depending on your viewpoint.

From junior on down through the minor hockey levels, Kamloops was a divided community. North Kamloops and Kamloops vied for local supremacy. On one hand, it gave more players an opportunity to play at the rep level, while on the other hand, it weakened the local teams when they played against other communities. The Kamloops area remained provincially competitive despite the division, revealing the depth of talent that was being developed.

The new kids on the block — the Kamloops Kraft Kings Juniors. (c. Riverside Coliseum Wall of Fame)

A big factor in the North Shore's emergence was its new Sports Centre officially opened in October 1965.

The Kamloops Rockets were replaced in the Okanagan league by a new team sponsored by Kamloops Pulp and Paper and operated by the Kamloops Amateur Hockey Association.

Andy Clovechok took over a team that had many returnees from the Rockets but more than a few significant losses. The Begg brothers were back along with Dale Sandyke, Eric Shishido, Charlie Cook, Ken Rodgers, Joe Bedard, Robbie Jamieson, Ricky McShane and Harvey Budarick in goal. Trying out for the squad were Roy Sakaki, Robbie Osborne, Brent Campbell, Jim Stewart, Wayne Laveay, Wally Deneault (goal) and Bob Haywood (goal). Terry Shishido was gone and Ken Rinaldi was off to Cranbrook in the WIHL.

Don Brown and Kenny Stewart emerged on the North

Shore heading up the new North Shore Totems of the Pacific Coast Junior Hockey League along with the New Westminster Royals, Prince George Pee Gees, Vancouver and Coquitlam.

Both teams had less than favourable starts but, for the Totems, the start and their circumstances were too much. After lopsided losses to New Westminster and Vancouver, they joined Coquitlam in dropping out of the league.

The Kraft Kings started with dead weights around their legs, too, losing their first three games before beating Penticton 4-2. From then on, it was a seesaw battle for position with Kelowna gazing back on the others in its rear-view mirror. Although the Kraft Kings captured second place, they were only one point ahead of Penticton and a full 16 behind the Buckaroos. The late-season reacquisition of Rinaldi from Cranbrook proved helpful. Added to the team by the time playoffs rolled around were Don Anthony and Jack Moores.

Eric Shishido had again run away with the scoring title with teammate Sandyke coming in second.

The last-place Vernon Blades had managed only nine points all season and fell to the Kings easily in four straight. Kamloops now faced the daunting task of going up against heavily favoured Kelowna. A clear reversal of last season's situation.

In the 10 games the teams had played, Kelowna had won nine and outscored Kamloops 65- 35. In Game 1 before 2,000 expectant Kelowna fans, however, the Kings dropped the Buckaroos 6-4 in overtime on the back of Sandyke's winner. Back in Kamloops, 2,500 fans turned up to see McShane score two and lead the Kings to a 3-2 victory. Returning to Kelowna, the Buckaroos got some life back with a 3-2 win but they were burned again in Kamloops when McShane netted a hat trick in the Kings 6-4 victory. Clovechok's boys were now in a position to upset the regular season champs right in their own backyard.

Despite being outshot 14-10 and taking five of the eight penalties in the first period, Kamloops had a 2-0 lead going into the second. The Bucks stormed out in the second outshooting the Kings 17-9 but, at period's end, the Kings remained in the lead at 3-1. Kelowna pulled out all the stops in the third. Outshooting Kamloops 18-9 they finally pulled to within one when they got one behind Budarick. The Kings were just holding on when Kenny Begg was called for a high sticking penalty at the 19 minute mark. Clovechok put out Laveay, Rodgers, McShane and Osborne and could only watch the seconds tick away.

They came through and Kamloops captured its fourth league championship in five years.

Fourteen years earlier, Clovechok had been a part of the Kamloops Elks squad favoured to make a run for the Allan Cup but was upset by a Kelowna team that had finished 25 points behind them. Last season, the Rockets had been in similar situation only to be upset by these very same Buckaroos. For Clovechok and the fans of Kamloops, revenge was sweet.

1965-66 Kraft Kings — Provincial junior finalists. Andy Clovechok Back Row: (l-r) "Dynamite" Don Anthony, Ken Rinaldi, Ken Rodgers, Jack Moore, Robbie Jamieson, Robbie Osborne, Wayne Laveay, Fred Doubt. Middle: Bush Jackson (Ast. Coach), Dale Sandyke, Wally Denault, Joey Bedard, Paul Smith, Ken Begg, Roy Sakaki, Gary Osborne, Rick McShane, Barney Lucas (Sponsor) Front: ? , Eddie Begg, Andy Clovechok, Harvey Budarick, Guy Pressy, Eric Shishido, Ross Jardine. (c. Andy Clovechok)

They had achieved their goal against a team that had brought in more than a few imports while Kamloops stuck with local talent. The Sentinel gloated "Kelowna's defeat in the final series is considered this season's biggest upset in the Okanagan area."

Poetic justice to be savoured.

The Kings now went up against the Trail Juniors. Outshooting the Kootenay team 38-18 in Game 1 they came away with a 5-2 victory at Memorial. In Game 2 Budarick shone in a

4-0 shutout. Up 2-0 in the best-of-five series, they had to get their third win in Trail.

Sakaki had the honour of scoring the winning goal in the 5-3 series-clinching win. For the fourth time in five years, they were going to the British Columbia Junior final and, once again, their foes were the New Westminster Royals.

In the ominous confines of Queen's Park, the Kraft Kings were rocked 13-1 and 7-4. Back on friendly ice at the Sports Centre, they made it close but still lost 3-2. They were down to their last game. New West was too much and, with their 6-2 win, they grabbed the Mowatt Cup for the second straight time. Even with the loss in the final, it had been a great comeback season.

Although the Chiefs had become history, Kamloops was not without a senior team as their place was taken by the North Shore Intermediate A Totems of the Okanagan Mainline Hockey Association along with the Vernon Luckies and the Salmon Arm Aces. The team had a familiar ring about it is as many of the players were longtime stalwarts of the Chiefs.

Nick Pyevach started as coach but later in the season was replaced by veteran Buddy Evans. Showing he still had a lot left Evans took to the ice and scored a hat trick in a 13-3 drubbing of the Luckies at the Sports Centre. At season's end, North Kamloops took first place three points ahead of Vernon. Glen Madsen won the scoring title and eight of the top 10 scorers were listed with the Totems. Panagrot was top goalie.

Vernon, with Peter Sasaskamoose in its lineup, faced off against the Totems for league bragging rights. The Luckies lived up to their name as they took Game 1 3-1 at the Sports Centre. The Totems didn't help their cause by dropping the next game in Vernon 4-2 and it got worse when the Luckies took the Totems again on home ice 4-2. The Totems recovered to stave off elimination in Game 4 4-2 in Vernon, but the Luckies maintained their form in taking Game 5 and the series with a 5-2 victory in Kamloops. It was hardly an upset given the closeness of the season standings but disappointing nonetheless.

Still, the Totems had put the North Shore on the hockey map and they were not the only North Shore team to make waves that season.

Peter Sasaskamoose's old team, the Kamloops' Braves, again won the B.C. Indian Hockey Championship at Salmon Arm. Braves' Ronnie Gottfriedson had the honour of holding the championship trophy and smiling for the camera man of the Kamloops Sentinel.

Kamloops' hockey prodigies were reaching into the professional levels and garnering the interest of NHL squads. Peter Sternig and Gary Schall were with Montreal's farm team in Muskegon while Don Newman was in the Boston system at Jacksonville. The big news, however, was that a local had cracked the NHL and looked like he was going to stay.

He left Kamloops for the Edmonton Oil Kings for the 1962/63 season and had the thrill of winning the Memorial Cup. He remained with same team that demolished his home town's Rockets the season after and made it to the Memorial Cup again. From there, he went to the Memphis Red Wings for one season before moving up to the Pittsburgh Hornets of the AHL the season after. He was only there for a few weeks before he got the call. Not only did he become a regular but he challenged Toronto's Brit Selby for the Calder Trophy (rookie of the year award). To top it off he went to the Stanley Cup final with the Wings that season.

Bert Marshall did the city proud over the course of his lengthy NHL career. He starred as a regular with Detroit, California and the New York Islanders for 14 years before hanging up his skates at the end of the 1978-79 season.

The well spring that had produced Marshall continued to make hockey waves.

The North Shore midget Totems, coached by Buddy Evans and sporting Randy Rota in their lineup along with Grant Evans and Rick Beauchamp, took out Penticton in the Okanagan final to advance to the provincials and a crack at the Cromie Cup. Their opponents were, not surprisingly, from Trail. A team that had won the Cromie Cup for three straight seasons and were looking for their fourth.

The first game at the Sports Centre was a close 9-8 Totems victory with neither team giving the impression of dominance.

Bert Marshall — The first Kamloops product to make the NHL. (c. Riverside Coliseum Wall of Fame)

Another win and the Totems would have the Cromie Cup.

Kamloops fell behind 2-0 in the first period, but the two teams were tied 3-3 with 33 seconds left in the period. At that point, the goal light went on, fortunately at the Trail end. Rota gave the Totems their first lead of the game. They were up 6-3 by the 4:41 mark of the second when Ernie Deadmarsh scored two goals to complete his hat trick and pull Trail to within one. Then, with a minute left in the second, Trail tied it up on Deadmarsh's fourth. It did not stay tied for long. Once again the final minute of the period was disastrous for Trail. Beauchamp scored what proved to be the winner.

The third belonged to the Totems who grabbed a 12-7 win and the Cromie Cup. Rota finished with four goals and four helpers, Gerry Vachon three goals and two assists and Bob Gill two goals and three assists.

Buddy Evans' North Kamloops Totems — Provincial Midget Champs for 1966 and winners of the Cromie Cup. Bottom: (l-r) Rod Calder, Bob Gill, John Bade, Rick Beauchamp, Dave Cochrane, Bob Shmyr, Ken Tarnow. Middle: Bud Evans, Doug MacLeod, Randy Rota, Grant Evans, Tosh Tabata, David Craig, Jim Carson, Doc Calder (manager) Back: Bill Waller, Rick Dyer, Bud Lloyd, Gerry Vachon, Paul Backman, (missing from photo is Roy Mabbett) (c. Buddy Evans/Randy Rota)

North Kamloops' entry into the hockey realm could not have been more successful. Evans had his third provincial trophy in four years and the Kamloops area had its fourth Cromie Cup.

Far off in Estevan, the Bruins were finishing their final year in the Saskatchewan Junior Hockey League with another league championship. Big changes were afoot. Western junior hockey was about to undergo a change which eventually expanded its hockey influence farther than ever before. Kamloops would, in time, be a big part of it all.

Before all that happened however, Kamloops was to have one of its own parade on to the national stage again.

When the Edmonton Oil Kings took out the Estevan Bruins for the Abbott Cup in six games, they snatched up Ross Lonsberry, Ted Hodgson and Kamloops' own Jimmy Harrison for their seventh straight run at the Memorial Cup. Their opponent in the best-of-seven final played at Maple Leaf Gardens was the Bobby Orr-led Oshawa Generals.

In the sixth game, with the Oil Kings up three games to two, it proved to be Estevan Bruins night. Hodgson and Harrison got Edmonton's two goals in their 2-1 Memorial Cup-clinching victory. Harrison joined Marshall as Kamloops' contribution to a Memorial Cup champion and he wasn't through making news yet.

1966 Edmonton Oil Kings — Memorial Cup Champions. Picked up from the Estevan Bruins, Kamloops' own Jimmy Harrison (middle row third from the right) played a big role in the Edmonton Oil Kings 1966 Memorial Cup victory. (c. Edmonton City Archives)

23

Junior Grows Up ____________ 1966-67

1966-67 saw changes that occurred outside Kamloops but were soon to have an impact upon the face of junior hockey in British Columbia.

A new league, the Western Canada Hockey League, unsanctioned and outlawed by the Canadian Amateur Hockey Association, set up shop on the Prairies. The Edmonton Oil Kings (now the Portland Winter Hawks), Weyburn Red Wings, Calgary Buffaloes (now the Tri-City Americans), Saskatoon Blades, Regina Pats, Moose Jaw Canucks and Estevan Bruins (now the Kamloops Blazers) formed the pioneering franchises.

It all seemed very far away as the Kraft Kings, still under the guidance of Andy Clovechok, set about their second year. Ten players were lost to age restrictions. Harvey Budarick, Ken Begg, Robbie Osborne and Joe Bedard came back and Bob Law came up from Merritt. Rookies trying out included Ron Hay, Don Clovechok, Duane Popp, Wally Deneault, Dennis Daws, Stacey Whiting, Rick Trent, Gerry Janicki, John Oldham, Frank Rossi and John Hughes.

The coach noted the other teams had sponsors who helped to cover their costs, which in turn, allowed them to enhance their local talent by bringing in more imports. Being under the sponsorship of the local minor hockey association, Kamloops was unable to compete. It soon became apparent.

The Kings lost their first eight games and struggled all season against teams in the Interior league and, in interlocking play, against coastal squads. One of the highlights of the dismal season was an upset win over the Edmonton Canadians which was leading the Alberta league at the time. Budarick led his Kings to a 3-0 whitewash in front of 700 fans.

In sole possession of last place the Kings had to face the Kelowna Buckaroos which had remained a powerhouse and taken the league again. Though they made it respectable with a 9-7 loss in Game 1, they were drubbed 8-0 in the second game. They did exact some damage by winning 4-3 in Kelowna but then bowed out four games to one.

It was obvious without a sponsor they were not on a level playing field.

The North Kamloops Intermediate A Totems began play in the revamped Okanagan Mainline League that included the Vernon Luckies, Kelowna Molsons, Revelstoke Selkirks and Salmon Arm Aces. Kenny Stewart was originally scheduled to be the coach but he left before the season began. He was to reappear elsewhere on the hockey scene.

The imbalance between the teams became apparent. In one game, the Totems demolished Revelstoke 21-1. At season's end, they were the class of the league but it was not as the Totems. In January 1967, they accepted sponsorship from Molson's [illegible] and officially became the North Kamloops Old Stylers.

There was reason for optimism starting the playoffs because in addition to finishing first, Dale Sandyke led the league in scoring with Old Stylers taking the next four positions, too. John Panagrot was the top goalie. They cruised by Salmon Arm and Vernon to take the league and then turned their attention north to the Prince George Mohawks. Minus star player Freddie Gaber, who stayed home to coach his bantam squad, the Old Stylers fell in two straight, but close, games by scores of 3-2 and 4-2.

Kamloops' players continued journeyman hockey in the WIHL where Murray Owens and Skip Holmes were part of an all star team that defeated a touring Russian squad in Trail in December.

The North Kamloops' midget Totems were again a force to be reckoned with. Stewart was behind the bench and Randy Rota and Ken Tarnow led the way as they got past the Kamloops' midget Elks, Penticton and Vanderhoof to reach the provincial final against North Vancouver. The favoured Totems had hopes of representing British Columbia in the Centennial Cup. Stewart had noticed some weaknesses in the team, perceiving it was slightly less powerful than the year before but they were still confident.

North Vancouver must have read Stewart's notes for they took Game 1 7-4 and forced North Kam to make up the three-goal difference in Game 2 of their two-game, total-points final. Tarnow did his bit by scoring four times in an 8-6 win but the Totems still went down 13-12 in total points. The Cromie Cup was North Vancouver's.

The North Vancouver team picked up Rota from the Totems to help bolster their squad for the nationals.

The North Kamloops Peewee Totems ended their season in a tight series against Kelowna with future NHLer Don Ashby in their team colours.

Gaber's bantams finished the regular season undefeated and then rolled over Revelstoke, Kelowna and Prince George to reach the provincial final against Trail. Despite hosting the series at Memorial Arena, they fell to Trail in two straight games by identical scores of 4-3.

It remained for the Kamloops' Braves to bring Kamloops its provincial championship that season as they took the Provincial Indian Championship for the third straight time. An all-star squad from the B.C. tournament, composed largely of Kamloops area players and coached by Gus Gottfriedson, subsequently won an invitational tourney in North Battleford, Sask. over 10 other teams from B.C., Alberta and Saskatchewan. Peter Sasaskamoose was joined on the squad by former Chief Freddie Sasaskamoose.

In Estevan, Jimmy Harrison had begun to make a name for himself. On Dec. 4, 1966, he set a league scoring record , that still stands, for the fastest three goals. In a regular season game, he got three goals in 24 seconds against the Regina Pats in a dramatic come-from-behind victory. Other future NHLer's joined him in the team photo. Greg Sheppard, Greg Polis and Dale Hoganson wore the B that year as the Bruins carried their successful ways into the new league.

Estevan Bruins Jim Harrison whose star was continuing to rise. (c, Ross Portrait Studio/Estevan Bruins)

24

Blast Off — 1967-68

Kenny Stewart, Don Brown and the Rockets returned in 1967-68 under the sponsorship of Ernie Davies' Central Hotel, adding Frank Rota as team trainer.

More than 40 local players plus four imports turned up at training camp. The season saw Randy Rota, Grant Evans, Ken Begg, Marv Ferg (from Cranbrook), Joe Bedard, Ken Tarnow, Bill Tarnow, Wally Deneault (goal), Robbie Osborne, Gerry Janicki, Jim McNeil (from Cranbrook), John Bade (goal), Rick Beachamp, Lyle Harp, Don Steinke, Greg Scriver and Larry Morry suiting up in Rockets' colours. A number had followed Stewart from his highly successful North Kamloops midget Totems. Don Clovechok started out with the squad but ended up with the Winnipeg Jets of the WCHL.

Grant Evans with trophy to commemorate record setting game. (c. Buddy Evans/Sentinel)

Rocket Star Randy Rota, on his way up. (c. Randy Rota)

Tarnow, Rota and Evans led the reborn Rockets offence. Rota finished third in scoring and Evans pulled off an historical night in front of the home-town fans.

On Jan. 13, 1968, the Rockets were entertaining the New

Westminster Royals at the North Kamloops' Sports Centre. In the stands to watch was ex-Rocket Jimmy Harrison who had come back home from Estevan to recuperate from a back injury. He was the home-town boy who was making his presence felt on the Prairies and who had set a junior hockey scoring record the previous season for the fastest three goals; 24 seconds.

In a close match, Evans was already starring having scored both Kamloops' goals going into the third. He was far from done. At 4:19 he got his third. Four seconds later he bagged his fourth. Then at 4:35 he notched his fifth. He had three goals in 18 seconds, surpassing Harrison's seemingly untouchable record and with him, by absolute coincidence, sitting in the stands. A remarkable accomplishment and coincidence. Evans was still not done as he scored two more for a seven-goal night. The only bad side was that New Westminster scored nine to take the game. Ephraim Steinke later donated a trophy in honour of Evan's incredible feat.

The newly formed British Columbia Junior Hockey League included Victoria Cougars, New Westminster Royals, Kelowna Buckaroos, Penticton Broncos and the Vernon Essos all vying for provincial honours . The opening game of the season had the Cougars visiting with a familiar face in goal. It was Murray Finlay, who had some years earlier sailed into town with a Trail minor league team and stopped Kamloops cold in its tracks on the road to the provincial final. Some 1,000 fans at the Sports Centre saw Finlay again play an outstanding game stopping 40 of 45 shots sent his way but, unfortunately for him, his Cougars could only manage three goals. Kamloops took the first recorded game against Victoria 5-3.

The Broncos proved themselves the class of the league with everyone else playing catchup. The Rockets finished above .500 and earned the privilege of meeting archrival Kelowna in the first round; the same team that had sent the Kraft Kings packing last year.

It started poorly for the Rockets with a 3-1 loss in Kelowna but the heroics of Deneault and Morry in Game 2 saw them knot the series with a 6-5 win. Some 1,600 Kamloops fans at Memorial Arena saw their squad outshoot the Bucks 40-33 in Game 3 but still lose 6-1. When they lost Game 4 7-5 and were headed back to Kelowna for Game 5 it looked like it was all over.

The expectant Kelowna crowd was silenced by Tarnow's hat trick and the Rockets' 8-1 victory to prolong the series. The Kelowna fans had even more disappointment ahead as their Bucks fell 6-2 in Game 6 to set up a seventh and deciding game in Kamloops.

Some 2,300 fans packed into the Sports Centre. Their hopes were dimmed when Gene Carr's goal held up at the end of the first as the only tally. In the second, Carr had Kelowna up 2-0 before the three minute mark. This time, the Rockets answered within 19 seconds on a goal by Evans. Tarnow tied it at 13:56 in a period which had the Rockets outshooting Kelowna 21-10. They entered the third tied.

Ferg gave Kamloops its first lead but Kelowna tied it to force overtime. There was little on the shot clock to show much difference between the two teams; however, a problem with the scoreboard showed the home side ahead 4-3. The teams changed ends and played with the error on the board. Perhaps it was an omen because at 9:05 Begg put home the eventual game winner on a goal-mouth scramble. Ferg's goal 15 seconds later was icing on the cake and Kamloops took the series. It was a great game to finish off a great comeback.

The Sentinel recorded Stewart as saying, *"I thought they'd had it after the first period. But they came back with the same old fight."*

They had indeed, and in doing so, reclaimed some damaged pride.

It would take much more to upset the Penticton Broncos and it started poorly with a 7-4 loss. The Broncos soon learned Kamloops still had that "same old fight" as the Rockets rebounded on home ice to take Game 2 6-2. Just as in the Kelowna series Kamloops dropped the next two games to go down 3-1 in the series and face a comeback challenge starting on unfriendly ice. Some 1,800 Penticton fans were on hand expecting the coronation. The Rockets called up Billy Tarnow from the junior B's and he made the most of his opportunity scoring two goals in a Rockets 5-3 victory. Could it be Kelowna all over again?

Not this time. Some 2,600 fans jammed the Sports Centre hoping to see their heroes extend the series. The Broncos poured it on firing 42 shots at Deneault. He stopped 39 but his teammates only got two behind the Penticton goalie. The final read 3-2 and the Broncos advanced. They had been impressed enough with Deneault that they took him along for their run at the Mowatt Cup.

In the Broncos run for the Memorial Cup, they were not yet through dealing with the Kamloops minor hockey system.

The Kamloops junior B Teamsters made their appearance that season under the direction of GM Melvin Recchi and coach Bob Gannon. As the Rockets' affiliate, they joined Kelowna, Vernon and Penticton in the Okanagan league.

As with junior A, the Penticton squad, known as the Combines, took the regular season. Kamloops garnered second and had to take on Vernon in Round 1. They waltzed over the North Okanagan squad in four straight, outscoring them 25-7 and were rewarded with a final round matchup against the Combines.

The Combines took the first three games and it looked like the Teamsters were going to go the way of the Rockets. At least they hoped to salvage some pride with a win in Game 4 on home ice. They did more than that. They took the next three games 3-1, 2-0 and 5-3 to set up a seventh and-deciding game in Penticton.

While brother Ken was contributing to the Rockets comeback Billy Tarnow did the same. His two goals and one assist sparked the Teamsters to a 3-0 series clinching win in Penticton. They had surpassed even the 3-1 series comeback accomplishment of the Rockets. They had even thrown in two shutouts to make it more impressive.

A tired crew now headed to Nelson for the semifinal series.

After a disappointing 4-3 loss in Game 1, the Teamsters were on the verge of elimination in the best-of-three. Down 4-1 in Game 2, they surprised their hosts and stormed back to tie the game at four. Misfortune then struck as the ref called a penalty on Robbie Osborne for playing without a helmet. His had been knocked off during the course of play and he, as did his coach, thought he could continue until a stoppage of play. Concern was warranted as Nelson scored on the ensuing power play and did not give up the lead this time. Their last goal was in to an empty net.

The Teamsters, despite the loss, had started with the type of play traditions are built on.

The Intermediates started out in a three team league involving the Kelowna Molsons and Vernon Luckies but Vernon dropped out in November. Kelowna and the Kamloops Old Stylers played out a season and then faced each other in a best-of-five playoff. With George Uyeda and Buddy Evans in the lineup, Kamloops took the series and advanced against Quesnel. They got no further as they fell in two games straight. There were to be some fine Coy Cup battles in the years ahead against Quesnel.

The Kamloops midget Elks won the regular season in the

Okanagan league and then put away Penticton to advance to the provincial semifinals against Prince George. Taking out the Northerners in two straight by scores of 6-3 and 6-5, they faced off against Kimberley for the provincial title. Their quest ended there in two one sided losses but another trip to the provincials didn't hurt Kamloops' minor hockey reputation.

In the NHL, Bert Marshall was still a regular, though, it was to prove a trying year. Traded by Detroit to the expansion Oakland Seals for former Toronto stalwart Kent Douglas, he later suffered a season ending injury. In the long run, being traded to an expansion team worked out very well as he landed on one of the greatest of them all, the New York Islanders.

Jim Letcher, Harvey Budarick, Murray Owens and Larry Roberge were toiling in the WIHL and Don Clovechok had stuck with the WCHL Winnipeg Jets.

Kamloops was not to be without a provincial trophy that season as the Kamloops Braves captured their fourth straight First Nations title. In recognition of their fourth win in the seven years the trophy had been competed for, two trophies were presented. One to be defended next season and the other for the team's permanent possession. Peter Sasaskamoose had again starred and, in the final game, netted five of Kamloops' six goals.

Across the Rockies, Estevan was on its way to establishing a new watershed mark for the franchise and Kamloops was well represented in the achievement.

In the second year of the WCHL, Estevan finished second behind the Flin Flon Bombers, which was led by Bobby Clarke and Reggie Leach. The two had finished first and second in league scoring without a single Bruin in the Top 10. Perhaps it showed the Bruins balance as they won 45 and lost only 13.

Estevan advanced past Winnipeg and Moose Jaw without losing a game and came face-to-face with Flin Flon. Maybe it was team concept over stars but, whatever the reason, they disposed of the Bombers four games to zero with one tied. Despite losing only eight games all season, the Bombers had dropped four to their southern rivals.

The Top 5 playoff scorers showed four Bruins with Jimmy Harrison at the very top. He had scored a league leading 13 goals and 22 assists in 14 games.

On its way to the Memorial Cup, the Bruins, with Kamloops minor hockey system product Harrison, disposed of the Penticton Broncos.

Though they finally lost to the Niagara Falls Flyers four

games to one the Bruins had taken the franchise farther than ever before. In so doing, they began a legacy that was to see the franchise, in its various forms, reach the pinnacle of junior hockey 11 times in 28 years. No other western franchise has even come close to matching that achievement since the 1967-68 season.

Had Harrison not been seriously impeded by injury in that first appearance who knows what might have been? Scotty Munro and Ernie McLean had reached a new pinnacle and they were soon to become known to Kamloops hockey fans more intimately.

25

Crash and Burn — 1968-69

The 1968-69 season started with ominous overtones for Kamloops' number 1 team, the Rockets.

Only five players were listed as returning. Randy Rota had been grabbed by Scotty Munro's Calgary Centennials and Grant Evans had gone to league competitors Victoria Cougars along with local Gerry Bond. Interior teams complained Victoria was drawing away Interior players and pointed to six examples. This compounded the existing problem of star players being taken by the WCHL.

Kenny Stewart and Don Brown were back with the Ernie Davies sponsored team. Suiting up that season were Lyle Harpe, Rick Beauchamp, Dale Ciochetti, John Bade (goal), Gary Osborne, Larry Simon (from Prince George), Marv Ferg and Don Stanley (from Cranbrook), Don Stewart, Bruce Johnson, Bill Tarnow and Larry Morry. Complaints were made the team had junior B calibre players and could finish last.

Evans and Bond had excellent years in Victoria. Evans particularly excelled when he went up against his old squad. Poor performance on the ice led to poor attendance and only 250 fans were on hand for the season-ending 5-4 victory over Penticton at the Sports Centre. By that time, Kamloops had already been eliminated from the playoffs by virtue of finishing fifth.

Although it wasn't suggested at the end of the season, it came to pass, legendary Kenny Stewart stepped down and a new era began. It began with a face from the north who brought with him a connection with the dynamic Munro.

The junior Teamsters, with star John Senkpiel, fared better but not well as they lost out on first place to Penticton. After getting by the Merritt Copper Kings in the first round, they were stopped by the Combines in the Okanagan final.

The intermediate Old Stylers never got off the ground. For the first time since the 1947-48, there was no senior hockey team challenging for the Coy Cup (with the exception of the year Kamloops was suspended from play). Players had to content themselves with play in the Kamloops Commercial Hockey League.

The midget Elks, with Ed Dempsey in their lineup, got as far as far as the Okanagan final before being stopped by Penticton.

The Kamloops' Sports Shop bantams put out Merritt on the way to the Okanagan final and then went up against Penticton. They took Game 1 4-3 in Penticton and were in a position to win the Okanagan on home ice. Duane Monteith was the local hero as he scored the winning goal in overtime to give the squad a 5-4 victory and restore some measure of civic pride. Monteith was injured and not available for the next challenge in Prince George. After tying Game 1 it was anybody's series going into the second game. Prince George carried the day.

Still at the minor hockey league level, a development occurred in the early spring that was destined to have far reaching effects on Kamloops' hockey reputation internationally. In the April 3, 1969 Sentinel, a full-page ad appeared announcing the first annual Bantam Ice Hockey Tournament which was being sponsored by the North Kamloops Minor Hockey Association. A photo of the North Kamloops team included future stars Terry and Bill Tarnow, Don Ashby and team captain Don Hay. The tournament, which listed teams from Vancouver, Kelowna, Quesnel, Vernon, North Vancouver and Penticton, eventually grew into the present day Kamloops' International Bantam Ice Hockey Tournament. The world-renowned tournament is a story unto itself.

Local fans could still draw some satisfaction in the exploits of Evans and Bond as they starred on a Victoria team which won the provincial title. Randy Rota, Don Clovechok and Ken Tarnow represented Kamloops in the WCHL and Murray Owens was still starring in the WIHL. Harvey Budarick and Robbie Osborne took the colours overseas and were leading a Dutch championship team.

Bert Marshall remained as a regular in the NHL but he had to share the glory with another Kamloopsian.

Jim Harrison grabbed the headlines in the local boy makes good category. After being rated by the press and scouts as Canada's top junior hockey player the previous year he began his pro career with the Central Hockey League's Oklahoma City Blazers. Despite his ratings and last years' selection as the western league's MVP, he was not picked to make it to the parent Boston Bruins with any regularity that season. Local columnist Lou Desmarais claimed his only chance was if he was called up due to injuries. Well, the opportunity came.

When Derek Sanderson went down with an injury, Harrison got his chance. Munro had claimed he would make the NHL that season and the words of Boston coach Milt Schmidt suggested the same.

"He's one of the best back checkers on the club. We really like him because he plays the puck instead of the man. The goals will come eventually."

On Jan. 18, 1969, the paper reported Harrison's first goal in a 5-5 tie with Toronto. He was destined to get many more before his pro career ended. He starred for 12 years in the NHL and WHA, primarily with Boston, Toronto and Edmonton until back injury problems eventually ended his career.

The Estevan Bruins soldiered on and, even without Harrison, managed a 40-20-0 season to finish second behind the Flin Flon Bombers. After eliminating Brandon in Round 1 they came up against Bobby Clarke's Bombers which eventually won the league. Three Bruins, Greg Polis, Brian Marchinko and Greg Sheppard, made it into the Top 10 scorers. Two other future NHLer's filled out the team photo. Dale Hoganson was still with the team and a young rookie phenom Lorne Henning made his debut. He was destined to be part of a major change on the horizon as well as NHL stardom.

Although it had been a poor season locally, it was to prove only an interlude.

26

The Munro Connection____________1969-70

The Rockets of 1969-70 were different in more than one way. Not only had Kenny Stewart been replaced by the spitfire from Smithers, Joe Tennant' and Don Brown by local lawyer Dennis Coates, but few of last year's players would finish the season with this new squad.

Imported players predominated and the team took on an affiliation (unofficially) with a WCHL team. The fabled Scotsman, Scotty Munro, was the first of the triumvirate to make his presence felt in Kamloops as his Calgary Centennials were the parent team.

Tennant and Munro had had a professional relationship for some time before he brought his act with the Smithers Bruins to Kamloops. Tennant had been coaching in Smithers for the previous four years and brought a few of his charges with him. The BCJHL had made it clear there was to be no working relationship between teams in their league and the WCHL, so the Rockets had to walk a fine line. It was not always easy or successful.

Derek Black - His promise tragically cut short. (c. Reno Commazetto)

Scotty Munro - The legend whose golden touch fell on Kamloops. (c. Estevan Bruins Hockey Club)

Munro had sold out from the Estevan Bruins and taken half the team with him to Calgary where he took over the Calgary Centennials (present Tri-City Americans) but he maintained his connections with Tennant. His relationship with Tennant and the Rockets was challenged and criticized by both the league and other teams but he and Joe certainly made for lots of colour.

Coming with Tennant from Smithers were Bernie Doan (father of future Blazer Shane Doan), Wayne Gibbs (brother of NHLer Barry Gibbs), Irvie Miller, Bill Goodacres (goal), Don Oulton, Murray McNeil, Ron Homeniuk and Ernie Wurmlinger. David Mitchell, who had been with Vanderhoof last season, also made the journey. They were joined by locals Ron Forester, Derek Black, Lyle Harpe, Craig Redmond and John Senkpiel. Imports included Arnie Pederson, Allan Stocks, Mark Atkinson (goal), Jim McMaster, Larry Iralson, Marv Ferg, Timber Peck, Peter Kay, Oliver Steward, John Snodgrass, Don Wilson and a 17-year-old from Hinton, Alta. named Bobby Nystrom.

The controversial season started well and Kamloops was vying for first place. As the season progressed, claims were made the Rockets were using illegal players and there were threats the team would be suspended. This led to a claim by the WCHL if this happened, they would put a team in Kamloops. Indeed city council was already talking about putting in a new arena that would make such a move possible. In the end, Kamloops lost seven points due to the claims and the team remained in the BCJHL.

Penticton Bronco coach and former Kamloops' Elk Jack Taggart complained that Munro was directly influencing the team. He accused the Rockets of playing a *"Chippy Munro type of Prairie hockey,"* to which Tennant responded Taggart and his team should expect more of the same. Tennant had shown, and would show again, he was not afraid to get involved in verbal battles and aggressive behaviour on and off the ice. He brought an intense competitiveness to the team.

In the end, they did not capture first; it went to the Vernon Essos. Kamloops had to settle for making the playoffs. They went up against second place Victoria Cougars. Games 1 and 2 were slated for Kamloops and the team split the matches. The winning goal in Kamloops' 3-2 victory came off the stick of Senkpiel, who had been knocked unconscious for five minutes earlier in the game.

In Victoria, the Rockets surprised the Cougars 4-1 in Game 3 but were smashed 10-1 in Game 4. Doan's two goals in

Game 5 were not enough as Kamloops went down 5-3. Down 3-2 in games, the Rockets had to take Game 6 on home ice just to stay alive. The teams skated to a 2-2 tie at the end of regulation and took it to overtime. In OT, a player, who was to become famous for his overtime goals with the New York Islanders, saved the day. At 3:30 of the second overtime period, Nystrom, on helpers from Gibbs and Oulton, gave the Rockets the game and kept them alive.

The 1969-70 Rockets featured future NHL star Bobby Nystrom. Front Row: (l-r) Rick McDonald, Bernie Doan, Joe Tennant (coach) Don Oulton, Dennis Coates (Mgr.) Wayne Gibbs, Mark Atkinson. Back Row: Frank Rota (trainer) Tim Peck, Lyle Harpe, John Senkpiel, Jim Kinsman, Bob Nystrom, Ken Wright, Gary McConnell, Andy Laramee, Dave Mitchell, Oliver Stewart, Marv Ferg. (c. Doris Rubel)

The seventh-and-deciding game went in Victoria. The storybook ending should have had the Rockets winning the game, but Victoria sealed the series with an 8-4 victory. It had been an exciting season and there was room for optimism for next year.

Developments were occurring involving the Vancouver Centennials and the WCHL that were to eventually have a direct impact upon Kamloops. The BCJHL Centennials agreed to consider joining the WCHL and, although it didn't happen immediately, the die was cast. The WCHL was soon coming to British Columbia.

Both Black and Nystrom were to be called up to the parent Calgary Centennials the following season but their futures were to prove, tragically, quite different. Both were eventually drafted by the New York Islanders and played in their minor pro organizations but, from there, fate took them separate ways. Nystrom went on to be a key part of the New York Islanders incredible four straight Stanley Cup seasons during his 13 years in the NHL. Black was dealt the black ace after being diagnosed with inoperable cancer. At only 21 years of age, he died at Royal Inland Hospital on Jan. 10, 1974.

The Kamloops Junior B Teamsters under coach Bob Gannon and assistant Ev Miller had a sensational regular season led by the likes of Gary Donaldson and George Aulin. The team lost only one game and outscored their opponents 110 to 26. They looked good for a shot at the provincials when they went up against the Merritt Copper Kings in Round 1.

Merritt shocked Kamloops by taking Game 1 6-4, but the Teamsters were back on track in the second and took it 5-0. On home ice, they were expected to win and advance. The game went into double overtime before the Copper Kings upset the Teamsters and eliminated them. Their fantastic season came to an inglorious end.

The intermediates were reorganized by Tom Endean and coached by Buddy Evans. The Stars had to settle for exhibition play with no league for them to play in. Vernon proved to be their downfall in the playoffs and they were eliminated in a series that had to go the full five games.

That season, local players in the WCHL included Randy Rota who was skating for Munro's Calgary Centennials. He claimed Rota would be in the pros next season even though he still had a year of junior eligibility. Sports writer Lou Desmarais claimed that Munro had found a gold mine in Kamloops as attested to by both Jimmy Harrison and Rota. Having his fingers in the Rockets franchise could only help him mine that talent better

Munro claimed that Rota "may be short, but he's got that powerful body and since, he's been with us he's learned how to take the rough body checking when the going gets rough."

Rota finished the season fifth in scoring with 90 points and won the league's most sportsmanlike player award.

Harrison, meanwhile, had been traded to the Toronto Maple Leafs for Wayne Carleton. Now, local fans could see more of him on Hockey Night in Canada telecasts.

Bert Marshall continued in the NHL but also brought his act back to Kamloops where he teamed up with former Elk/Chief Andy Clovechok to operate a summer hockey school.

Jim Letcher was in Salem with the Virginia Rebels and Wally Deneault, Don Clovechok and Rick Beauchamp were lacing up the skates in the WIHL.

The 1969-70 season was not kind to Estevan as they had their first sub .500 season in many years. Regardless, they finished second in their division and Greg Polis finished only seven points behind Reg Leach for the league scoring championship. Lorne Henning landed in fourth place. Winnipeg ended its season in the first round, but it would be back.

At season's end, it had become apparent that the BCJHL was a development league for the WCHL despite that league's inability to play for the Memorial Cup because the CAHA had outlawed it. The following season was to see this formally acknowledged and set the stage for the WCHL to cross the Rockies.

The local Kamloops product had become a community export at the junior level and beyond. There were no guarantees local stars would be on a local team regardless of their talent. This was made strikingly apparent the next season with Gary Donaldson and a few years later with Ed Dempsey. Junior teams had now become composites with players drawn from around the province and the Prairies. Locals made their names elsewhere and at many levels. What had once been unusual when Bert Marshall faced off for the Edmonton Oil Kings against his hometown Rockets was now commonplace.

Although it may have been a bit frustrating to have local talent playing against the home team, it showed the respect Kamloops players and the local minor hockey association had throughout the hockey world.

Kamloops Hockey talent together. Andy Clovechok's 1969 hockey school. Left to Right: Andy Clovechok, Bert Marshall, Joe Watson, Don Clovechok, Randy Rota and Jim Harrison. (c. Randy Rota)

27

First Glimpse — 1970-71

When the Kamloops fans watched their Rockets take to the ice for the 1970-71 season, none would have thought they would be getting a glimpse of a team that would become junior hockey's most storied franchise. Nor could they have imagined that the epitome of its success would occur in their own town.

It had come out in the open BCJHL teams had working agreements with WCHL teams. Scotty Munro's ownership of the Rockets made it clear who they were associated with. The association had been to Kamloops' benefit as Munro paid off the $11,000 debt the Rockets wracked up the previous year. Of the eight teams in the league, only Victoria, Vancouver and New Westminster did not have an affiliation. Curiously enough they were the three British Columbia communities destined to get WCHL franchises next season.

As part of this new association, BCJHL teams were to get the opportunity to go up against WCHL squads in exhibition play. Notice came that Ernie McLean's Estevan Bruins were coming for a pre-season match.

The Bruins took the Rockets 4-1 in their first match, played at Merritt, in a game where the Kamloops side managed to skate with the physically tougher Estevan team for the first half. Game 2 went in Kamloops before 700 fans at the Sports Centre. It proved a much closer game despite the fact New Westminster skated away with a 6-3 victory led by Bernie Lukowich's two goals. Joe Tennant was more than pleased with how his boys had stood up to the heavier and more experienced Bruins team.

At the outset, Calgary took Bernie Doan, Derek Black, Bob Nystrom, Wayne Gibbs and Don Oulton. Their places were eventually taken by Gary Howatt, Curt Brackenbury, Kelly Pratt and Jerry Holland. Returnees included Timber Peck, Lyle Harpe, Ollie Steward, John Senkpiel and Mark Atkinson. Also suiting up for the team that season were Stephen Gramms, John Phillips, Carson Baldwin, Wayne Bianchin, Terry Tarnow, Russ Weichnuk, Ken Wright, Gord Girard, Marty Kissel, Sam Clegg (goal), Gary Johnson (captain), Larry Simon and Jim Evans (goal). For a brief time, it looked like they were going to scoop future NHL goalie John Davidson but Munro took him up to the Cents.

A local hopeful, Gary Donaldson, attended camp but was cut early. He signed with Penticton and the Rockets rued the day they did not take him every time the two teams played. He finished sixth in scoring in the league and eventually landed in the Chicago Black Hawks organization. Kamloops' own Gerry Bond was still with Victoria and was joined by Darryl Fedorak.

Call-ups by the parent Calgary Centennials contributed to an up and down season. It was a situation that was incurable until Kamloops could get its own major junior team.

Interestingly enough, Kamloops established a working relationship with the Merritt Copper Kings junior B team while Penticton did the same with the Kamloops' Teamsters. It made for the unusual situation where called-up players could spend one game playing for Kamloops and the next against it. It spawned some rather divided loyalties.

All season Kamloops battled with Penticton for first . In the end, the Broncos took the league and Kamloops had to settle for third. The Broncos were off to the interprovincial finals leaving the other league teams to battle for the Mowatt Cup. Kamloops drew Vernon in the first round.

A special night was held that season for Ernie Davies, the Rockets' loyal sponsor. He was reluctant to take the credit for the success of junior hockey in Kamloops and claimed if it wasn't for the efforts of Kenny Stewart an Don Brown junior hockey just wouldn't have happened. Asked to pick his all-time, all-star team he was hard pressed. He finally settled upon Jim Letcher in goal, Terry Shishido (his all-time favourite) and Buck Crawford on defence; Glen Madsen or Eric Shishido at centre; Randy Rota and Murray Owens on wings. Honourable mentions went to Jimmy Harrison, Bill Steinke, Larry Bedard, Ken Rinaldi, Larry Roberge, Rick Beauchamp, Bob Nishamura and Glen "Cowboy" Richards.

In the first round of the playoffs, Evans shut out the Essos in their own building 3-0 and back at the Sports Centre before 1,500 fans, they took game two 5-1. Intensity mounted and, in Game 3, even the fans got into the fights in a 5-1 Vernon victory. Returning to the Sports Centre, the Rockets went up 3-1 in games with a close 5-4 win. One more win and the Interior championship was theirs.

Howatt opened the scoring in the first minute to silence the Vernon crowd, but they were soon on their feet cheering as the Essos came back to take a 2-1 lead at the end of the first and extend it to 3-1 by the end of the second. It was looking like Game 6 in Kamloops. The Rockets were not yet done though. Harpe tightened the game at 2:50 of the third and then Holland netted two goals to turn the tables on the Essos. Peck got a much needed insurance goal that turned into the winner as Vernon crawled back to within one. It was Kamloops' game and they were going to the provincial final.

1971 Provincial Junior Champs - The Kamloops Rockets. Top Row: (l-r) Kelly Pratt, Steve Grams, Gord Girrard, Carson Baldwin, Curt Brackenbury, Jerry Holland. Middle Row: Gary Mowatt, Oliver Stewart, Wayne Bianchin, Terry Tarnow, Tim Peck, Lyle Harpe. Front Row: Marty Kissel, Ron Lyon, Jim Evans, Joe Tennant, Russ Weichnik, Gary Johnson. (c. Doris Rubel)

Holland led the squad with two goals in an opening game 6-4 victory in Vancouver but the Centennials returned the favour in Game 2 in overtime by the same score. Fifty-five Rockets shots in Game 3 gave them a 5-2 victory and, when they took the next game 6-2, they were within one win of reclaiming the trophy they last held in 1964. The Cents were not prepared to go down easily and staved off elimination with a 5-3 victory.

Some 2,400 fans filed into Memorial Arena in Kamloops in the hopes of seeing a provincial championship. Kamloops took a 3-1 lead, with Bianchin potting two goals, but Vancouver tied the game before the period ended. It wasn't until the third that Howatt claimed the game winner and later added the final goal in the Rockets' championship-clinching 6-3 victory.

Howatt was destined to move on to the WCHL the following season and spend 10 full seasons in the NHL; mostly with the New York Islanders. He enjoyed sipping from two of its Stanley Cups.

Speaking of the team's victory, trainer Frank Rota was quoted in the Sentinel as saying *"The Kamloops fans were pleased also. They stayed in the arena for a long time after the game and there were still a few hanging around when the B.C. junior champions pulled away."*

As Penticton, by virtue of winning the regular season, had gone on to represent B.C. there was no more play for the provincial champs. Kamloops had to satisfy itself with Donaldson carrying the city's colours in a seven-game series loss to the Red Deer Rustlers.

The junior B Teamsters were back for their fourth year and included Ed Dempsey, Mickey Fritz and George Aulin in their lineup coached by Ev Miller. That season Duane Monteith had a career night getting seven goals in one game against Merritt.

In the playoffs, they rolled over Vernon and came up against Merritt for the league. Memories of last season's upset would have been hard to shake and a close 4-3 win in Game 1 would not have given a lot of comfort. This time, there was no upset and Merritt fell in three straight giving Kamloops the Village Hotel Trophy.

Their next battle was with the Prince George Texacos in Prince George and a 6-3 opening game loss was not a good omen. The Teamsters bounced back to take the next two games by close scores of 6-5 and 5-4 and advanced against the Kootenay champs. They swept the Trail squad and took on Victoria Cubs in a battle for the provincial championship in Kamloops. To the winner went the Cyclone Taylor Trophy.

A fine season came to a disappointing close as Kamloops went out in two straight by scores of 7-5 and 6-5. The paper sang the praises of the team and commented on how it had gone up against a bigger and more experienced team in the final.

The North Kamloops Kiwanis midget Totems took out Vernon for the Okanagan championship and then faced off against Quesnel. After losing Game 1 7-5 in a two-game, total-point series, they squeaked by 6-3 in the second game to advance. The team that took them to the Charles Anderson Trophy had some names to be heard from in the near future. Don Hay, Don Ashby, Rick Hodgson, Mac Zinger (captain) and Larry Lestander had some great nights ahead of them.

The Kimberley midgets ended the Totems' quest for the provincial titles winning the two-game, total point series 9-6, despite Don Ashby's three goals and two assists.

The North Kamloops Kinsmen bantam Totems took out Revelstoke and Penticton on their way to winning the Okanagan championship and the Jack Robertson Memorial Trophy. This earned them the right to go to the provincial round robin series in which, despite faring well, they did not bring home the hardware.

The success of the minor hockey rep teams was already considerable but there was frustration the true strength of Kamloops was not being represented because of the North South division. A proposal brought forward by Bud Mabbett of the North Kamloops Minor Hockey Association to have a joint rep team was turned down by the Kamloops Minor Hockey Association, much to relief, I am sure, of other minor hockey associations in B.C.

An intermediate team turned up that season and, after exhibition play, took out Vernon in their quest for the Coy Cup. Then, they simply disappeared from the sports pages.

Much hockey activity did not make it into the papers, though, its presence was obviously there. Most notably absent was women's hockey, though, there was passing mention that season of a women's hockey team graced by some well known surnames. Jane Clovechok , Brenda Rota, Milly Poeschek and Allison Watters were listed as skating for a newly formed Kamloops Women's team in 1970.

On the intercollegiate front, word came Kamloops Caribou College had been accepted for league play next season in the Pacific Intercollegiate Hockey League.

The pro circuit still harboured Jimmy Harrison and Bert Marshall but Randy Rota was now knocking at the door, too. Drafted by the Oakland Seals, he spent the season toiling on their Providence Reds American Hockey League team. Harrison's prominence was reflected in the awarding of the Jimmy Harrison Trophy to Bianchin as the Rockets most valuable player. Bianchin was destined for a six year-stint in the NHL with the Pittsburgh Penguins after moving up to the WCHL the following season.

Grant Evans was playing pro with the Seattle Totems while Marv Ferg was skating for his home-town Cranbrook Royals of the WIHL.

The Estevan Bruins, in their final season on the Prairies, finished in first place with a 41-20-5 record. Lorne Henning was their leading scorer with 110 points, good for third place in the league. Regular season success did not follow them to the playoffs where they were upset in the first round by Winnipeg.

During the 14 seasons in Estevan, five had been in the WCHL. During that short stint, they had won the league once and gone to the Memorial Cup; finished first once; had only one season under .500 and produced 11 players who went on to solid NHL/WHA careers, including Kamloops' own Harrison. Prior to that, they had nine years in the Saskatchewan Junior Hockey League during which time they won the league four times.

They left the house the Bruins built in 1957 and headed west for the intimate confines of historic Queen's Park Arena in New Westminster. Old Humboldt Indian Ernie McLean was still at the helm along with Bill Shinske and together they took the franchise to even greater heights, setting records that last to this day.

The New Westminster Bruins were to impress themselves upon the provincial and national scene like no other B.C. hockey team; professional or amateur, had ever done before. Kamloops was not untouched by their presence.

28

Westward Ho! 1971-72

The defending Mowatt Cup champs paid the price for success.

When they played an exhibition game against the parent Calgary Centennials, Wayne Bianchin, Matt Kissell and Russ Wiechnik were on the other side. Star Jerry Holland was called up later in the season. On the good side, the losses gave some new players a chance.

Locals Don Hay, Rick Hodgson, Mac Zinger, Don Ashby, Duane Monteith, Stan Johnson and Larry Lestander all got opportunities alongside returnees Steve Gramms, Curt Brackenbury, John Phillips and Timber Peck. Ernie McLean's son, Brian, came to camp along with Garth Malarchuk, Ron Burgess and Ken Gassoff. Later in the season Butch Owchar, Ray Tyler, Ernie Wurmlinger, Bob Lindberg and Jack "Hayrack" Patterson suited up.

During the exhibition season, the Rockets locked horns with the New Westminster Bruins who trampled them 11-2 at the Sports Centre. The Bruins joined new kids on the block the Vancouver Nats and the Victoria Cougars in the WCHL.

Controversy and the Rockets seemed to go hand in hand. The team was temporarily suspended for not paying its registration fees and then colourful coach Joe Tennant managed to get himself suspended more than once for his behaviour and comments.

During the course of the season Hay came up from the Teamsters and was so impressive he stayed. Put on a line with Holland and Peck the Sentinel characterized him as *"One of our most hustling players right now."*

The defending champs managed a sub .500 season but still snuck into third place in the six team league. Second place Penticton was the first round opponent. Down two games to one in the series, Gassoff and Patterson led the team to a 5-1 series-tying win at the Sports Centre with series' intensity measured by the fights in the stands as much as on the ice. They were dealt a double blow in Game 5 where they not only lost 7-0 but also lost top scorer Peck with a broken ankle. Game six before 1798 fans at the Sports Centre ended it all with a 3-2 loss.

Despite the loss, the Rockets had to be pleased with their performance given the loss of players and the expanded roll rookies had to take on. Graduate Brackenbury went on to 10 years in the WHA and NHL enjoying his best seasons with the Quebec Nordiques, with whom he won the AVCO Cup (WHA championship) in 1977.

The junior B Teamsters easily won the regular season in a diminished league that had only two other teams: Revelstoke Mountaineers and Merritt Copper Kings. The Teamsters went undefeated . They also made the logical move of moving their affiliation to the home-town Rockets.

In the playoffs, they rolled over Merritt in two games straight to win the Okanagan and then took on the undefeated Prince George Chiefs. The Teamsters kept their undefeated streak alive by taking out the Chiefs in two straight. The season ended, ingloriously, in two straight playoff losses to the Cranbrook Colts.

The Caribou College Chiefs made their appearance that winter and, despite finishing fifth in the seven team league, showed its commitment to remain and to become more competitive. Local players who had gone to teams elsewhere, such as Gerry Bond and Don Clovechok, returned to suit up for the new squad. The team also demonstrated it could draw a reasonable crowd as seen by the 800 who turned up for a game against the University of British Columbia.

On the professional front, Jimmy Harrison was still with Toronto but rumour had it he was headed to the fledgling World Hockey Association. Bert Marshall remained a regular and Randy Rota had been traded to the Montreal Canadian organization where he played for the Nova Scotia Voyageurs in the American Hockey League. Ken Tarnow laboured in International league with the Oklahoma City Blazers.

The WCHL sported Derek Black, Bob Nystrom, Gary Howatt, Marty Kissel, Jerry Holland, John Senkpiel, Kelly Pratt and Wayne Bianchin, all of whom were either local products or players who had moved through Kamloops on their way up.

As for the two franchises that were to have direct ties with Kamloops, they were going in entirely different directions.

The Vancouver Nats, a spanking new franchise, started at a disadvantage to its neighbours the New Westminster Bruins which had inherited the already highly successful Estevan franchise. It showed.

The Nats finished last while the Bruins forged a 40-27-1 record for third place. Lorne Henning landed seventh in scoring with 114 points. The playoffs proved less than kind, however, as their old nemesis the Edmonton Oil Kings dropped them four games to one in the first round.

The WCHL was in B.C. and sniffing around.

29

The Dempsey-Hay Season_______________1972-73

Years later, they combined behind the bench of the Kamloops Blazers but, in the 1972-73 season, Ed Dempsey and Don Hay were on-ice foes in the battle for junior hockey supremacy.

Hay was in his second year with Joe Tennant's Rockets while Dempsey was in his first with the Penticton Broncos. He was joined by Greg Milliard, son of former Elks/Chiefs star Johnny Milliard. Their season-long battle and playoff exploits made for an exciting campaign.

The 1972-73 Rockets - Back Row: (l-r) Terry Tarnow, Bill Kelts, Brian McLean, Paul Mulvey, Neil Lyseng, Rick Hodgson, Chris McMaster. Middle Row: Wayne Morin, Don Moores, Rick Shinske, Don Hay, Mark Severyn, Ken Dodd, ? ,Rick Lalonde, Len Hewer (trainer). Bottom Row: Frank White (stick boy), Garth Malarchuk, Eldon dever (owner), Butch Owchar, Joe Tennant, Ken Wilson, Ephraim Steinke, Brian Edgington, Rick Fuoco (stick boy). (c. Riverside Coliseum Wall of Fame)

The Rockets included Rick Shinske, future New Westminster Bruin star and son of New West GM Bill Shinske, in their 1972-73 lineup. He was joined by all stars Rick Hodgson, Chris McMasters and Garth Malarchuk (goal) and a roster that included Don Ashby, Don Hay, Butch Owchar, Mac Zinger, Ivan Christianson, Steve Tarnaski, Brian Edgington, Don Moores, Jack Patterson, Brian McLean, Steve Gramm, Terry Tarnow, Neil Lyseng, Bruce Greig, Rick Lalonde, Ken Dodd, Wayne Morin, Ken Wilson, Ron Longlitz and Dave Walker.

The league expanded to add the Nanaimo Clippers and the Bellingham Blazers. When the first team with the name Blazers hit Memorial Arena that season, they fell to the locals 11-2.

Penticton started the season strong, taking the first two games against Kamloops 6-4 and 2-1, to forge, by late November, a nine-point lead over the favoured Rockets. Later that month, Kamloops invaded Penticton and stole a 3-2 victory. Meeting again in Penticton in December, they won 7-6. By mid-December, they were within four points of first. Despite winning 12 straight, they found themselves back nine points again as the month neared the end.

By mid-January, they managed to briefly tie the Broncos for first. Later that same month, the two teams met at Memorial in front of 3,202 fans. Kamloops came back in the game to tie it at 2-2 and force overtime. At 6:11 of OT, Shinske potted the winner that put Kamloops in sole possession of first place for the first time. Penticton was one point behind with two games in hand.

They met again in February with the Rockets on another winning streak that was to go 13 games. With 3,200 fans looking on, they once again took Penticton, this time 5-4, with Owchar scoring the winner. Hay, who had caught the attention of Cents Scotty Munro, notched a goal, too. The two teams remained neck-and-neck the rest of the month. When they met again, Kamloops held a slim one-point lead but had injured Shinske returning to the lineup. Their games to date had all been close affairs and there was no reason to believe otherwise for this one.

Hay's leadership was affirmed when he went out on the first shift and decked three Broncos. Kamloops went on to take the game 4-1 and, from then on, Penticton was unable to make up enough ground to catch them. The Rockets took the league, and with it, the Kamloops Elks Trophy. They also won the season tilt against Penticton 5-3-1 and, more importantly, dominated in the last half of the season.

The first-round playoff against Vernon proved to be a heated affair. After taking Game 1, the Rockets went into Vernon and were leading 5-3 when a fan attacked Lyseng late in the game. The officials forfeited the game to Kamloops on the grounds that Vernon could not control its fans. The league overruled the officials and required the game be played out. It was played, after Vernon had won the next game to tie the series. The delayed game was won by Kamloops as was the following contest and the Rockets held a 3-1 series lead. Shinske and Hay starred as the Rockets took the final game 4-1 over the Essos to earn the right to go up against Dempsey's Penticton Broncos.

After taking Game 1 in Kamloops 5-2 and winning 5-4 in Penticton in overtime, the Rockets were looking to wrap the series up early. Penticton came back to take the next two games by decisive scores. The Rockets put Penticton on the ropes by winning the next game, but the Broncos wouldn't quit. They came back to win Game 6 in Penticton and force a seventh-and-deciding game in Kamloops.

Some 3,500 fans filled Memorial Arena and watched their Rockets outplay and outshoot the Broncos but, in the final minute, their heroes were down 3-2. Guarding the Penticton net was Glen Buekerct and patrolling the blueline was Dempsey. Tennant pulled his goalie and sent out his top players: Hay, Hodgson, Shinske, Ken Dodd, McMaster and Severyn. Dempsey, who had scored the opening goal, gathered in the puck in the dying seconds and sent it down the ice to kill the last few seconds and seal the upset series victory.

Future coaches with the Memorial Cup Blazers, Don Hay and Ed Dempsey were on ice foes in the 72-73 season. (c. Kamloops This Week)

Penticton went on and Kamloops hung up their skates. The relationship between the two hockey communities was destined for change next year.

Moving on to the WCHL were Hay and future pros Hodgson, Alex Tidey, Morin and Ashby. Hay was destined to return home to Kamloops and share in Memorial Cup championships with the Blazers as well as coach the Canadian juniors to a World Championship but not before he had the chance to suit up as a New Westminster Bruin first. Hodgson had a cup of coffee in the NHL with both Atlanta and Hartford and skated for a few years with the Tulsa Oilers of the Central Hockey League. Tidey and Morin enjoyed brief stints in the WHA. The greatest rise and most tragic fall was saved for local product Ashby.

Drafted number 6 in the first round in 1975, by the Toronto Maple Leafs, his star was rising. In his sixth season he had five points in only six games with the Colorado Rockies before a car accident in 1981 cut short his life and promise.

The Caribou College Chiefs, with Grant Evans, George Aulin and Lyle Harpe on its roster, improved dramatically to a 15-1 record and won the Totem Conference. The only loss was to Selkirk College.

First round draft pick Don Ashby as a Toronto Maple Leaf. (c. Jim Ashby)

Randy Rota as an Edmonton Oiler. (c. Randy Rota)

On the professional front, Bert Marshall was upstaged by Jimmy Harrison who, having moved over to the Alberta Oilers of the WHA, set a Guiness World Book of Records feat that stands to this date. On Jan. 30, 1973 he scored three goals and garnered seven assists for a 10-point evening against the New York Raiders. The performance was tied three years later by Darryl Sittler of Toronto in a game against Boston.

Randy Rota remained with the Calder Cup winning Nova Scotia Voyageurs but got some quality playing time with the parent Canadians. In his first call-up, he gathered a goal and an assist. A later chance saw him score the game-tying goal in an exhibition match at the Forum between the Canadians and the Moscow Selects. Randy went on to six solid seasons in the NHL and WHA enjoying his best years with the Kansas City Scouts

Gary Donaldson had jumped up to the Dallas Black Hawks, farm team of the Chicago Black Hawks.

Former Rockets Bob Nystrom and Gary Howatt quickly moved from the New Haven Night Hawks to the parent New York Islanders and became regulars. Curt Brackenbury signed with Philadelphia.

The New Westminster Bruins managed fourth place and again dropped out in the first round to Edmonton. Vic Mercredi placed in the Top 10 scorers preceded by former Rocket Wayne Bianchin, who was now playing in Flin Flon.

The Nats had an even worse season than the year before. They lost 55 games and, more importantly, lost a lot of money for their owner. He decided to sell.

Kamloops was about to join the major junior hockey world.

30

Big Time Junior ____________ 1973-74

For years, the best juniors in Kamloops were snatched up and taken off to major junior A teams on the Prairies.

Sometimes they came back to haunt Kamloops' teams, as in the case of Bert Marshall. Other times their absence simply hurt the advancement of the local junior team as with Jimmy Harrison and Randy Rota.

The 1973-74 season saw major junior hockey arrive in Kamloops. It afforded local fans the opportunity to see top-flight hockey while local talent had the chance to play at the highest level of junior hockey right in their own backyard.

Kamloops' First Tier 1 Junior team — the Chiefs. Front Row: (r-l) Johnny White (stick boy) Row 2: Terry MacDonald, Jim McAloney, Tim Priestley, Joe Tennant, Lloyd Saar, Jack Patterson, Mel Zinger Row 3: Bob McConnell (trainer) Randy Andreachuk, Ron Poole, Wayne Krebs, Neil Lyseng, Gordie Stewart, Alex Tidey. Row 4: Chris McMasters, Dwight Bailey, Dave Robinson, Rob Flockhart, Wayne Morin, Darryl Ferner, Dave Okrainee. (c. Doris Rubel)

The Vancouver Nats were sold to new owners in Kamloops, including Andy Berna, Ephraim Steinke and Ernie Rempel, and moved to the intimate confines of Memorial Arena. It was a franchise that had only known failure and had a long way to go before opposition teams would give it any competitive respect. The remaining Nats of the first two years were joined by a host of new players and more than a few were Kamloops' products. Greg Milliard, Mac Zinger, Chris Dyer, and Donnie Moores all suited up in Kelly green at some point in the season. Darryl Ferner joined the squad as did ex-Rockets Timber Peck, Neil Lyseng, Chris McMasters and Jack Patterson. Future NHLer Don Murdoch put in some games before being returned to Junior B and towering Barry Beck came up from Langley for one game. Others skating in the Chiefs' colours that season were Allan Young, Lloyd Saar (goal), Al McLaren, Dave Orianek, Brian Arnold, Dale Dreich, Ron Poole, Ron Boskil, Brian Day, Randy Andreachuk, Gord Stewart, Alex Tidey, Mark Severyn, Rob Flockhart, Rod Dyck and Wayne Morin. Don Hay did not make the cut but he would be back.

The old relationship between Kamloops and Scotty Munro's Centennials was apparent when the season started. Suiting up at the start for the foothills city were Rick Hodgson, Don Ashby, Mel Zinger, Jerry Holland, Terry Tarnow, Brian McLean, Larry Lestander, Garth Malarchuk, John Phillips, Rick Shinske and Craig Enfield. The Chiefs took on those familiar faces in their first outing where, despite being outshot only 30-26, they lost 4-1. They lost Game 2 7-1 to Medicine Hat and the inaugural season was looking grim with the New Westminster Bruins next on the schedule.

Some 1,300 fans looked on at Memorial as the Bruins, with Don Hay and Ken Dodd in their lineup, skated out against the underdog Chiefs. It was a slaughter. On the strength of two goals by McMasters, the Chiefs took it to the Bruins 8-1 for their first victory and it was against the franchise that was to eventually take its place in the hearts of Kamloops fans.

After the euphoria of their first win died down, they went on the road. The long and winding road was a difficult and discouraging trip for they went the entire season without a win.
By the time they met the Bruins again, they were on a modest two-game unbeaten streak. They stunned the Bruins once more, this time 4-1.

As the season progressed, the Bruins began to get the upper hand in games and the Chiefs spiralled towards a dismal season with only 13 wins. It was clear they were destined for last place with their only realistic goal being to improve over the last season in Vancouver. In the end, they accomplished it with three more wins. Four of their victories came over the New Westminster Bruins. John Senkpiel's franchise record 31 goals was passed by both Patterson and Randy Andreachuk.

As the team's performance steadily slipped so did attendance and, at season's end, the awards banquet had to be called off due to lack of support. Word had it that Joe Tennant would not be back next year and, in response, some players spoke up. They pointed out 16 of their losses had been by only one goal and they had one of the best farm systems in the league. To prove this, they pointed to the success of farm clubs in Langley, Penticton and Smithers. The claims were not unfounded as the following season demonstrated.

That future must have seemed a long way off to a team struggling with a 13-49-6 record, poor attendance and talk they may not even make it to the next season.

The other Chiefs in town, those from Caribou College, lost all of their regulars from the previous season but still wound up winning the Totem conference and representing British Columbia in The Four West Tournament.

Jimmy Harrison ranked amongst the top scorers in the new WHA with the Alberta Oilers while Bert Marshall continued as an NHL regular. Randy Rota danced up and down between the NHL and the minors. Gary Donaldson got a brief callup with the Chicago Black Hawks and former Rockets Nystrom, Howatt and Brackenbury solidified their NHL career prospects.

Ed Dempsey left Penticton for a hockey scholarship in the United States He was destined to return home. Don Hay was drafted by the Minnesotta North Stars, but he and Dempsey were destined to reunite at home.

The New Westminster Bruins fared better with a second-place standing in the regular season and advanced past Medicine Hat in the first round. Munro out dueled Ernie McLean in the second round as they fell to Calgary.

Hardly noticed that winter was the word in February 1974 the old exhibition barn, so proudly unveiled in 1925, was scheduled for demolition to make way for a road into Exhibition Park. Its rafters had been there for the baptism of local hockey but could not withstand the winds of time that swept it away. Like the oldtimers who had played the game within its confines, it moved off into the pages of history and Kamloops hockey continued to progress.

Here Come the Chiefs ______________ 1974-75

If there is one good thing with a team starting off with a bad record, it is there is no where to go but up. It also gives them plenty of scores to settle. The 1974-75 Chiefs forged the best season to date for the four-year-old franchise, finishing above .500 for the first time.

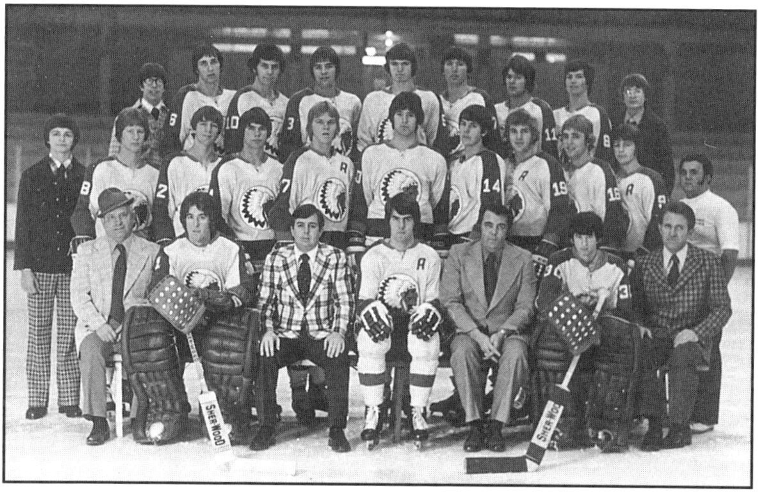

The 74-75 Chiefs.
Front Row: (l-r) Ephraim Steinke, Mike Priestner, Harvey Roy, Terry MacDonald, Jack Tennant, Mark Earp, Ernie Rempel, Middle Row: ?, Reg Kerr, Jamie Gallimore, Dave Hatheway, Neil Lyseng, Jim McAloney, Barry Melrose, Mal Zinger, Chris Dyer, Darryl Ferner, Nick "0". Top Row: Bernie Roy, Wayne Morin, Don Moores, Craig Toplinsky, Dave Robinson, Rob Flockhart, Brad Gassoff, Allen Young, ?.
(c. Doris Rubel)

They started off under a new coach, former Estevan Bruin Harvey Roy, and Jack (not Joe) Tennant as GM. Joe Tennant landed on his feet as coach of the Vernon Vipers of the BCJHL and remained as controversial as ever.

NHLer's Jim and Joe Watson helped out at training camp where locals Chris Dyer, Kirk Aulin, Kelly and Darryl Ferner also laced up skates. Don Murdoch moved over to Medicine Hat in a trade that brought Brad Gassoff while Barry Beck landed in New Westminster. A young Barry Melrose and his cousin, Gary, came out along with a promising rookie named Reg Kerr.

Others suiting up included Neil Lyseng, Don Moores, Rob Flockhart, Allan Young, Dave Hatheway, Jamie Gallimore, CraigTopolinsky, Brian Henderson (goal), Mark Earp (goal), Wayne Morin, Mike Priestner (goal), Kevin Marinos, Mac Zinger, Jim McAloney, Dave Robinson, Terry MacDonald and Tim Priestly. Down on the farm they had a budding star in Langley by the name of Ryan Walter. His rising career was to parallel the rise and fall of the Chiefs in Kamloops.

The season started on the road which was an unfriendly environment last year. Even in this season's exhibition play, the Chiefs had not managed a road win. This time it started much better as they got the monkey off their back right away. In their opener MacDonald's two goals led them to a 5-1 victory in Lethbridge.

In their home opener before 2,249 fans, they demolished last season's regular champs, the Calgary Centennials, 9-0. Their second game on home ice saw them down the reigning Memorial Cup champion Regina Pats 7-1. No one was making fun of the Chiefs anymore. When they next went out on a major road trip, they took their first four games in a row.

Gassoff was starring regularly with Flockhart, Moores, Darryl Ferner and MacDonald putting in big nights, too. On Dec. 2, 1974, the paper noted a silver lining in a 5-3 loss. Walter, called up from Langley, scored all three Chiefs goals. They had a star on their hands.

Even with the on-ice success, there were some disturbing signs that had shown up earlier with the Senior A Elks and Chiefs. The Chiefs lost $60,000 their first year and needed an average of 2,100 fans just to break even. With 2,500 seating capacity at Memorial Arema, it did not leave much wiggle room. Calls went out for a new arena.

With 1975 approaching, New Westminster and Kamloops were battling it out for second behind front-running Victoria. The year was coming to a close on a positive note with a much anticipated exhibition match against an undefeated Czechoslovakian touring team. However, before the game took place, a near tragedy occurred.

On an icy road outside of Jasper, with the team savouring a 6-4 win in Edmonton, the team bus overturned. Unlike a similar incident years later involving the Swift Current Broncos no one died; however, six people were injured. Coach Roy and CFJC's Earl Seitz were the most seriously hurt. Others included Melrose, Topolinsky, Darryl Ferner and McAloney.

The Chiefs called up Kelly Ferner and Walter for the exhibition match and New Westminster contributed former Rocket Rick Shinske to the cause. It was an appropriate gesture as he led the Chiefs to a 5-4 victory in front of 3,400 fans at Memorial Arena.

Walter was making the most of his call-ups. In January, he scored his seventh goal in six games and it was a big one as the winner in a 5-4 victory over first place Victoria. Victoria was to figure prominently in the Chiefs' season and were Kamloops' opponents in the first round. It was the first time the franchise had made the playoffs.

The Chiefs landed fifth overall and fourth in their division, only three points out of second. Their 38-24-8 record was their best ever. However, they were going up against a Victoria team 15 points ahead of them, playing in their own rink to start and which had lost to the Chiefs only once all season.

Gassoff was a one-man wrecking crew in Game 1 as he scored the winning goal on a slapshot and the insurance goal into an empty net in the Chiefs' 6-4 win. As if that wasn't enough, he potted the winner in overtime in Game 2's 4-3 victory. Melrose had tied the game to force overtime. Amazingly Kamloops was heading home up 2-0 in the series.

Victoria hadn't finished first for nothing and showed up for Game 3. They outshot Kamloops 42-22 and pounded them 7-2 to take the air out of the crowd. Some 3,400 turned up for Game 4 hoping Kamloops could return to the form that had given them the first two games. The match was closer but Victoria skated away with the 5-3 victory to tie the series. Now, it was a best of three with Victoria having home-ice advantage again.

The Chiefs tightened up in Game 5 but still lost 3-2 .Kamloops fans lost heart and it was a disappointing crowd that turned up to see the Chiefs end their season with a 3-0 loss. It remained a season of accomplishment despite its end and the diminished fan support. Victoria fell to New Westminster which went all the way to the Memorial Cup to start an amazing run of Memorial Cup appearances.

The prospects for 1975-76 were uncertain as Kamloops lost Zinger, Gassoff, Lyseng, Morin, Darryl Ferner and McAloney. But there was still Walter.

Gassoff went on to play parts of four seasons with the Vancouver Canucks and was destined to reappear before Kamloops fans in enemy colours.

The Caribou College Chiefs, coached by Cliff Russell, iced a team but did not enjoy the success of their previous two years.

The Kamloops midget Bucks' Oil Kings, sporting future NHLer Doug Lidster, had more than a passable year. When they were eliminated in the final by Vernon, coach Craig Sturgeon gave vent to his frustration that Kamloops' best players were not all available given the practice of dividing the talent between North and South Kamloops. It was hard to argue against his point and the advantage that similar-sized communities enjoyed in the divided Kamloops strength.

Doug Lidster as captain of the Buck's Oil Kings midget team. (c. Dave Lidster)

The greatest success in the minor leagues came from the bantams. The Okanagan final came down to a contest between the North Kamloops Toyota bantams and the Jardine bantams. Team Toyota took the series and advanced all the way to the provincial round robin tournament. The Don Clovechok team led by Glenn Merkosky's 40 points won seven straight games to become provincial champs. Their victories were as tight as 5-4 over the North Shore Winter Club and as crushing as their 19-1 pummelling of Kimberley.

The three year drought of provincial championships came to an end.

In the pros, Jimmy Harrison was traded to the Cleveland

Crusaders and ex-Rockets Kelly Pratt (Pittsburgh) and Jerry Holland (New York Rangers) got ice time in the NHL. Randy Rota and Bert Marshall remained and Gary Howatt and Bob Nystrom continued with the New York Islanders. Sam Clegg was playing goal with Nova Scotia in the AHL while Gary Donaldson remained with the Dallas Black Hawks.

In the WCHL, Don Ashby landed fifth in scoring despite being on the worst team in the league. Don Murdoch, who had resisted playing in Kamloops, finished third in scoring but Kamloops was not displeased with the player they got in return, Gassoff.

When the playoffs rolled around, the Bruins hit their stride. After disposing of Victoria, they took a hard-fought, seven-game series against Saskatoon 4-3 and headed for the franchise's second Memorial Cup. The cup went to the legendary but dying Toronto Marlboros; however, the Bruins were not through. For the next three seasons, they were to come from the West to challenge for the cup.

Punch McLean was still steering the franchise that initially set sail in Humboldt almost 30 years before. His best sailing was ahead of him.

The Kamloops Team Toyota midgets — Provincial Champs in 1975 with future pro Glenn Merkosky in the lineup. (c. Riverside Coliseum Wall of Fame)

32

National Dream 1975-76

1975-76 saw the Chiefs reach higher than ever before and, for the first time, people were talking about the Memorial Cup seriously. It did prove to be a season when Kamloops skated out on to the national stage for the second time.

Harvey Roy's roster included the WHY line composed of Ryan Walter, Dave Hatheway and Allan Young playing behind the top line of Rob Flockhart, Darryl Ferner and Larry Lestander. Other locals on the squad included Mike Urquhart, Kelly Ferner and Chris Dyer. Reg Kerr, Donnie Moores, Barry Melrose returned. During the course of the campaign, Don Bliault, Mark Taylor (grandson of Cyclone Taylor), Dan Clark, Brian

The 1975/76 Chiefs with future NHL star Ryan Walter in the lineup. Front Row: (l-r) Brian Henderson, Ernie Rempel, Darryl Ferner, Harvey Roy, Allen Young, Andy Berna, Mark Earp. Middle Row: Dell Udell, Kelly Ferner, Larry Lestander, Don Moores, Jamie Gallimore, Ryan Walter, Dave Robinson, Mike Urquhart, Reg Kerr, Nick "0". Back Row: Dave Hatheway, Dave Johnson, Barry Melrose, Dan Clark, Rob Flockhart, Dwayne Lowdermilk, Bernie Roy. (c. Doris Rubel)

Henderson, Mark Earp(goal), Rocky Saganuik and Elmer Ray skated for the squad. Roy brought up Larry Playfair, Leonard Dies and Errol Rause for the playoff run.

The season opener was against Lestander's old team, the Calgary Centennials, and he had the pleasure of scoring the game-tying goal in the Chiefs' 3-2 victory. After a start that had them playing .500 hockey, they began to gather momentum and, by late October, were challenging for first. The Nov. 7, 1975 Sentinel boasted, after bombing Lethbridge 13-1 and Brandon 7-2, the Chiefs were tied for first with New Westminster. By Dec. 1, 1975 the team that had gone a complete season without winning a single road game had gone unbeaten in 12 straight and was eight points up on New Westminster in first. Nationally ranked, they were now talking of a shot at the Memorial Cup.

The two teams met in New Westminster in December before almost 4,000 fans at Queen's Park. The fans, described as almost as belligerent as the Bruins, saw Rick Shinske lead their heroes to a 4-3 victory. The rematch in Kamloops was a sellout but also a cold shower for the Chiefs as the Bruins took them 7-1. The hot streak went cold, and by month's end, New Westmisnter had regained first. They did not let it go and by season's end were 26 points up on their nearest competitor. Kamloops had to fight it out for second with Medicine Hat and Victoria.

The two rivals met again in late January 1976 and the Chiefs stunned the Bruins with two shorthanded goals in a 6-5 victory. In February, 2,600 Kamloops fans saw their Chiefs hand New Westminster its first shutout loss of the season as they prevailed 6-0. They stood third overall in the league. Although they had to concede first to the Bruins, they knew they could beat them.

The battle with Medicine Hat for second went down to the wire and was finally settled at home before 2,600 fans. In the last game of the season, they downed The Hat 8-4 to clinch second. They finished with a 40-26-6 record and outscored the opposition 365 to 285. Almost every record in the franchise's five-year history was broken. They went into the playoffs as favourites.

They took on the Winnipeg Clubs in Round 1 and won Game 1 4-2. They were in tough in Game 2. Down 5-4 in the third Kerr was awarded a penalty shot. He made good on it and, at 16:53, Hatheway nailed the game winner. Up 2-0 in the series, they were off to Winnipeg.

The Clubs bounced back with an 8-5 win on home ice

and the fans were enjoying a 3-1 lead in Game 4 with only five minutes remaining. Taunting Walter with chants of "Walter" proved to be a mistake as he scored the game-tying goal in a 3-3 final. The Clubs managed a 3-3 tie in Kamloops in Game 6 which put the Chiefs up 6-4 in points and within a win of advancing. The Clubs could not prolong the series as the Chiefs took the next game 6-3 and advanced to the second round for the first time in franchise history.

The Saskatoon Blades had finished 10 points ahead of the Chiefs and had future St. Louis star Bernie Federko in their lineup. CFCR carried the game back to Kamloops and the cheers from across the Rockies must have helped as the Chiefs surprised the Blades 5-3. Although Saskatoon took Game 2 6-2, Kamloops had done what it needed to do; take a road game to get home ice advantage. They used it in Game 3 to win 7-2 and take the series lead. The Blades thundered back in Game 4 with a stunning 12-4 victory to take the series back to the Prairies tied. The Blades won 4-2 to put Kamloops on the edge of the golf season, but at least the next game was in Kamloops.

The Kamloops faithful saw their Chiefs fading as the Blades built up a 4-0 lead and looked to be cruising into the next round. Kamloops showed it had more than a little heart. Goal-by-goal they clawed back until they tied the game and then went ahead 5-4. It was a fantastic comeback. However the Blades answered with the tying goal and, when the light went on for the eleventh time, the Chiefs best season ever was over.

In addition to setting new team records, the Chiefs had three-all stars in Flockhart, Kerr and Earp. Despite the loss of Earp, Darryl Ferner, Lestander and Melrose for next year, there were enough returnees and future prospects to be optimistic.

Melrose turned up next season with Cincinnati of the WHA and spent nine years in the WHA and NHL before moving on to the coaching ranks. In 1993, he reached the Stanley Cup finals against Montreal as coach of the Wayne Gretzky-led L. A. Kings that also sported Kamloops' own Tim Watters.

The dark cloud that hung over the horizon had nothing to do with the talent and desire on the ice or the good farm system. Owner Ephraim Steinke had lost big bucks in the first two seasons. December brought the news that the WCHL had turned down his attempt to move the franchise to Portland. Then there was talk of returning the team to Vancouver. By the end of the month, word had it he had decided to keep the franchise in Kamloops but the rumours just would not die. Despite the uncertainty, the team had excelled. It was to face more of the same the following winter.

The local minor hockey scene was as active as ever. The midget Buck's Oil Kings became the star attraction as they advanced farther than any other minor league team from Kamloops ever had.

The 1976 Provincial midget champs Buck's Oil Kings with Tim Watters and Doug Lidster in the lineup. A trip to the Nationals.
(c. Dorothy Watters)

Touting a lineup with future NHLer's Tim Watters and Doug Lidster, they dominated provincial play. By early December, they had six of the Top 10 scorers with Murray Matheson, Doug Watt, Ray Rempel, Kevin Chaben, Lance Lestander and Watters. They were also in the running to represent British Columbia in the National Wrigley's championship. To get there, they had to advance through regional and provincial playdowns.

In the regionals, they waltzed over Salmon Arm 22-2, Oliver 15-0 and Vernon 6-4. In the provincials at Trail, it was closer as they lost their opener 7-5 to Quesnel but then went on to beat Saanich 6-4 and Kimberley 9-2. They were the B.C. reps for the Calgary tournament. They later avenged their loss to Quesnel by defeating that team in the final game of its own midget tourney by a score of 5-1.

Coach Craig Sturgeon expressed frustration other teams in the national tournament had stacked their squads and Kamloops was playing with the added liability of its talent being divided between North and South Kamloops. The Oil Kings went 2-3 in their division and did not make the finals but their performance was more than credible.

Their season was not over and back in B.C. their 14-3 season-ending victory over Merritt capped a perfect 15-0-0 campaign. It came as no surprise they made the provincial final and won the round robin with seven straight wins to take the midget championship and the Cromie Cup.

The Oil Kings were not the only squad bringing provincial championships to the Thompson that season. It was a banner year.

Don Clovechok's North Kamloops Team Toyota bantams won the Doug Grimston Memorial Trophy as provincial champs and the Kamloops South Peewee Chiefs, under Don Busch, won the province and the William Mott Trophy. Further recognition came Kamloops' way when it was reported in January 1976 it had the largest minor hockey association in Western Canada.

The Caribou College Chiefs added Danny Rota to its roster and had a credible if not a championship-winning campaign.

In the pros, Jim Harrison, Bert Marshall, Randy Rota, Bob Nystrom, Gary Howatt and Curt Brackenbury were joined by Terry MacDonald (Kansas City Scouts NHL), Neil Lyseng (Phoenix Roadrunners WHA), Wayne Morin (Toronto Toros WHA) and Alex Tidey (San Diego Mariners WHA). Don Hay, Brad Gassoff and Mac Zinger were toiling in the minor league pros.

The New West Bruins stopped the Saskatoon Blades and advanced for the second time to the Memorial Cup where they fell in the final to the Hamilton Fincups. Ernie McLean must have felt snake bitten. Three times to the final and no Memorial Cup.

Sadly, one of the cornerstones of the franchise's development was not destined to see them and his friend Ernie finally take the Cup. Scotty Munro, at the age of 57, died of cancer in September 1975. He had been in hockey for 40 years and seen the franchise through its formidable years in Humboldt and Estevan. A major force in the development of the WCHL, he eventually left his stamp on the local hockey scene through the Kamloops Rockets and impressed himself upon many local players who went on to the pros. Harrison, Rota, Don Ashby, Derek Black and Rick Hodgson were but some of the players whose careers and lives were influenced by the fabled Scotsman.

His name lives on in the Scotty Munro Trophy awarded to the WCHL regular season champs. First named after him in 1966, his own Calgary Centennials took it in 1972 and, in the season of his death, his buddy McLean captured it with the Bruins. In the years ahead the Kamloops Blazers would garner it seven times by 1995.

For now however, no one would ever have guessed Kamloops, on the edge of losing its existing team, would ever be in a position to win anything.

33

Demise ______ 1976-77

If 1975-76 had been a steady rise, the following season was a roller coaster of play and emotion.

The last season in Kamloops for the Chiefs. The 1976-77 Chiefs. Front Row: (l-r) Gary Nakrayko, Harvey Roy, Ryan Walter, Ephraim Steinke, Allen Young, Andy Berna, Brian Henderson. Middle Row: Reg Kerr, Jamie Pearson, Dwayne Lowdermilk, Greg Dunn, Dan Clark, Ryan Hatfield, Dave Robinson, Len Dies, Mike Boychuk. Top Row: Tim Watters, Clint Eccles, Gary Soetaert, Steve Zanatta, Anthony Thomas, Jamie Gallimore, George Wright, Errol Rausse. (c. Doris Rubel)

Ivan "the Terrible" Prediger, another former Estevan Bruin, came on as head coach while Harvey Roy moved over to GM. Local players sprinkled in the lineup included Tim Watters, Glenn Merkosky, Mike Urquhart, Anthony Thomas and Mike Boychuk. They joined the season's roster of Ryan Walter, Jamie Gallimore, Reg Kerr, Brian Henderson (goal), Gary Nakrayko, Allan Young, Errol Rause, Clint Eccles, Dave Robinson, Duane Loudermilk,Greg Dunn, Steve Zanatta, Ryan Hartfield, James Pearson, Gary Soetart, Dan Clark, George Wright and Len Dies.

Rumours about the team going to Portland finally died if only because the age-old Edmonton Oil Kings beat them to it. That franchise, so steeped in history and tradition, that had stoned the Kamloops Rockets in the '60s and been the Bruins' staunch rival, pulled up stakes and moved south of the border. Though they were destined to field some great teams in the years ahead, they have never regained the supremacy the franchise had once known. However, that season they were very much a factor in the fortunes of the Chiefs as the two struggled for second place. New Westminster was the clear favourite for the regular season.

The reason for that choice was apparent in the Chiefs' season opener as they were shocked 11-3 at Queen's Park.

Their home opener was against the new Winterhawks and the Chiefs looked good on the rebound. Rause got two goals in a 6-1 victory. It looked even better when they took their second game against Portland 6-2.

Despite the success, talk of the team moving persisted. Edmonton and Seattle were cited as likely destinations. The rumours hurt attendance which only added to the difficulties. Problems piled on problems as injuries plagued the squad and coach Prediger managed to get himself suspended for 20 games. Despite all this, they remained around the .500 mark and were giving their fan club, the "Chief Believers" something to hold on to.

As the season neared its climax, Portland was staying ahead of the Chiefs and they needed a solid winning streak if they were going to grab second. By late March, it was clear the two squads would be facing each other in the playoffs. The only uncertainty was who was going to have home ice.

In a remarkably strong finish, the Chiefs clinched second place when they went into the Royal city and stole a game to run their record in the last 19 games to 13-4-2. It was a good thing they won that one because in their final game of the season in Portland, they were bombed 10-2. Second was theirs by one point.

Game 1 of the playoffs was a disappointment for the 2,400 Kamloops fans as the Chiefs dropped the hard-fought game 3-2 in overtime. On the strength of Young's three goals, however, they rebounded to take Game 2 4-3 before only 1,700 faithful. Some 3,500 Portland fans saw former Chief Dave Hatheway score a shorthanded goal and the game winner in Game 3 as the Winterhawks took a 5-4 decision. The pattern of close games ended, unhappily for the Chiefs, when Portland stormed out to take game four 7-0. Kamloops was on the edge of elimination.

Some 2,000 fans turned up at Memorial Arena knowing all too well their Chiefs were not coming back next year and they might be seeing their last game in Kamloops' colours. The end came as expected. Portland won the day 5-1. The Sentinel lamented the loss but noted Walter, in particular, battled to the very end and scored the Chiefs' only goal. His fortunes exceeded that of the team's as he went on to stardom in Seattle and eventually got to sip out of the Stanley Cup with the Montreal Canadians.

In its four years in Kamloops, the team put together three back-to-back .500 seasons and, despite adversity in its final year, had melded into a squad to be reckoned with. This did not survive their move to Seattle where it took them 13 seasons to collect three .500 seasons. Even today, the franchise can look back to its years in Kamloops as the most successful in its history.

The legacy of the Chiefs was not lost on the pros. Rause flirted with the Washington Capitals for three seasons while Kerr had a solid four seasons in the NHL. Larry Playfair had an 11 year stint, mostly with Buffalo; Rocky Saganiuk toiled for six seasons in the NHL; Rob Flockhart for parts of five; and Mark Taylor put in five. First round draft choice Walter more than fulfilled his promise over the course of 15 years at the top.

1976-77 also marked the return of junior B hockey to Kamloops with the birth of the Kamloops Braves, a team also owned by Ephraim Steinke and affiliated with the Chiefs. Their inaugural season was a tumultuous one and featured names that would grace NHL rosters. Chief amongst these was 15-year-old Andy Moog in net but it also included Kamloops own Tim Watters and Glenn Merkosky. They were joined by Peter Dineen of the well known Dineen hockey family. Don Busch was initially to coach the squad but his place was taken by Craig Sturgeon.

Their home opener was against last season's provincial champs the Nanaimo Clippers. The 400 plus fans who took in the game saw Merkosky and Moog lead their team to a 4-3 win. In the early going, these two led the squad to some promising victories but then the roof caved in. They went 10 games without a win.

Topping it off was the return of Joe Tennant as coach of the Merritt Centennials, a team which managed to lure away Kamloops' products Kirk Aulin and Wade Jowett to their side. The cagey old coach was to prove a thorn in the Braves' side as the two teams battled for the final playoff position.

The Braves slowly began to regain some respectability and, by early February, had a six point lead on Merritt. Moog was leading the league in saves percentage at 90 percent. Yet, in the closing games of the campaign, they were only two points ahead of Merritt and the Cents had a game in hand. Luck was with the Braves when the Abbotsford Flyers stopped Merritt 4-1. Kamloops could now do no worse than tie for the final playoff spot and battle it out in a sudden-death tie-breaker. That, in fact, was what happened.

Normally, the final playoff spot would have been decided on goals for and against differential, which would have favoured Kamloops, but not that year. Instead, they were to play a sudden-death tie breaker at Logan Lake, a neutral site. Somehow this got changed and the game was set for Merritt. Still, the Braves, backed by Moog, went into Tennant's own backyard and took the game 5-2. They were in or so they thought.

Tennant was not about to let mere defeat on the ice stop him. Not only had his team benefited by avoiding elimination on the goals for and against differential, not only had they benefited from moving the tie breaker from Logan Lake to Merritt; he also found a way to deprive the Braves of advancement despite their clear 5-2 victory. He complained the Braves had used an ineligible player, Grant Reid, in the final game. The league sided with Tenant and Merritt, not Kamloops, advanced.

The 1976-77 BCJHL Kamloops Braves. Top Row: (l-r) Lance Lestander, Glen Merkosky, Scott Rauch, Norm Meyer, Dennis Warawa, Rauno Saarnio, Peter Dineen. Middle Row: Andy Moog, Jim Crosson, Tim Watters (captain) Lawrence Angus, Shane Clark, Reg Rempel, Ward Sparrow. Front Row: Curtis Billy, Phil Logan, Doug Watt, Greg Duncan, Ken McNabb.

Given the fate of the Chiefs and the Braves, it was no wonder Kamloops hockey fans felt a little ill-treated that season. Still, the Braves had come back from a bad start and next season, as the number 1 act in town, they had some reason to feel optimistic.

At the college front, the Caribou College Chiefs, under the guidance of Terry Bangen, came up with one of its best seasons ever. Finishing the regular season with an 11-0-1 record they eliminated Selkirk College to go to the western final for the third time. They made it to the championship game before being put out by Red Deer. It was their best run yet.

The Buck's Oil Kings, with Doug Lidster still on the roster, made it all the way to the provincial final but could not duplicate last season's championship. Tim Watters moved on and was to eventually enjoy a 14-year pro career split between Winnipeg and Los Angeles. With former Chief Barry Melrose at the helm, Tim got to the lip of the Stanley Cup in the 1993 final against Montreal.

Harkening back to a legendary past in local hockey was an oldtimers' game in January, that saw Vernon, led by Tom Stecyk, beat the Kamloops Oldtimers 6-4. Fred Gaber, Bill Donaldson, Ross Jardine, Don Busch, Ev Miller, Lorne Lussier (goal), Bud Schollen, Buddy Evans, Cliff Russell, Al Ritchie and 62-year-old Kenny Stewart carried the local colours. For the fans, it was a reflective skate down memory lane.

Tim Watters — 14 years in the NHL and a glance at the Stanley Cup. (c. Dorothy Watters)

The New West Bruins were not to be denied. They rolled over Portland in four straight and lost only one game in their conquest of Brandon. For the third straight year, they won the west and were headed to the Memorial Cup.

Ernie McLean had taken his teams on the quest for junior hockey's holy grail three times before but had always drawn up short in the final match. Not this time. His Bruins took home the hardware with a thrilling 6-5 win over the Ottawa 67's at Pacific Coliseum and they were not done yet.

34

Return of the Chiefs ______________ 1977-78

1977-78 saw the Kamloops Chiefs again carrying the junior colours for the city; however, it was the junior B franchise of the BCJHL. The renaming of the Braves did not change their ownership by Ephraim Steinke nor did it alter their affiliation with the former Tier 1 Chiefs which had become the Seattle Breakers.

The Chiefs sported an impressive lineup, if future pros are any indication. Andy Moog, Tim Hunter, Doug Lidster, Glenn Merkosky and Peter Dineen all had pro careers ahead of them. They were joined by Norm Meyer, Doug Merkosky, Jay Kozak, Peter Gerlinger, Brian Graves, Paul Phee, Clint Fehr, Murray Matheson, Steve Blyth, Barry Huber, Darryl Moen, Dennis Warwa, Mike Mesic, Gary Skuta, Ward Sparrow, Kevin Quin, Don Suraki and Randy Will. Coach Craig Scott was replaced by Ken Rodgers part way through the season.

Despite the talent the team started slowly. Andy Moog and Ward Sparrow were unhappy and wanted out. Eventually Moog was traded to the Penticton Vees for Ralph Andreeson and goalie Shawn Chisholm. If this wasn't bad enough, now there were rumblings this team might be transferred to Salmon Arm.

Moog's incredible star was to shine for 18 seasons in the NHL, capturing two Stanley Cups in Edmonton and appearing in three other finals.

Even before the trade, the Chiefs were beginning to show some life but they were doing it in cardiac fashion. The Feb. 17, 1978 Sentinel noted they had tied four games in the last minute and won three of them in overtime. Later the same month, they reached the .500 mark for the first time in the team's brief history. When they came up against Penticton and their two former teammates, they were riding a nine game, home-ice unbeaten streak. Their streak went to 10 with an 11-7 victory.

Their strong second half earned them fourth place and the right to face Kelowna in the playoffs. A playoff between the Kamloops Chiefs and the Kelowna Buckaroos sounded like a voice calling from the old Senior league days. Kelowna took Game 1 9-6 but the Chiefs evened the series up at one. Merkosky was a one man act in the third game scoring four goals in a 6-4 victory. Kelowna never recovered and the Chiefs advanced. They had to savour their series victory because they went out quickly in the final four straight. Their improvement was visible and there was promise if Kamloops could just hang onto the team.

Merkosky moved on to a pro career that saw him playing five partial seasons in the NHL but his star was to shine the brightest in the American Hockey League. So prominent was his role with Adirondack Red Wings he became the first player from that team to ever have his number retired when his on-ice career ended.

The Caribou College Chiefs, still under coach Terry Bangen, were excited about the prospects for the new season as word had it many local stars, including John Senkpiel, Don Hay, Gary Donaldson and Larry Lestander, were coming on board. However, a new act in town stole that thunder.

Despite the disappointment, the Chiefs still won the Totem Conference and went to the Western Canadian final for the fourth time in its short history.

The new act in town was the rebirth of senior hockey. Contending that Kamloops was one of the premier hockey communities in British Columbia, a number of businessmen, including David Robertson and Mike Mortimer, paid $5,000 for the old WHA Calgary Cowboy uniforms and let it be known they were putting together a challenge team for the Coy Cup. The Cowboys' first contest was against the Prince George Mohawks which had a Kamloops connection.

The Mohawks were coached by Don Wilkie, who had been the first Kamloops player to advance into major junior hockey. Former Rocket Grant Evans was also skating in the lineup.

When the two teams met in Prince George, they faced a familiar face in net. Glen Buekerct, who had made the difference in the series between the Kamloops Rockets and Penticton Broncos in 1973, guarded the pipes. This time Ed Dempsey was playing for his home-town Cowboys and was in the company of Hay. The Mohawks took both games and the third in the series in Kamloops before 1,800 fans. Some, 1,200 turned up the next night as the Cowboys got their first win, 5-0. They ended their exhibition play with a 5-5-1 record and the expressed intention of joining a new senior league next season.

In the playdowns, the Cowboys rolled over a challenge team from Kelowna and then had to go up against Prince George in the semis. They went out in two straight against the more experienced Mohawks but there was talk even more former Kamloops' players were to be returning to the fold next year.

More players with ties to Kamloops made their way into the pros. Dan Clark and Clint Eccles were picked up by Philadelphia and sent down to Milwaukee; Dave Robinson and Jamie Gallimore were in Flint; Brad Gassoff was with Vancouver's farm team in Tulsa and Barry Melrose was a regular with the WHA Cincinnati Stingers.

The New Westminster Bruins barely scraped their way into the playoffs despite having a .500 season but had to get by Portland which had finished 34 points ahead of them. That they did and eventually made it to the Memorial Cup for the fourth straight time. Ernie McLean got the satisfaction of taking the cup for the second straight time. The success of the Bruins appeared to be an act almost impossible to follow.

The Seattle Breakers, which had predicted it would do 25percent better than last year, didn't make the playoffs, getting four points fewer that last season.

The prospects for hockey in Kamloops had some bright spots in the future but some dark years were to come in between.

35

Fire Up the Rockets — 1978-79

The 1978-79 season saw a new owner but an old name for the juniors. Jim Mullen took over the team and brought back the Rockets. There was fuel in the tank and they were headed higher.

Returning to the squad was Doug Lidster, Doug Watt, Clint Fehr, Jay Kozak and Murray Matheson. Peter Gerlinger, Tim Hunter, Shane Clarke and Norm Meyer headed off to Seattle's training camp. Hunter did not return. Ian McEachern, Jim Crosson, Randy Kirby, Brad Duncan, Elton Allen, Al Radke, Brian Henderson (goal), Allan Graves and Glen Sorenson skated in the team's colours that season. Toward the end of the season three players-Gordie Miller, Kenny Gannon and Ralph Charlton-were brought up from the highly successful Weycan juveniles.

Hunter stuck with Seattle and went on to a 16-year NHL career largely with Calgary and Vancouver. He sipped from the Stanley Cup with the Flames in 1989 and came within a game of doing it again with the 1994 Canucks.

Peter Dineen's future saw him enjoy a few games with L.A. and Detroit.

The team started slowly again and there was a coaching change. Ken Rodgers stepped down, complaining the owner was interfering too much, and was replaced by the familiar Harvey Roy, who was, in turn, replaced by Craig Sturgeon. On the ice, the team had recovered to the .500 mark by December and was fighting with Merritt for second place. Concerns were being raised about attendance and money in much the same way as they had with the Tier 1 Chiefs. Still, the team was performing on the ice seemingly oblivious to the distractions.

When businessmen Francois Lambert, Jack Kennedy and Howard Webster took over the team, it looked as if matters were finally secure. The Rockets captured second place behind the Merritt Centennials and were to meet Vernon in the first round.

Only 450 fans were on hand to watch Fehr, with three goals, lead the Rockets to an 8-4 victory over the Vernon Vikings. Despite a close battle in Game 2 in Vernon Kamloops was unable to break the Vernon jinx and came up on the short end of a 5-4 score. Game 3 went to double overtime but once again Vernon took the one-goal game. Back in Kamloops, the Rockets poured it on to win going away 8-2 and then rubbed salt into the wound with a 12-2 victory. Up 3-2 in games, they headed back to Vernon. Again the game went into overtime but this time Vernon could not pull it out. The Rockets won to advance against Merritt.

The series started poorly for the Rockets as they lost 7-2 in Merritt and then 4-2 at Memorial Arena before 1,300 fans. Only the goaltending of Henderson kept them in the game. It did not look good going back to Merritt down 2-0. The lines of Kirby/Radke/Allan along with Fehr/Kozak/Graves starred as the Rockets took a 4-3 decision to get back in the series. At home they came up with a nail biting 3-2 win in front of 1,500. It didn't stop there as they returned to Merritt and beat the Centennials again, this time 3-1. Graves, with his hat trick, proved the hero in Game 6 at Memorial Arena as his Rockets beat Merritt 7- 4 to take the Okanagan. They had once again moved a notch up from the previous year's performance.

Their next task was the Bellingham Blazers, a team that had dominated the BCJHL all year. The Nat Bailey Trophy at stake. The Blazers could not compete for the Mowatt Cup because they were not from British Columbia. It was no contest as the Rockets bowed out easily in four straight. They still had a chance at winning the Mowatt Cup, however.

To do so, they had to go up against the Richmond Sockeyes of the Pacific Coast Junior Hockey League. The league was considered inferior to the BCJHL and so the Rockets had every reason to be confident. Kozak scored a hat trick in Game 1 and the Rockets took it 5-3. It looked like it was all but over for the best-of-three.

Richmond saw it otherwise and surprised the Rockets 4-1 in Game 2. In Game 3 the Rockets fired 50 shots at goalie Paul Fricker but it was the Sockeyes that came away with the upset 5-3 victory and the Mowatt Cup.

New York Ranger Doug Lidster became the second Kamloops product to have his name on the Stanley Cup. (c. Dave Lidster)

The Rockets had improved again and, if they could just manage to survive in Kamloops, the future looked good. Star defenceman Lidster moved on and was destined to sparkle for 15 seasons in the NHL, 10 of which were with the Vancouver Canucks. Before his career ended, he reached the ultimate goal of holding the Stanley Cup as a member of the 1994 New York Rangers, which ironically, beat out the Canucks in a seven-game final, and again in 1999 with the Dallas Stars.

The Cowboys took to the ice for training with Don Ashby back to help out. Don Hay took on the position of player/coach and even Randy Rota, whose pro career had ended, suited for some games.

In the four-team Caribou Interior Hockey League, the Mohawks and the Cowboys fought it out for first with Quesnel as the also ran. Williams Lake was a distant fourth and did not finish the season. During the campaign, Cowboy goalie Mark Earp got to go up against his brother, Brad, in goal for Quesnel.

After finishing second to Prince George, the "Pokes" started their series against the Quesnel Kangaroos in Quesnel. They took the first two games easily and finished off the best-of-five at home before 900 fans at Memorial. The Mohawks were rested and waiting but they also had another big advantage.

The Cowboys had lost eight of 11 games to the Mohawks and were in an uphill battle in any event. In addition, they were informed they would only get two home games even if the series went the full seven. The team shot off a letter to league president Buddy Evans claiming they would not return to the league next season because of the move.

The Cowboys turned their anger to good use as they went into Prince George and took Game 1 4-3. Although they lost the next game, they had taken an important road win. Back at Memorial, it began to look good as they won 4-2 and took the series lead. The Mohawks took the crucial fourth game to tie the series. All three remaining games were road games for the "Pokes."

Heading up the Prince George coach Hay, in an interview, took time to give credit for some of his success to the great coaches he had played under. Included in his list were Joe Tennant (with the Rockets), Scotty Munro (with Calgary Centennials) and Ernie "Punch" McLean (with the New Westminster Bruins).

The unfriendly confines of Prince George were even more depressing as the Mohawks took the next two games and put the Cowboys out. Despite their protests, the "Pokes" were to return the next season.

At the minor league level, the Weycan juveniles dominated. After leading their rep league all year, they took silver at the B.C. Winter Games held in Kamloops. They won the Okanagan and went up against Prince Rupert in the semis. Rupert fell in two straight and the juveniles took on the White Rock Rebels at Memorial for the Monarch Cup. White Rock fell 6-3 and 6-5 to give Weycan the provincial championship.

Another juvenile team, that had not received much attention before, brought home its third straight provincial championship. The Kamloops First Nations juveniles won at the provincial tournament by an overwhelming score of 21-3 over Salmon Arm.

The Caribou College Chiefs played in the local commercial league and gained entry into the Western College championships but fared poorly outside of B.C.

The New Westminster Bruins finished above .500 again but there were stresses in the seams of the dynasty made worse by a brawl at Queen's Park in a game against Portland. The matter went to criminal court and five Bruins were suspended from play until Dec. 1, 1979. Elimination in Round 1 of the playoffs was nothing compared to the indignities the proud franchise was to suffer next season.

The light of junior hockey began to fade in both Kamloops and New Westminster but the fates were at work to relight the torch.

36

Rockets Away 1979-80

Coach Darryl Ferner and assistant Allan Young began the Rockets season with Jay Kozak and Norm Meyer returning from tryouts with Regina and Tim Jordan as a local rookie hopeful. Al Radke, Elton Allen and Dave Kirby returned, too. On the ice, it looked like one of the best years yet.

Unlike other years, the team started strongly and was turning heads. Unfortunately, it was not drawing fans. Financial pressures mounted and, by early December, rumours the team was going to Revelstoke were being taken seriously. By mid-December, the prospect was even more probable and Colin Day was brought in to try to spearhead a move to keep the franchise. He was not successful, but in the not too distant future, he was to be involved again in another bid to save a Kamloops' franchise and this time with better results.

Colin Day. He would be back trying to save another franchise in the not too distant future. (c. Colin Day)

The decision came down the team had to fold or move; it was up to the players. In the end, they decided on the move but they had to do it without Darryl Ferner or Allan Young who opted to remain in Kamloops. Their final game as the Kamloops Rockets was against the Nor West Caps at Memorial. They pummelled the Caps 10-3 to take their record to 19-10-1. A three minute standing ovation from the fans echoed through the arena; there were only 350 there to see the Rockets last game. Revelstoke became their new home.

For the first time in 19 years, there was no junior hockey team in Kamloops.

The Cowboys now had the chance to be the main attraction in town. For a brief while, the sun shone on the seniors. Their season began with the return of a familiar face in Grant Evans. Having developed locally and played on the junior Rockets, Victoria Cougars and Edmonton Oil Kings, he had gone on to two years of senior hockey with the Edmonton Monarchs. His career then took him to Prince George where he led the Mohawks to four Coy Cups and one national championship Hardy Cup victory. His return to Kamloops was as the coach under team owner and GM Mike Mortimer.

The British Columbia Senior Hockey League included the Prince George Mohawks, Quesnel Kangaroos and North Delta Hurry Kings as well as the Cowboys.

The Cowboys suited up Ed Dempsey, Don Hay, Larry Lestander, Shane Clarke, Darrell Zelinski, Al Glendenning, Rod Danchuk, Gary Donaldson, Benoit Couture, Donnie Moores, Gregg Agar, John Flann, Wayne Henry, Doug Swaine, Ferner, Wade Jowett, Dave Robinson, Bryan James and Bill Tkachuk (goal) for the season.

Partway through the campaign controversy struck as Evans stepped down, reportedly due to conflict with the players. He was replaced by playing coach Hay who was assisted by Wally Deneault. Grant later rejoined the team and contributed to the season's success.

The success included chasing the Hurry Kings for first throughout the season while Quesnel and Prince George lagged behind. In January, before 800 fans, they took the Kings 5-3 and then took Game 2 6-1 to close to within two points of the front runners. They returned to North Delta with the chance of catching the Kings. On their home ice, it was a different story and the Kings essentially locked up first with two wins.

At season's end, Kamloops finished second. Donaldson won the league scoring championship.

The first round of the playoffs had the Cowboys going up against Vernon of the North Okanagan Intermediate League. Surpassing that hurdle, they went up against the third-place team from their league-the Quesnel Kangaroos.

On home ice, the Pokes took Game 1 6-2 but were then upset 4-3 in Game 2. They now headed to Quesnel with the series tied. It didn't look very promising when they were downed 4-0 in Game 3. They regrouped though and, after taking Games 4 and 5 on Quesnel ice, they were headed home with a chance to wrap up the series. Quesnel showed it, too, had some character as they forced Game 7 with a 5-4 overtime victory.

Some 1,000 fans turned up for Game 7. They got to see James score two goals as the Cowboys downed Quesnel 4-2 and went on to battle the Hurry Kings.

The Kings took the first two games in North Delta and then put Kamloops on the ropes with a 3-0 Game 3 victory at the Sports Centre. It was now four straight or lights out for the Cowboys. They came through with a 5-2 victory to stay alive and then, with a 6-4 victory, made a series out of it. Now, it got even harder because the remainder of the series was to be played in North Delta. Showing home ice didn't have to matter, the Cowboys rode into the Kings' turf and took Game 6 6-4.

The seventh-and-deciding game was over quickly and unhappily as the Kings finally regrouped and put Kamloops out with a 9-0 triumph. The comeback had fallen short but it was exciting and hopefully more fans would come out the following season.

At the local minor league level, the Syd Smith Chevy bantams had the best run under the direction of Craig Sturgeon and Harvey Roy. They had a future Kamloops Junior Oilers star in their midst in Mark Ferner. Taking out Kelowna to win the Okanagan, they then disposed of Fuller Lake to make it to the provincial round robin championship. Beating out Prince George and Castlegar, they came up against Burnaby in the final game. Down 8-2 at one point, they pulled to within two at 8-6 before finally bowing out 9-6.

The Knights of Columbus peewee team made a mark for themselves in the Guinness Book of Records when they scored seven goals in two minutes and 22 seconds against the Prince George Vikings on Jan. 25, 1980.

One of the biggest games of the season had nothing to do with league play but still pulled out 3,000 fans. The Montreal Canadians Oldtimers came to town and Kamloops called out its own oldtimers for an exhibition game. The Canadians beat the locals, whose lineup included Freddie Gaber, Murray Owens, Bud Schallen, Ev Miller and Lorne Lussier, 7-3.

Don Ashby still skated in the NHL but was now with the Edmonton Oilers. Reg Kerr was up with the Chicago Black Hawks. Former Rockets Bob Nystrom and Gary Howatt got to see their names engraved on the Stanley Cup.

On a sad note, hockey and general sports vet Grant MacLeod died at the age of 58. He had been one of the original Hub City Leafs and had played at the intermediate level for many years. His name became so synonymous with sports in Kamloops that he is honoured on the Sports Wall of Fame at Riverside Coliseum.

Where once there had been two junior teams and a senior team, Kamloops was now reduced to one senior squad. With senior hockey being so tenuous in the province, there was uncertainty if they could even hold on to that level.

If times had gone a bit sour for Kamloops, they had also bottomed out for the New Westminster Bruins. In the worst season since joining the WCHL, they finished last in their division and, were it not for the abysmally unsuccessful Great Falls (Montana) Americans, they would have been dead last. Consolation would have to come from former Bruins Gordie Lane and Lorne Henning getting their names on the Stanley Cup with the Islanders.

The Bruins finished 10-61-1, a full 39 points behind Seattle, which itself did not get above 500.

The Bruins were experiencing serious bad times for the first time in their history while Kamloops pined for major junior hockey. Two great rivers were moving toward convergence.

37

Cowtown________________________1980-81

The 1980-81 Cowboys — A reflection of local talent. Top Row: (l-r) Brian McMillan, Gary Scircia, Ron Ellis, Jay Kozak, Darrel Zelinski, Rod Danchuk, Grant Evans, Doug McQueen. Middle Row: Wally Deneault, Donnie Moores, Dave Robinson, Rick Hodgson, Bucky Buchanan, Norm Meyers, Chris Dyer, Laurie Norstrom, Ed Dempsey, Gary Donaldson. Front Row: Greg Hays, Greg Agar, Mike Mortimer, Al Glendenning, Don Hay, Wayne Harvey, Brian Henderson. (c. Rick Hodgson)

The Cowboys were the big show for the 1980-81 season. After coming within a game of winning the league last year, there was some valiJ optimism.

Their training camp roster included Donnie Moores, Gary Donaldson, Al Glendenning, Larry Lestander, Wayne Harvey, John Flann, Dave Robinson, Rod Danchuk, Grant Evans, Chris Dyer, Ed Dempsey, Greg Agar, Norm Meyers, Gary Sciria, Jay Kozak, Darrell Zelinski, Gerry Bond, Doug Buchanan, Don Schultz, Stuart Gale, Gord Fitzer, Steven Penrose and Laurie Nordstrom. Battling for goal were Brian Henderson, Greg Hayes, Ron Ellis and Bill Tkachuk. Local product Rick Hodgson, who had been in the Hartford system, was also being counted on to join the squad. Don Hay remained the team's playing coach with help from Darryl Ferner.

The team was awaiting new uniforms. This time they were coming a la Washington Capitals.

Although the Hurry Kings were initially seen as the team to beat, it soon became apparent there was a new force in the North to be reckoned with. It had some links with heady days for Kamloops hockey fans and a family act that was hard to surpass. The Quesnel Kangaroos' lineup included Don and Brian Festerling, Jim and Tom March, Rick and Mike Szabo, and most importantly, the Gassoff brothers: Gary, Ken and Brad. Local fans were hard pressed to forget the exploits of Brad Gassoff who starred with the old Tier 1 Chiefs. This time around they did not love him.

The league's tenuous hold on life began to show signs of weakening. Partway through the season the former flagship Prince George Mohawks folded. The Hurry Kings were having trouble icing a full team. Though Kamloops remained alive, the Cowboys were playing to disappointing crowds.

The league was realigned and started a round robin elimination to determine what team was to advance against the Kootenay champs. The once favoured Hurry Kings, after a number of losses, saw the light and dropped out leaving Quesnel and Kamloops to fight it out. The teams battled back and forth to determine who was to get home ice advantage in the playoffs. In the end, it came down to one game and that was at Memorial. Enter the Gassoffs.

Ken Gassoff scored three goals and Brad two as the "Roos" took the "Pokes" 6-3 and gained home ice. Brad Gassoff added insult to injury as he razed the crowd by riding down the ice on his stick, a la Tiger Williams, after scoring a goal.

The playoffs started in Quesnel and not well for the Cowboys. Rocked 11-3 in Game 1 they were bounced 5-2 in the second tilt. The second game was not at all mannerly as Ed Dempsey got his nose broken by Brad Gassoff and Don Hay was put out for the series with a shoulder injury. Fights resulted in suspensions to all three Gassoffs and Lyle Inglis of Quesnel while Al Glendenning, Donnie Moores, Allen Young and Laurie Nordstrom were lost to Cowboys

When Game 3, at Memorial Arena went to the Kangaroos 5-2, it was last year all over again. Some 1,300 fans turned out for Game 4 in the hopes they could see some revenge against the Gassoffs. Showing the type of character they needed, Dempsey turned up, playing with a broken nose. This time there was no great comeback. The season ended in disappointment with a 6-2 loss.

That was enough for Hay. Having guided the team for three seasons, he stepped down, telling the press "I'ts time for a change. After a while under the same guy, the players get stale."

Sports writer Mike Reimer commented "Nobody cherishes winning more than Don Hay" and claimed he had resigned out of frustration.

Hay would only say "After three years of never winning, you start doubting. I know I am going to miss it."

Of course, history went on to show Hay had a coaching future ahead of him which was the envy of every junior hockey bench boss in the country. As coach of the Kamloops Blazers, he enjoyed the thrill of two Memorial Cups and took the Canadian junior team to a world title in Red Deer. As an assistant coach with the Blazers, he had another Memorial Cup.

The Cowboys' connection with success did not end there as Dempsey, Moores, Glendenning and Henderson all found their ways into the Blazers' organization.

In minor hockey, the Evans Products midgets starring Mark Ferner and coached by Joe Tennant, ended up second in the provincial championship round robin to Prince George.

The bantam Chevies, under Terry Bangen, also reached the Provincial finals and finished with a 3-21 round robin-record.

Randy Rota took the Knights of Columbus peewee team to the provincial championship. In his lineup was a familiar hockey name. Mark Recchi led his side to the provincial championship. The latest product of one of Kamloops' greatest hockey families was destined for true NHL stardom.

The Three Recchis — Mark, Mel and Ron — 1998. (c. Glen Cowley)

Off in the NHL, Bob Nystrom, Gary Howatt, Lorne Henning and Gordie Lane were again having their names etched on the Stanley Cup.

Kamloops, as a drawing card for hockey, was not lost on people in the know and so it wasn't surprising when rumbling began about a higher calibre of play coming in. It came in two forms with a twist no one expected.

In mid-January, rumours began Vancouver was looking at moving its farm team from Phoenix to Kamloops and Cowboy GM Mike Mortimer had been contacted. Chances of a minor league pro team were small if the WHL returned.

Harvey Roy was a driving force behind efforts to grab a WHL franchise and eyes were turned on three prospects. The Billings Bighorns and the Spokane Flyers were the front runners but there was talk the Seattle Breakers might even return.

The funny twist was in late January 1981 when the Sentinel recorded the New Westminster Bruins were unable to use Queen's Park Arena due to a CUPE strike. There was talk the Bruins, struggling at the gate, might play out the season using Memorial Arena as their home base. GM Tracy Pratt ruled that out, advising they had made arrangements to play their home games out of Bellingham, Wash. Though admitting the team was doing poorly, it was emphasized there was no thought of leaving New Westminster.

Matters didn't go as planned and New Westminster ended up playing their home games at a number of different arenas. The suitcase Bruins brought their act to Kamloops on Feb. 10, 1981 to take on the Brandon Wheat Kings. Coach Muzz MacPherson's rookie-ladened squad, 13 in all, had a tough night of it.

Brandon took it to them 12-4, but the 900 fans gave their temporary home team a warm welcome and cheered them on as their own. Roy was impressed so many fans would turn up on the night of the NHL All Star game, especially given this was just a "one night" home team. If only they had known.

Mike Reimer wrote "most encouraging was the fan reaction whenever the Bruins scored. No one in the press box could remember the last time a Kamloops crowd cheered a New Westminster team."

Veteran CFJC announcer Earl Seitz, who called the action live back to Brandon and who did the play-by-play of games back in the Tier 1 Chiefs' era, put it best. "I've never seen it and neither has Adam."

Next season, Kamloops fans were to be cheering on the franchise as their own.

The New Westminster Bruins saw their record improve over the previous dismal year but, at 17-54-1, it was not great. They managed to tie for the last playoff spot with the Spokane Flyers but then lost the tie-breaker to finish out of the playoffs for the second straight year. It seemed the once mighty franchise had been humbled and could be taken lightly by teams that had looked upon them with respect in the past. Ernie McLean and Bill Shinske had gone. Could it be the mystique that had typified the team throughout its history had come to an end? Had the most successful franchise in the WHL become ordinary?

Already successful in the Saskatchewan Junior Hockey League before the start of the WCHL, they had become one of its founding franchises in 1966. In the 15 years since that time, they had finished over .500 12 times, won the league five times and the Memorial Cup twice. No other team had matched that record.

Thirty-five years ago a budding franchise had started in Humboldt, Sask. and grown into a dominating junior hockey force. Two years later, Kamloops got artificial ice and began building a minor hockey system second to none. Like two great rivers, they grew with the passing of time. Every so often they flowed together. Jim Letcher, Don Newman, Jim Harrison, Don Hay and Rick Shinske all imparted a bit of Kamloops into the franchise's history.

The 1981-82 season saw the two great rivers converge. The franchise was given new life while bringing Kamloops a forum to draw national attention to its hockey tradition and talent. The franchise became the Montreal Canadians of junior hockey and a model for every other franchise in North America. First, as the Junior Oilers and, then as the Blazers, they took the already legendary franchise to even greater heights.

The Wind and Ice had met at the confluence of the North and South Thompson rivers and the howling was heard across Canada. The "Franchise" had arrived.

Mark Recchi —The third Recchi on the ice reached the ultimate prize with Pittsburgh. (c. Mel Recchi)

38

The Franchise Arrives_____________1981-82

When it arrived, the "Franchise" was humbled. It had just gone two sub .500 seasons back-to-back and its mentors, Ernie McLean, Bill Shinske and Scotty Munro, were all gone.

Up to 100 hopefuls turned up at the Valleyview Arena in August hoping to attract enough attention to earn a chance on the rebuilding squad. Harvey Roy as GM, Lyle Moffatt as coach and Joe Arling as director of player personnel began the task.

The Sentinel recorded: "Optimism prevails among former Bruins players contacted by Arling now that there is no tie left to the black-and-gold team that finished dead last."

Arling was later quoted as saying, " For such a long time, that black-and-gold represented a winning philosophy from Estevan to New Westminster to Memorial Cups. But, the last two years, it's really been lost. They once had an aura about them, but now it's lost. For the players, that's a good point. They come here with the air clear."

Yet Arling was wrong. The winning tradition, whatever its source, was waiting like a durable seed for the chance to grow again. The seed fell on the fertile soil of Kamloops. What had been a shoot in the Prairies had become a spreading bush in New Westminster and grew into a towering oak along the Thompson.

Local fans were already excited about the team and 500 seasons tickets were sold before the sales campaign even started.

Thirteen players were scheduled to return but trades and cuts pared down that number. A trade brought local hero Mark Ferner over from Regina, and former Bruin Doug Kostynski was awarded the captain's C. When the season began, five former Bruins remained. In addition to Kostynski; Trav Gibson, Larry Bumstead, Ron Amyotte and Doug Thompson became a part of the rebirth of the legend.

Although the first season saw scant improvement from the year before, it was to be the team's last losing season until 1996-97. When the wind hit the ice against Portland that fall evening in October 1981 and fell behind 4-1, they gave notice the winning tradition remained. Their first gift to Kamloops; a 5-4 comeback victory with former Bruin Doug Thompson netting the winner.

The success of the "Franchise" in Kamloops has known no equal since.
instantly

Doug Kostynski

Larry Bumstead

Ron Amyotte

Doug Thompson

The torch carriers from New Westminster to Kamloops. (c. Doris Rubel)

Trav Gibson

39

Final Whistle

Wind and ice.

The dance of skates upon nature's glass and the contesting of youthful will in hockey glory had begun innocently in the bygone days of the tiny river settlement of Kamloops.

Over the years, especially after the coming of the railroad, it had begun its slow rise. Ever dependent upon the uncertainties of weather, local hockey had ebbed and flowed with the inconsistencies of our winter season. Even with the building of the first arena in 1925, its natural ice left Kamloops at a disadvantage against its colder rivals.

When artificial ice arrived, hockey success came soon after and never looked back. Locals took a back seat behind imported stars from the East but, in time, the two forces came together to create and solidify the hockey tradition so integral to Kamloops' image. The stars from the East and the exuberance of the local players formed the basis for what was to become one of the most widely admired minor hockey organizations in Canada.

It was, in fact, a team of local players, the Kamloops High School Ramblers, who brought the city its first provincial accolades in 1949 when they won the Provincial High School Championship.

Over the years, the teams have come and gone. The Hub City Leafs, which became the Elks which became the Chiefs, brought excitement and trophies. The Besette Loggers brought the Coy Cup while numerous other senior teams made their way to provincial finals. What the Chiefs had been to the seniors the Rockets were to the juniors as they, in their many forms, brought provincial accolades. The midgets, bantams, juveniles and peewees all shared in bringing provincial titles home to a city proving itself as a hot bed of hockey year after year. First Nations teams dominated the provincial scene, in one case, they were given the original league trophy to keep.

All of this, combined with commercial, oldtimer and women's hockey, have demonstrated the depth of the sport in the city.

Its hockey ambassadors have been many. Bert Marshall, Jim Harrison, Randy Rota, Doug Lidster, Rudy Poeschek, Tim Watters and Mark Recchi have carved out long-term careers in the big leagues. Glenn Merkosky became so synonymous with success with the American League Adirondack Red Wings that his sweater was retired and he returned to coach. Others have made their mark in the many pro leagues throughout North America as players and coaches. Its teams have nurtured others whose careers passed through the city on their way to the top. Andy Moog, Bob Nystrom, Ryan Walter, Gary Howatt and Tim Hunter all got to display Stanley Cup rings while others, such as Wayne Bianchin, Barry Melrose, Reg Kerr and Curt Brackenbury, carved out solid big league careers. After the 1981-82 season, the list just kept on growing.

There had been those who brought their skills and commitments to Kamloops both as players and within the minor hockey organizations. Arthur Gagne' (Kamloops' first genuine hockey hero), Kenny Stewart, Paul Thompson, Andy Clovechok, Johnny Milliard, Buddy Evans, Hec MacKenzie, Don Reid and a host of others brought tradition, skills and the willingness to share.

Rudy Poeschek, another Kamloops product who toughed it out to become a solid NHLer. (c. Jerry Poeschek)

When we take in a Blazers' game, watch a local hero playing in the big league or marvel at the success of the local minor hockey organization, it is important to remember the present did not just happen. It grew out of the past and, in that past, there are many fond memories and achievements that give depth to the present. When I look up at the rafters at Riverside Coliseum, I see many invisible banners hanging down and along the catwalks the faces of Kamloops' hockey past smiling and shaking their heads in amazement at what has come to pass.

And smiling the widest is old Angus Nelson, like father time himself.

40

The Player

He is old now.

He feels his bones complain as he stands. His back aches. He gazes upon withered hands with failing eyes, but not failed yet.

Silence fills the great cavern as he steps out on to the ice.

Stumbling ever so slightly he feels the joy of freedom touch his nerves. He glides and finds the kiss of the wind in his thinning hair, the flow of blood warms his soul and he soars on timeless wings.

A dull roar grows in the crowd.

Looking about he sees the people rise as one.

They clap.

They chant.

They laugh and they cry.

There is no age, there is no language, no race, no colour, no religion, no distance. There is only freedom and the language of hockey. They are all as one in the moment and the memories.

There is only Wind and Ice.

The Sources

Balf, Mary - (History Committee, Kamloops Museum) - Kamloops 1914 to 1945. Published 1975

Cuthbert, Chris & Russell, Scott - The Rink (Stories from Hockey's Hometowns) Penguin Books - Toronto - 1997

Guinness Book of Records - 1989 - edited by Donald McFarlane

Humboldt & District Museum and Art Gallery, Humboldt, Saskatchewan

Inland Sentinel - 1880-1916

Hollander, Zander (Editor) - Inside Sports Magazine Hockey 1997 Visible Ink Press, Detroit, Michigan

Kamloops Sentinel Standard - 1916-1924

Kamloops Sentinel - 1924-1982

Lapp, Richard M. & White, Silas - Local Heroes (A History of the Western Hockey League) Harbour Publishing, Vancouver - 1983

Lapp, Richard M.& Macaulay, Alec - The Memorial Cup - Harbour Publishing Vancouver - 1997

Lowe, Kevin & Stan & Shirley Fischler - Champions (The Making of the Edmonton Oilers) Prentice Hall Canada Inc., Scarborough, Ont. 1988

National Hockey League Stanley Cup Centennial Book - Edited by Dan Diamond McClelland & Stewart, Toronto - 1992

Total Hockey - Encyclopedia of the NHL - edited by Dan Diamond - Andrews McNeels publishing, Kansas City, 1998

Western Hockey League 95/96 Guide

Western Hockey League 94/95 Yearbook

The People - Andy Berna, Larry Candido, Andy and Molly Clovechok, Dennis Coates, Sinclair Dalgleish, Colin Day, Len Demarchi, Ted Desireau, Buddy Evans, Grant Evans, Ed Dempsey, Jamie Durr (Estevan Bruins SJHL), Keith Gagne, Jim Harrison, Don Hay, Brian Henderson, Ernie McLean, Gloria Micciaro, Greg Micciaro, Doris Rubel, Kerry Rubel, Ken MacDonald (Estevan Bruins SJHL), Randy Rota, Ken and Jean Stewart, Earl Seitz, Ephraim and Ida Steinke, Clarence Ulveland, Eric Shishido, Don Wilkie

The Players

With the coverage of each season or time period only the players from the dominant teams were covered as fully as information sources allowed. For those looking for the names of others the following were recorded in the course of researching the book. Unfortunately many names will have been missed and some misspelled given that I could only be as accurate as my sources allowed.

1917/18 - Fred Carr, Clifford MacDonald, S. Gatin, J. Wilson. (town team)

1918/19 - C. Falconer (goal), B. McCall; Richard & Doug Palmer; Sinclair, Harry and R. Dalgleish (Juniors)

1920/21 - Cliff MacDonald (goal), Allan Milton, M.. Sault, Ted Buse, Alex Swanson, Andy Bruce, Zar Shaw, Eddy Malone, Herbert (Bert) Peacock (Kamloops Junior Brotherhood)

1921/22 - C. Falconer, Cliff MacDonald (goal), Dalton Walker, Harry Dalgleish, Ted Buse, Sinclair Dalgleish, Richard Palmer, Lee Weatherby, Bert Smith, Eddie Docker, Tom Slater, Bert Peacock (Seniors)

1922/23 - Cecil MacDonald (goal), Lee Weatherby, Sinclair Dalgleish, Frank Gisborne, Allan Milton, Richard Palmer, Bert Peacock, Frank Gale, ? Reid, Eddie Docker and Dalton Walker (Seniors)

1924/25 - Sinclair & Bert Dalgleish, Dalton Walker, Tom Slater (goal), Lee Weatherby, Eddie Docker, Robert Cail, ? Choate, Zar Shaw, Allan Milton, Frank Gisborne, M. Irvin, Jim Craig & Bert Smith (captain) - (Seniors) Ray Chapman, C. Shaw, ? O'Brien (goal), Jim Craig (captain), Robert Cail, Dave & Bruce Dalgleish, George Craig & M. Chater (Juniors)

1926/27 - Allan Milton (goal), Sinclair Dalgleish, Eddie Docker, Tom Slater (goal), Buster Todd, Bert Wolfe, Lee Weatherby, Frank gale, Robert Cail, Jim Craig, Frank Gagne', Dalton Walker, Zar Shaw and Fred Irwin (Seniors)

1928/29 - ? Dempster, Allan Milton (goal), Lee Weatherby, Frank Gisborne, Bert Wolfe, Wally Turnbull, John& George Craig, Sinclair & Bruce Dalgleish, Joe Hamm. ? Stewart, Jack Coates, Percy Fraser, Fred Irwin, Roy Sparks and Zar Shaw. (Seniors)

1929/30 - Allan Fraser (goal), James Weatherby, ? McCurrach, A. Burr, Percy Fraser, Jack Coates, Bert Wolfe, ? Taft, ? Tymich, ? Stokes, ? Huston and Reg Burton (Juniors)

1931/32 - Allan Fraser & Allan Milton (goal), Buster Todd, Bert Wolfe, Percy Fraser, Jack Coates, ? Tymich, Ed Anderson, ? Saunders, Bruce & Dave Dalgleish (Seniors)

1932/33 - Allan Fraser(goal), Bruce Dalgleish, Eddie Anderson, Robert White, Percy Fraser, K. Roberston, George Stinson, ? Boyd, Jack Coates, Roy Sparks, Buster Todd, Peter Luback and ? Corbin (Seniors)

1933/34 - Bruce Dalgleish, Howard Portman, Eddie Anderson, ? Davies (goal), Buster Todd, Robert White, Zar Shaw, Peter Luback, Bert Wolfe, Jack Coates & ? Coghlan

1935/36 - ? Beruschi (goal), Joe Hall, Bruce Dalgleish, Eddie Anderson, Jack Coates, Robert White, Howard Portman, Stan Moffatt, Jim Burtnick, Zar Shaw, Allan Fraser (goal), Bill MacEwan, ? Leadbeater, T. Anderson and Cy Young.

1936/37 - Fred Irwin (then aged 43), Buster Todd, Bert Wolfe, Allan Fraser (goal), Joe Hall, Stan Moffatt, Robert White, Cy Young, John Anderson, Mike MacDonald, Gordon Cahilty, Dave Dalgleish and Les Moore (Seniors)

1937/38 - Roy(Ron) Sparks, Joe Hall, Allan Fraser, Beruschi(goal), Robert White, Cy Young, A. Whiteman, Stan Moffatt, Tom Slater, Jim Burtnick, ? Kozak, Howard Portman, "Box Car" Thompson, Bill MacEwan, Bill Cook & Mike MacDonald (Seniors) - John & Frank Basaraba, Roger Roberts, Herb Young, Ken Sproule, Earl Klinck, ? O'Connor, Grant Sumners and Harold Persons (Juniors)

1938/39 - Allan Fraser(goal), Peter Luback, Bill MacEwan,

Stan Moffatt, Hec MacKenzie, Jim Burtnick, Jack Bloom, Howard Portman, ? Leadbater, Ken Sproule, Stewart Peterson, Mike MacDonald, Herb Young, Jack Coates, Joe Hall, A. Whiteman, Earl Klinck, Jim Baird, Robert White, John Basaraba (goal), Tom Slater, E. O'Connor & Murray Querns (Seniors) - Bill Mcdermid, N. Worral, Bill Peterson, Leland Leslie, Robert Esselmont, Murray Querns, Keith Gagne', Walter Wasyikow, V. Boyd, Sam Corea, Frank Farmer, Earl Klinck, Stan Marriott, Stewart Peterson, Norm MacDonald, John Basaraba (goal), Ken Sproule, Frank Basaraba, Harold Person, Jack Bloom & George "Lefty" Marriott (Juniors)

1939/40 - Allan Fraser(goal), Roy Sparks, Stewart Peterson, Hec MacKenzie, Mike MacDonald, Keith Tomlin, Jim Burtnick, Robert White, Ray Pinchback, Bill MacEwan, Howard Portman, Peter Luback, E. O'Connor, Herb Young (Seniors) - Allan Corbin, Bill & Stewart Peterson, Grant Sumners, G. Williams, Jim Baird, D. Nell, Robert Esselmont, Harold Persons, G. Worral, William McDermid(goal), Keith Gagne', W. Worral & ? MacDonald (Juniors)

1945/46 - Len Scott (goal), Norm MacDonald, Sam Corea, Grant Sumners, Tom Green, Ken Moyer, ? Johnson, Robert Esselmont, Bill Marriott, Harold Wish, Eddie & Charles Small, Alf Morton, John Garay, Ron Humphrey, Ernest Houghton, Ray Pinchback, Stanley Taylor, Jack Glover & Lorne Clow (Seniors) - Murray Dyer, Roy Josephson(goal), Mike Hartline, Joe Desjardine, Dick Wood, Jim Ashby, Don Moyer, Jim Green, Jack Hardy, Maurice Clark, Harold Ulveland, Paul Prehara, ? Wood, Bill Marriott, Lorne Clow, Walter Tennant, ? Gaiten, ? MacDonald (juveniles) - Don Moyer, Jerry Brown, Maurice Clark, Lorne Clow, Stan Taylor, Tom Green, Peter Plastiras, George Prehara, Bill Marriott, Jim MacQuarrie, Ron Humphreys, ? Davis, Charles MacArthur & Ralph Ulveland

1946/47 - George & Bill Marriott, Don Moyer, Raymond Pinchback, John Brkick, ? Reynolds, Harold & Ralph Ulveland (Seniors) - Don Moyer, Fred Pippolo(goal), Morris Clark, Gordon Werts, Gordon McQuerrie, Currie MacKensie, Bill Zanowski, Tosh Takanaka, Allan "Peanuts" Ulveland, Jim Jardine, Jim Ashby, John Hendry, Gordon Clow, Ed Garay (Juveniles)

1947/48 - Robert Esselmont, Glen MacKay, Eugene Hakansen, E. Small, “Rocky” Ulveland, Jack Glover, Bill Marriott, J. Desjardin, Dick Johnson, John Yanisko, Sam Corea (Kamloops Aces)

1948/49 - Len Scott, Don Campbell, Grant MacLeod, Peter & Bill Schall, John Yanisko, Jack Beecher, Ralph Snider, Eugene Hakensen, Ole Birkeland, Bud Pettit, & Rocky, Clancey, Allan & Ralph Ulveland (Kamloops Merchants)

1950/51 - Cliff Mills, Grant MacLeod, Art Thomson, Guy Ludgate, Walter Malahoff (goal), Bob Irvine, Walter McIntyre (Kamloops Senior B All Stars)

1952/53 - Kenny Stewart, Guy Ludgate, Walter Malahoff (goal), Al MacDougall, John Ursaki, Cliff Mills, Al Swaine & Don Campbell (Besette Loggers) - Ev Millar & Don Wilkie (goal), Al Raymond, Ron Baker, Wally Wozniak, Dave Gilliespie, Kermal Singh (bantams)

1953/54 - Kenny Stewart, Stan Berry, Nick Pyevach, Bob Irvine, Walter Malahoff(goal), Grant MacLeod, Busher Jackson, Al MacDougall, Al Swaine, Guy Ludgate, Sonny MacDonald & Bill McQuay (Besette Loggers)

1954/55 - Busher Jackson, Buddy Evans, Stan Berry, Gary Candido, Al Black, Al Swaine, Al MacDougall, Gordie Kusumoto, Harold Ulveland, Jack Dunphy, Clare Indseth, Gordon Tansley (goal), Andy Clovechok (Kamloops Millionaires)

1955/56 - Walter Malahoff (goal), Mickey Spelay, Gordie Kusumoto, Bob Irvine, Stan Berry, ? Boxeur, Jack Dunphy, Ross Jardine, Ken Terry (Kamloops Balcos)

1956/57 - Sam Corea (manager), Kenny Stewart (coach), Busher Jackson, Walter Malahoff (goal), Don Jakes, Grant MacLeod, Bob Irvine, Al MacDougall, Ken Terry, Al Swaine, Stan Berry, Ross Jardine, Al Black, Tony Spelay, Gordie Kusumoto, Wally Hryciw, Cliff Pachal, Bruce Harrison, Bud Schollen, Ron LeBlanc (Kamloops Balcos)

1957/58 - Walter Malahoff, Lorne Slater (goal), Gordie Kusumoto, Grant MacLeod, Al MacDougall, Ron "Shorty" Stiles, Bud Schollen, Ross Jardine, Clare Indseth, Walter Hryciw, Bruce Harrison, Robert LeBlanc, Tony Spelay, Gordon Shaw, Al Swaine (Plaza B's) - Kats Kitamura, Bill MacEwan, Murray Owens, Gary Schall, Richard Bullock, Don Sherrett, Don Newman, Ray Holmes, Lyle Moffatt, Terry Shishido, Bert Marshall (bantams)

1958/59 - Grant MacLeod, Gordie Kusumoto, Ross Jardine, Bob Gannon, Fred Gaber, Gary Candido, Don Busch, Carman Candido, Melvin Recchi (goal), Kenny Stewart, Nick Pyevach, Busher Jackson, Al Swaine, Bob Irvine, Steve Gryshuk, Bud Schollen, Larry Sash, Ken Terry
(Senior B Rockets) - Peter Sternig (goal), Terry & Eric Shishido, Bill Steinke, Ricky Telford, Ricky McShane, Don Anthony, Will Moffatt, George Meridew, Clair Long, Butch Senkpiel, David Clark, Ken Takeuchi (bantams)

1959/60 - Gord Hudson (coach), Mel Recchi & John Panagrot (goal), Don Busch, Fred Gaber, Bob "Bongo" LeBlanc, Busher Jackson, Ev Millar, Walter Hryciw, Gordie Kusumoto, Ross Jardine, Grant "Digger" MacLeod, Al MacDougall, Bruce Harrison, Bud Schollen, John Jamieson, Ken Terry, Bob Irvine, Steve Gryshuk, Johnny Milliard (Central Caribous)

1960/61 - Doug Cousins (coach), Frank Bell (manager), Roy Sakaki, Dave Ferguson, Rick Trent, Billy Moores, Len Demarchi, Ron Hay, Jim Stuart, Bobbie Osborne, Kenny Rodgers, Ken Begg, John Oldham, Jim Harrison, Rick Nishizaki, Bob Haywood, Wally Deneault (goal), Joe Bedard (Jardine bantams) - Ron Recchi, Jackie James, Larry Bedard, Bill Bowles, Don Newman, Bill Cochran, Glen Madsen, Skip Holmes, Brian Smith, Bob Davoren, Bill Graff, Bob Bradley, Brian Stoodley, Larry Roberge, Glen Richards, Bernard Martin, Brian Wallace, Bert Marshall, Paul Madsen (coach) (juvenile Falcons)

1961/62 - Nick Pyevach (coach), Mel Recchi (goal), Fred Gaber, Don Busch, Bob Gannon, Ross Jardine, Buddy Evans, Gordie Kusumoto, Larry Berg, Bruce Harrison, Bob "Bongo"

LeBlanc, Don Busch (Senior B Chiefs)

1962/63 - Ross Jardine, Ev Miller, Buck Crawford, Bruce Harrison, Freddie Gaber, Bob Gannon, Gordie Kusumoto, Shorty Stiles, Don Busch, Bill Donaldson, Bud Schollen, Buddy Evans (player/coach), John Panagrot & Mel Recchi (goal), Nick Pyevach (coach) (Senior B Chiefs)

1963/64 - Freddie Gaber, Bud Schollen, Don Romeike, Ev Miller, Buck Crawford, Ross Jardine, Don Busch, John Panagrot & Mel Recchi (goal), Gordie Kusumoto, Bob Gannon, Ron "Shorty" Stiles, Buddy Evans (playing/coach), Nick Pyevach (manager) (Senior B Chiefs)

1964/65 - Nick Pyevach (manager), Ev Miller (coach), Ron Shorty Stiles, Ross Jardine. Bill Donaldson, Freddie Gaber, Bon Gannon, Skip Holmes, Terry Bedard, Glen Madsen, Bud Schollen, George McIntyre, Larry Roberge, Bob Nishimura, Brian Stoodley, Don Romeike & John Panagrot (goal) (Senior B Chiefs)

1965/66 - John Panagrot (goal), Freddie Gaber, Bob Gannon, Ev Miller, Bill Donaldson, Terry Shishido, Ken Moffatt, ? Malone, Cliff Sturgeon, Don Busch, Dale Cassel, George McIntyre, Glen Madsen, Bill Cochran, John Engelbrecht, Cliff Russel, Bob Nishimura, Nick Pyevach (manager) (North Kamloops Senior B Totems) - Buddy Evans (coach), Grant Evans, Randy Rota, Rick Beauchamp, Ken Tarnow, Rod Calder, Bob Gill, Bill Walker, Rick Dyer, Tosh Tabata, Bob Shmyr, Gerry Vachon, David Craig, Jim Carson, Doug MacLeod, Roy Mabbett, Bud Lloyd, Paul Backman, John Bade (goal) (North Kamloops midget Totems)

1966/67 - Eric Shishido, Ken Moffatt, Dale Sandyke, Eddie Begg, Bob Gannon, Fred Gaber, Gordie Kusumoto, Cliff Russel, Glen Madsen, John Panagrot (goal), ? Palmer, ? Anderson (North Kamloops Senior B Totems) - Ken Tarnow, Len Steinke, Dave Craig, Rod Calder, Dave Struch, Bruce Stewart, Les Eriksteen, Bob Gill, Lyle Harper, Roy Mabbett, Spud Maddink, Doug Pourier, Daryl Price, Randy Rota, Garry Lillow, Doug Smith, Bruce Johnson, Frank Rota (assistant coach), Kenny Stewart (coach) (North Kamloops midget

Totems)

1970/71 - George Aulin, Greg Toma, Bruce Johnson, Ed Dempsey, Tim Struch, John Flann, Ron Lefebvre, Brian Fuoco, Duana Monteith, Mickey Fritz, David Susak (goal), Barry Kelly, Doug Swaine, Doogie Anderson, Mark Evans, Dale Redekop, Stan Johnson, Frank Rossi, Bob Gannon (coach), Ev Millar (assistant coach), Lou Desmarais (manager) (Junior B Teamsters) - Don Ashby, Don Hay, Ken King, Jernal Dhaliwal, Mel Zinger (captain), Bob Klim, Dennis Bergeron, Fred Turner, Stan Johnson, Dave Caldow, Peter Poeschek, Kim Bostock, Larry Lestander, Dale Morry, Steve Chumm, Rick Hodgson, Dennis Zinger (coach), Craig Sturgeon (coach) Ken Holden (coach) (North Kamloops Kiwanis midget Totems) -Muray Owens, Wally Deneault, Fred Gaber, Larry Roberge, Glen Madsen, Bill Donaldson, Cliff Russell, Ribbie Osborne, Dale Sandyke, Ken Begg, Ev Millar, Ken Rinaldi, Ed Begg, Bill Steinke, Bill Tarnow (coach), Nick Pyevach (manager) (Senior B Stars)

1975/76 - Andy Moog (goal), Tim Watters, Glen Merkosky, Peter Dineen, Steve Zanatta, Doug Watt, Shane Clarke, Mike Urquhart, Ken Baerg, Norm Meyer, Murray Matheson, Ian MacEachern, Lance Lestander, Ward Sparrow, Greg Dunn, Chris Bulley, Phil Logan, Laurence Angus, Jim Crosson, Ray Rempel, S. Rauch, Craig Sturgeon (coach) Nick Pyevach (manager) (Junior B Braves)

1977/78 - Don Hay, Ed Dempsey, Gerry Bond, Doug Swaine, Brian Marchinko, Glen "Cowboy" Richards, Gary Donaldson, Kim Kriebiehl, John Senkpiel, Larry Lestander, Darrell Zelinski, Lyle Harpe (Senior B Cowboys)

1978/79 - Fenton Gale, Phil Roy, John Senkpiel, Gregg Robertson, Terry Tarnow, Don Hay (playing/coach), Mark Earp (goal) Peter Poeschek, Allan Young, Al Glendenning, Gary Donaldson, Wade Jowett, Lance Lestander, Ward Sparrow, Danny Rota, Neil Robinson, Craig Enfield, Ed Dempsey, Darryl Ferner, Laurie Norstrom, Ken Ellis (goal), John Flann, Doug Swaine, Bryan James, Kevin Chaben, Greg Agar, Darrell Zelinski, Mike Urquhart (Senior B Cowboys)

À mes parents,
à mon mari et mes enfants.
F. R.-F.

Conception et réalisation : Laurence Moinot
Conforme à la loi n° 49.956 du 16 juillet 1949
sur les publications destinées à la jeunesse

N° d'éditeur : 10098145
ISBN : 2-09-202219-9
Dépôt légal : mai 2003

EN GRANDE FORME

LA NAISSANCE

Dr. Françoise Rastoin-Faugeron
Illustrations :
Benjamin Chaud

NATHAN

Sommaire

C’est Noël ! Rémi et Lilou sont très occupés à ouvrir leurs cadeaux.
Ils ne se doutent pas qu’une autre surprise les attend.

8 – Nous avons une grande nouvelle à vous annoncer, dit papa. L'été prochain,vous aurez un petit frère ou une petite sœur.
– Super ! s'écrie Rémi.
– Moi, je veux une petite sœur, dit Lilou.

Mais pourquoi
faut-il attendre
l'été ?

10 Lilou est songeuse.
– Mais comment on fait les bébés ? demande-t-elle.
– Moi, je sais, dit Rémi. Les parents qui s'aiment se serrent très fort... et voilà !
– C'est un peu comme ça, dit leur maman, mais ce n'est pas tout.

Comment on fait les bébés ? 11

Pour faire un bébé, il faut que deux **cellules** minuscules se rencontrent : l'une venant du père, le **spermatozoïde**, l'autre de la mère, l'**ovule**.

Pendant que les parents font l'amour, le papa dépose des millions de **spermatozoïdes** dans le ventre de la maman où attend un **ovule**.

Un **spermatozoïde** entre dans l'**ovule**. Un petit œuf commence alors à se former. C'est le futur bébé qui va se développer pendant neuf mois.

Pour faire les bébés animaux aussi, il faut généralement un père (le mâle) et une mère (la femelle), mais pas chez tous. Parmi ces animaux, connais-tu celui qui est tantôt mâle, tantôt femelle ?

le chien

le chat

la souris

l'escargot

Réponse : l'escargot. On dit qu'il est hermaphrodite.

Maman sort alors de son sac une drôle de photo.
– C'est quoi ? demande Rémi.
– La photo du futur bébé, répond-elle en souriant.
Il a déjà deux mois, c'est un vrai bébé en miniature.
– Mais comment l'œuf devient-il un bébé ? demande Rémi.
– Eh bien ! regardez, dit leur maman en ouvrant un livre.

Comment l'œuf se transforme-t-il en bébé ?

Dans le ventre de la maman, il y a comme un petit nid prêt à recevoir l'œuf : l'**utérus**. L'œuf s'y fait un petit coin bien à lui. Il arrive que deux œufs se développent en même temps. Ils vont donner des jumeaux.

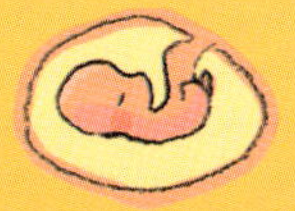

1 mois : l'œuf ressemble à une crevette. Il mesure 5 mm et porte déjà en lui tout ce qui deviendra un cœur, des os, de la peau, des poils...

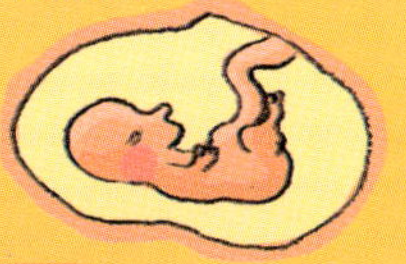

2 mois : le bébé est formé avec une tête, des bras, des jambes. Il mesure 3 cm et vit dans une bulle d'eau qui le protège, le liquide amniotique.

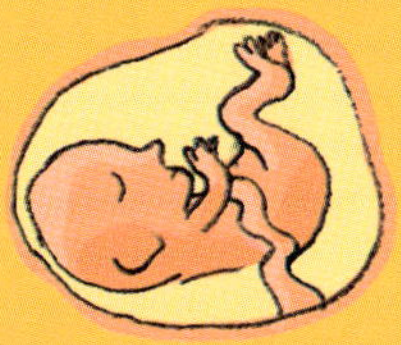

3 mois : les yeux et les oreilles sont formés. Tout est là ! Le bébé mesure 10 cm et commence à bouger.

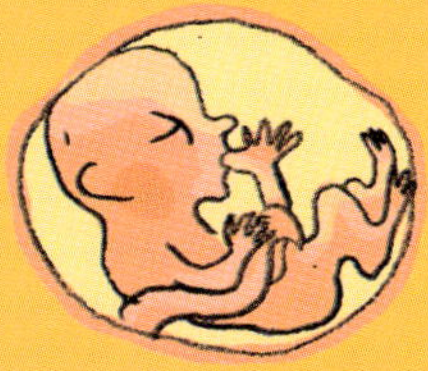

5 mois : le bébé mesure 25 cm. Il bouge de plus en plus.

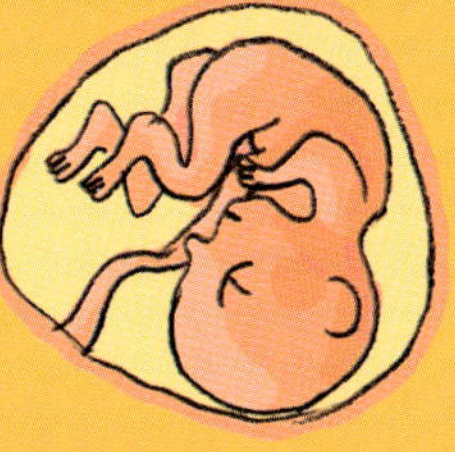

8 mois : le bébé mesure 45 cm. Il s'est retourné, la tête en bas.

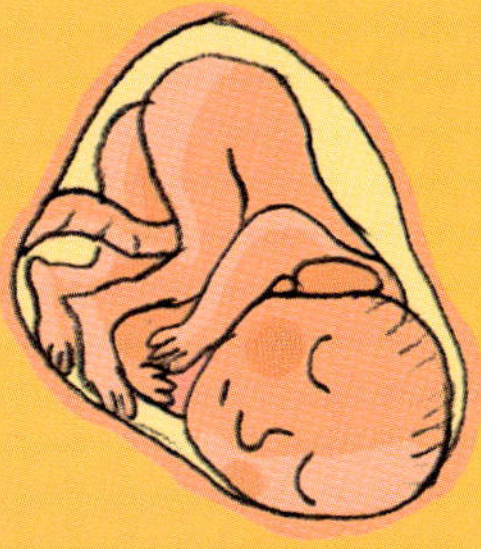

9 mois : il mesure 50 cm et il est prêt à naître...

Pour te faire une idée de la taille du bébé, compare les mesures indiquées ici à celles de cette règle.

14 C'est le printemps. Rémi, Lilou et leur maman prennent un goûter au square.

– Que c'est bon de manger quand on a faim ! dit maman. Ce bébé doit avoir bon appétit.

– Mais il mange ? s'étonnent Rémi et Lilou.

– Il ne mange pas comme nous, bien sûr. C'est moi qui lui apporte tout ce dont il a besoin pour vivre et grandir.

Comment mange le bébé et comment respire-t-il ? 15

Le **cordon ombilical** relie le bébé à sa maman. Ce qu'elle mange passe dans le sang du bébé après avoir été digéré. C'est aussi par le cordon que la maman fournit au bébé l'oxygène dont il a besoin, parce qu'il ne sait pas encore respirer.

Pour que le bébé soit bien nourri, la maman doit avoir une bonne alimentation pendant toute sa grossesse.

Le bébé fait pipi dans le liquide qui est nettoyé en permanence, mais il ne fait pas caca !

Parmi ces aliments, trouve celui qui est le meilleur pour la croissance des os du bébé.

l'eau — le lait et les laitages — les haricots verts

Réponse : le lait et les laitages. Ils apportent le calcium nécessaire à la construction des os.

16

Après une journée fatigante, maman se repose sur le canapé quand soudain :

– Ça y est ! s'exclame-t-elle, il bouge. Je sens ses premiers petits coups de pied.

– Il joue peut-être au foot, dit papa en riant.

– Même pas vrai ! s'écrie Rémi. Mais qu'est-ce qu'il fait toute la journée, ce bébé ?

Que fait le bébé dans le ventre de sa maman ?

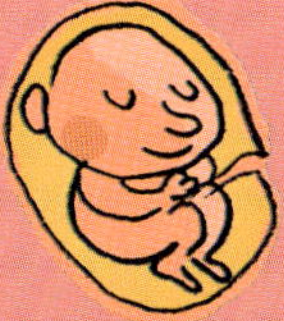

Le bébé dort presque tout le temps.

Et quand il ne dort pas, il fait des galipettes ou il joue avec son cordon.

Plus tard, il suce même son pouce.

Il aime déjà beaucoup les caresses.

Dans le ventre de sa maman, pendant qu'il dort, le bébé a les bras et les jambes repliés. Longtemps après, même quand on est grand, on aime s'endormir dans cette position.

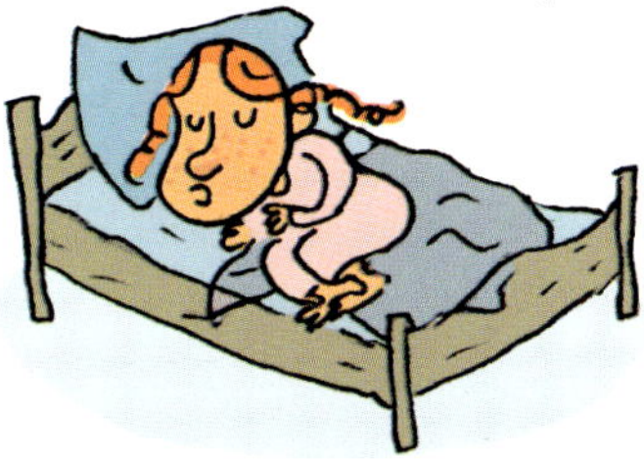

Et toi, comment t'endors-tu ?

Rémi approche du ventre de sa maman sa trompette et souffle dedans.

– Tu crois qu'il m'entend ? demande-t-il.

– Bien sûr qu'il t'entend. Il entend la musique, mais aussi les rires, les cris et bien d'autres choses encore. Certains bruits lui plaisent ; d'autres lui déplaisent.

Est-ce qu'il entend ? Est-ce qu'il voit ?

Dans sa bulle, le bébé entend surtout la voix de sa maman, son cœur, les gargouillis de son ventre...

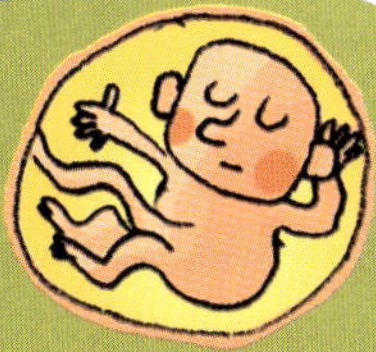

... mais aussi plein d'autres bruits venus de l'extérieur. Ce qu'il adore, c'est quand son papa lui parle.

À la fin de la grossesse, le bébé peut ouvrir et fermer les yeux, mais il ne voit pas grand chose.

Mon bruit préféré à moi, c'était celui de la voiture de pompiers !

Tu veux avoir une idée de ce que le bébé entend dans le ventre de sa maman ? Dans ton bain, mets tes oreilles sous l'eau, en fermant les yeux, et amuse-toi à écouter les bruits.

Mais ne le fais qu'en présence d'un adulte !

20 – C'est un grand jour aujourd'hui ! dit maman. On va avoir des nouvelles du bébé grâce à une autre échographie. Le médecin va savoir si c'est une fille ou un garçon. Mais votre papa et moi préférons garder la surprise.

– Moi, je veux savoir ! s'écrie Lilou.

– Il faudra patienter jusqu'à la naissance, dit papa.

Fille ou garçon ?

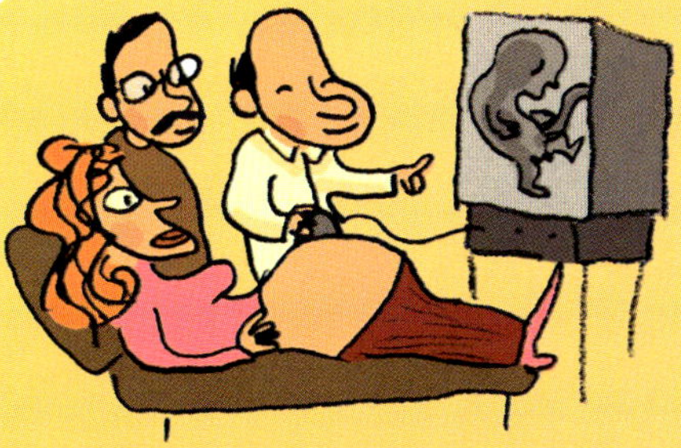

Après plusieurs mois de grossesse, l'**échographie** permet de distinguer si le bébé a un **sexe** de fille ou de garçon.

Tout se décide le premier jour de la grossesse.
C'est le **spermatozoïde** qui porte en lui ce qui fera un garçon ou une fille.

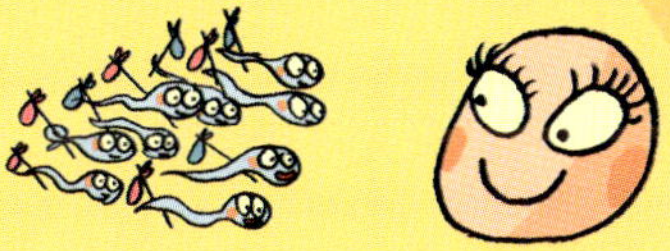

Souvent, les filles préfèrent jouer à la poupée et les garçons aux voitures, mais pas toujours.

Et toi, parmi ces jeux, lesquels préfères-tu ?

22

C'est l'été. Il reste maintenant peu de temps avant la naissance. Tout le monde prépare l'arrivée du bébé.

– Par où il va sortir, le bébé ? interroge Lilou.

– Tu te rappelles la naissance des chatons chez Tante Agathe ? Eh bien, ça se passe un peu pareil, répond sa maman.

Par où sort le bébé ? 23

Quand le bébé est prêt à naître, l'**utérus** s'ouvre peu à peu pour le laisser sortir. C'est l'accouchement. Pour que la maman n'ait pas mal, le médecin peut faire une **péridurale**.

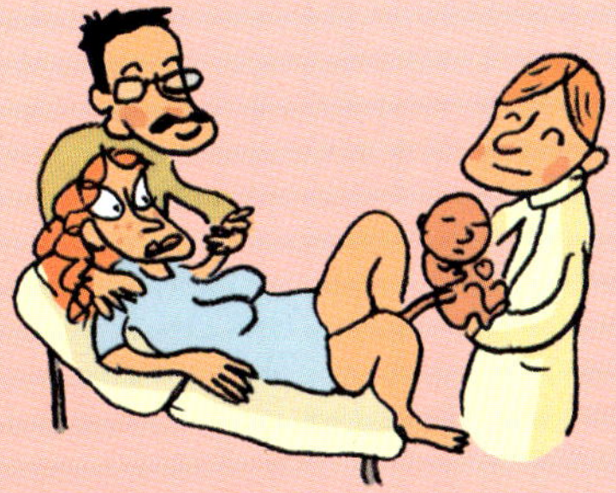

Le bébé sort le plus souvent par le sexe de sa maman. Quand il n'arrive pas à sortir de cette manière, le médecin fait une **césarienne**.

Dès qu'il est né, le bébé pousse un cri. C'est la première fois qu'il respire. Il n'a plus besoin du cordon pour vivre. On le coupe et le petit bout qui reste va former le nombril.

Mon 1er est le début de « maman ».
Mon 2ème est la planète de la vie.
Mon 3ème est la maison des oiseaux.
Mon 4ème est la fin de « tétée ».
Et mon tout est l'endroit où naissent les bébés.

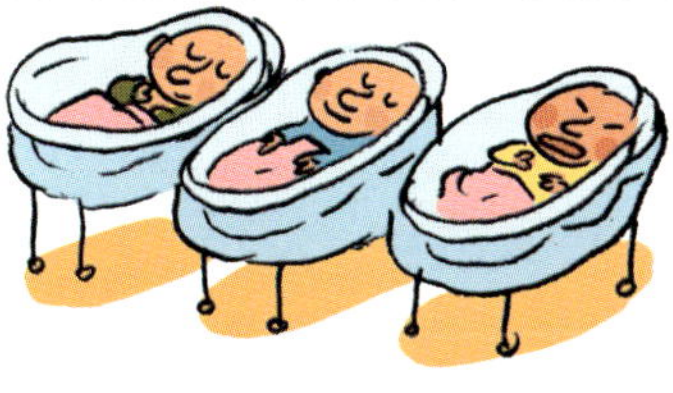

Réponse : maternité (ma-terre-nid-tée).

Ça y est ! le bébé est né. C'est une fille. Elle s'appelle Juliette et elle est en grande forme !
Rémi et Lilou sont impatients de la voir.

– Qu'elle est petite ! s'écrie Lilou. Elle tète déjà !
– Et elle a même l'air de beaucoup aimer mon lait, dit maman attendrie.
– Quand est-ce qu'on va pouvoir jouer avec elle ? demande Rémi.
– Laisse-la d'abord grandir un peu ! répond papa.

Le nouveau-né

En repartant de la maternité, Rémi et Lilou sont étonnés par tout ce qu'ils voient.

Une couveuse :

On met dans une couveuse les bébés qui sont nés trop tôt, pour qu'ils continuent à se développer en ayant bien chaud et en respirant du bon air.

Une maman qui donne un biberon :

Si le bébé ne tète pas le sein de sa maman, elle lui donne le lait dans un biberon.

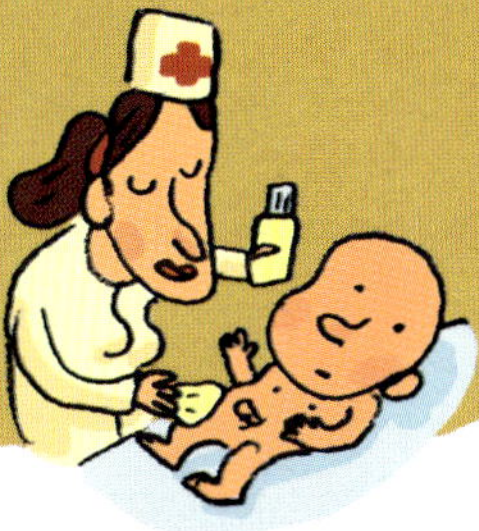

Un pansement sur le nombril :

Une fois que le cordon a été coupé, il reste un petit bout qui demande des soins jusqu'à ce qu'il tombe.

Ta naissance

Le jour de ta naissance

Date et heure :

....

Lieu :

....

Ton poids :

....

Ta taille :

....

Ton prénom :

....

Ton nom :

....

Ta photo

AVANT

La première personne à qui tes parents ont annoncé qu'ils t'attendaient :

....

Ta maman se rappelle-t-elle la première fois qu'elle t'a senti(e) bouger ?

....

Tes parents ont-ils voulu savoir s'ils attendaient une fille ou un garçon ?

....

APRÈS

Ton alimentation des premiers mois : le lait de ta maman ou le biberon ?

....

Ton sommeil : très bon, moyen...

....

À quel âge as-tu marché ?

....

Les mots difficiles

Les mots en gras dans le texte sont expliqués ici.

Cellule

La partie vivante la plus petite du corps. Il y a des milliards de cellules microscopiques dans le corps.

Échographie

À l'aide d'une petite boîte passée sur le ventre de la maman, l'échographie permet de voir le bébé à l'intérieur et de prendre des photos. Elle permet de surveiller le bébé tout au long de la grossesse.

Césarienne

Le médecin est parfois obligé de faire une petite ouverture dans le ventre de la maman pour faire sortir le bébé. C'est la césarienne.

Ovule

La graine de la maman qui lui permet de faire un bébé. Les ovules sont fabriqués par les ovaires.

Cordon ombilical

Sorte de long tuyau souple qui relie le bébé à la maman et lui permet de recevoir tout ce dont il a besoin pour vivre et se développer.

Péridurale
Par une piqûre dans le dos, le médecin injecte un produit qui supprime la douleur. C'est la péridurale.

Sexe
La partie du corps qui permet, quand on est adulte, de faire des bébés. Le sexe du garçon s'appelle le pénis, celui des filles le vagin, avec un petit orifice, la vulve. Le plus souvent, on donne au sexe un autre nom, comme le « zizi ».

Spermatozoïde
La graine du papa qui lui permet de faire un bébé. Les spermatozoïdes sont fabriqués par les testicules.

Utérus
Situé dans le ventre des filles, l'utérus ressemble à une petite poche. Quand la maman fait un bébé, c'est là qu'il se développe. L'utérus grossit en même temps que le bébé et c'est pour cela que le ventre de la maman s'arrondit de plus en plus.